Community Values and Legality Under Challenge

Europäische Hochschulschriften Recht

European University Studies in Law

Publications Universitaires Européennes de Droit

Band/ Volume **6279**

Simon P. Blätgen

Community Values and Legality Under Challenge

The Example of International Climate Change Law

PETER LANG

Bibliografische Information der Deutschen Nationalbibliothek
Die Deutsche Nationalbibliothek verzeichnet diese Publikation in der Deutschen Nationalbibliografie; detaillierte bibliografische Daten sind im Internet über http://dnb.d-nb.de abrufbar.

Zugl.: Berlin, Freie Univ., Diss., 2020

The research for this book was funded by the:
Deutsche Forschungsgemeinschaft (DFG, German Research Foundation)

Gedruckt auf alterungsbeständigem, säurefreiem Papier.

D 188
ISSN 0531-7312
ISBN 978-3-631-85235-4 (Print)
E-ISBN 978-3-631-87167-6 (E-PDF)
E-ISBN 978-3-631-87168-3 (EPUB)
E-ISBN (MOBI)
DOI 10.3726/b19446

Diese Publikation wurde begutachtet.

www.peterlang.com

To Leon and Lenn,
in the spirit of intergenerational equity.

Acknowledgments

"They threw me a whirlwind,
And I spat back the sea.
I took a battering but I've got thicker skin,
And the best people I know are looking out for me."
Frank Turner

This study was accepted as a PhD thesis by Freie Universität Berlin in the summer term of 2020. I want to thank my supervisor, Prof. Dr. Heike Krieger, for her guidance in writing this study as well as for many years of collaboration. I also want to thank Prof. Dr. Helmut Aust for his second review of my thesis.

My copy-editor Danielle Schmitz skilfully and patiently mitigated the fact that this book was written by a non-native speaker. Her cheerful and encouraging attitude was most helpful in the sometimes cumbersome process of getting the manuscript to the finish line.

My topic is closely related to the notion of 'community' in international law. It therefore only seems appropriate to thank the communities I was fortunate enough to become a part of. I am blessed with more people, both from professional and personal contexts, to be grateful for and thankful to than could reasonably be named in a few lines prefacing my thesis. That I feel inclined to name some of them here, I hope no one mistakes as disregard.

I would like to thank all the members, fellows and staff – present and former – of the Berlin Potsdam Research Group "The International Rule of Law – Rise or Decline?" for the enriching discussions and stimulating environment. I particularly thank Dr. Nina Reiners and Dr. Felix Lange for their very helpful comments on earlier drafts of the key chapters in this study. Especially, I am grateful for the encouragement and friendship of my fellow PhD candidates Alicia Köppen and Dr. Julien Berger, during what has certainly not always been an easy journey.

During my legal studies, the chairs of Professors Philip Kunig and Heike Krieger, where I was a student assistant, provided an inspiring environment. While working for Prof. Dr. Kunig, Dr. Despoina Glarou first encouraged me to pursue my interest in public international law.

I am indebted to all my dear friends, whose presence in my life sustains me every day. As they also helped with tireless proof-reading and/or substantial input on this book, Moritz Thörner and Bastian Benrath represent all others here. Special thanks to Clara Brockmeier, one of the few people without any professional reason to read and comment on my entire thesis.

Words cannot express how full of gratitude I am for my family and the backing they have given me. Thank you in particular to my father Paul as well as my grandmothers. I want to thank my mother Angelika, whose unwavering love, support and confidence has strengthened me not only during the years of working on this book, but also in every single day of my life. My brother Tobias was the best companion and guardian anyone could ever wish for growing up. Today, he and his family are a constant source of love, inspiration and purpose to me.

And last, but most certainly not least, I want to thank my partner in life, in crime and in everything else, Natalie. Not only did she tirelessly read my work through the various stages of its writing but also her bright and inspiring comments were crucial in the process of finishing it. But much more importantly, her love and partnership are the best encouragement I can imagine to embrace life and make the best of whatever it brings.

Düsseldorf/Berlin
October 2021

Table of Contents

List of Abbreviations

AJIL	American Journal of International Law
Am. U. J. Int'l L. & Pol'y	American University Journal of International Law and Policy
ASEAN	Association of South East Asian Nations
BASIC	Group of Brazil, South Africa, India and China
B.C. Int'l & Comp. L. Rev.	Boston College International and Comparative Law Review
BYIL	British Yearbook of International Law
CBD	Convention on Biological Diversity
CBDR	Common but Differentiated Responsibilities
CDM	Clean Development Mechanism
CDP	Carbon Disclosure Project
CFC	Chlorofluorocarbon
CMA	Meeting of the Parties to the Paris Agreement
CMP	Meeting of the Parties (to the Kyoto Protocol)
COEJ	Coalition on the Environment and Jewish Life
COP	Conference of the Parties (to the United Nations Framework Convention on Climate Change)
CSD	United Nations Commission on Sustainable Development
CUP	Cambridge University Press
DSB	(WTO) Dispute Settlement Body
ECHR	European Convention on Human Rights
ECJ	European Court of Justice
ECtHR	European Court of Human Rights
EIA	Environmental impact assessment
EJIL	European Journal of International Law
Envtl. Pol'y & L.	Environmental Policy and Law (Journal)
EU	European Union
Fordham Int'l LJ	Fordham International Law Journal
GATT	General Agreement on Tariffs and Trade
GHG	Greenhouse gas
Harv. Int'l. LJ	Harvard International Law Journal
ICC	International Criminal Court

ICCPR	International Covenant on Civil and Political Rights
ICJ	International Court of Justice
ICTY	International Criminal Tribunal for the former Yugoslavia
IDI	Institut de Droit International
IEL	International Environmental Law
IGO	Inter-governmental organisation
ILA	International Law Association
ILC	International Law Commission
INC	Intergovernmental Negotiating Committee (for the UNFCCC)
IPCC	Intergovernmental Panel on Climate Change
ISA	International Seabed Authority
ITLOS	International Tribunal for the Law of the Sea
J. Int'l L & Int'l Rel.	Journal of International Law and International Relations
MEA	Multilateral environmental agreement
Mich. J. Envtl. & Admin. L.	Michigan Journal of Environmental and Administrative Law
MPEPIL	Max Planck Encyclopedia of Public International Law
NDC(s)	Nationally determined contribution(s)
NGO	Non-governmental organisation
Notre Dame L. Rev.	Notre Dame Law Review
OECD	Organisation for Economic Co-operation and Development
OHCHR	Office of the High Commissioner for Human Rights
OIC	Organisation of Islamic Cooperation
OUP	Oxford University Press
PCIJ	Permanent Court of International Justice
QELROs	Quantified emission limitation and reduction objectives
RECIEL	Review of European, Comparative & International Environmental Law
RIAA	United Nations Reports of International Arbitral Awards
Stan. Envtl. LJ	Stanford Environmental Law Journal

S. Afr. YB Int'l L.	South African Yearbook of International Law
TFEU	Treaty on the Functioning of the European Union
UDHR	Universal Declaration of Human Rights
UN	United Nations
UNCED	United Nations Conference on Environment and Development
UNCLOS	United Nations Convention on the Law of the Sea
UNEP	United Nations Environment Programme
UNFCCC or FCCC	United Nations Framework Convention on Climate Change
UNGA	United Nations General Assembly
UNTS	United Nations Treaty Series
VCLT	Vienna Convention on the Law of Treaties
WMO	World Meteorological Organization
WTO	World Trade Organization
YB Int'l Env. L.	Yearbook of International Environmental Law

Part A: Introduction

I. A Decline of the International Law Established After the 'Cold War'?

The often-made claim that the international order established during and densified after the Cold War is facing challenges or even a crisis[1] does not seem audacious or even particularly pessimistic at the beginning of the 2020s. Recent years have brought about major setbacks for this order and its fundamental elements which previously had seemed to be solidly established. Authoritarianism and human rights violations in different parts of the world put a bold question mark behind the 1990s-narrative of economic prosperity, democratic progress and human rights orientation. Withdrawals from the International Criminal Court by African countries and even more threats thereof are salient examples of the pressure under which key institutions are put when States disregard institutional authority and questioning their legitimacy. In Europe and North America, populism, nationalism and anti-multilateralism are on the rise in countries which used to be the origin, center and backbone of modern international law and international relations. The 2016 US presidential election brought to power a leader who questioned century-old alliances and actively promoted[2] the abandonment of multilateral structures in favor of bilateral 'deals'. Yet, this again is only one example that gained public attention. It has become conventional wisdom that 'something' is going on with the international order.

These developments are worrying in and of themselves for those in favor of peaceful international relations based on the rule of law. The reasonable suspicion that they are in fact parts of a broader erosion of the existing international order makes them even more alarming. But while being concerned or alarmed are understandable reactions, they do not replace the necessary and nuanced analysis of *what exactly* is and/or will be affected by these apparent political trends. Which parts of international law will prove resilient? Have certain

---

1 See e.g., Richard Haass, *A world in disarray: American foreign policy and the crisis of the old order* (Penguin, 2017); G. John Ikenberry, "The End of Liberal International Order?", *International Affairs* 94, no. 1 (2018), p. 7 et seqq.

2 Kim Willsher, "Quit the EU for better trade deal, Trump reportedly told Macron", *The Guardian*, 29 Jun 2018; Daniel W. Drezner, "Why the Trump Administration Hates Multilateral Trade Agreements the Most", *The Washington Post*, 9 Mar 2017.

elements of international law itself even contributed to the problem and hence, will come under even larger pressure?[3] Are the occurring setbacks only a slight impediment in an overall progressive development or an actual sign of decline of international law?[4] In short, the 'something' needs to be scrutinized to find out what it is about. These broader questions drive the research agenda of the larger project in connection to which the present analysis has been elaborated.[5]

What advocates[6] and critics[7] of the development of international law since the 1990s have in common is the role of values as a focal point in their debates and narratives. For some, the new political circumstances were an opportunity for international law to move from a formal order of "correlative rights and obligations running between States" towards one that "incorporates common interests of the international community as a whole, including not only States but all human beings."[8] This idea is neatly captured in the notion of 'community values'. As will be elaborated, the idea that international law can accommodate and promote values transcending classical state 'interests' brings with it certain normative and structural implications. These include the questions of who is comprised in 'the international community', how its values are understood to be formed and by whom, and what the relationship between such values and legal norms should be.

---

3 cf. Heike Krieger, "Trumping International Law? Implications of the 2016 US Presidential Election for the International Legal Order," *EJIL: Talk! Blog of the European Journal of International Law*, https://www.ejiltalk.org/trumping-international-law-the-implications-of-the-2016-us-presidential-election-for-the-international-legal-order/ .3 January 2017.

4 Heike Krieger and Georg Nolte, "The International Rule of Law – Rise or Decline? Points of Departure", *KFG Working Paper Series* 1 (2016).

5 The Berlin Potsdam Research Group "The International Rule of Law – Rise or Decline?"; For more information on the group and its analytical framework, see http://kfg-intlaw.de/Research-Agenda/research-agenda.php?ID=1; The present author is a PhD candidate within the group and affiliated with the 'value-perspective' of the research agenda, led by Prof. Dr. Heike Krieger of Freie Universität Berlin.

6 E.g., Santiago Villalpando, "The Legal Dimension of the International Community: How Community Interests Are Protected in International Law", *EJIL* 21, no. 2 (2010), p. 392 et seqq.

7 E.g., Jean d'Aspremont, "The Foundations of the International Legal Order", *Finnish Yearbook of International Law* 18 (2007), p. 220 et seqq.

8 Bruno Simma, "Universality of International Law from the Perspective of a Practitioner", *EJIL* 20, no. 2 (2009), p. 268.

The centrality of values in the developments described above is the starting point of the present analysis. A study focusing on value-laden international law could be perceived as rather theoretical and of little practical use. But to the contrary, a focus on values in international law helps in understanding a significant general trend in the (recent) evolution of international law.[9]

II. International Climate Change Law – a Focal Point of Modern Developments in International Law

"Our collective responsibility to each other is nowhere more evident than in the huge challenge posed by climate change."
British Foreign Secretary Margarets Beckett[10]

The field of climate change law is a key example for the phenomenon of value-orientation and the structural challenges for international law relating thereto. Established in the 1990s, the climate regime entails many examples for the ambition that international law promotes community values beyond state interests. Because of its historical and structural overlap with the general development of international law after 1990, the climate regime will be the case study for the present analysis.

Climate change is a fundamentally cross-cutting issue, with community value implications at its very core. It impacts almost every aspect of human life and societies, from economic development to social standards, from human health to basic nutrition and water supply, from global inequalities to newly arising reasons for conflict. It exacerbates existing problems like in the field of migration[11] and is quickly creating new ones in almost every realm of human life. The crucial resource in avoiding hazardous climate change, namely, a stable atmosphere of the earth, shares the fate of all 'commons' famously discussed by Garret

9 As in, Villalpando, "The legal dimension of the international community", p. 419.

10 Statement by the Secretary of State for Foreign and Commonwealth Affairs of the United Kingdom of Great Britain and Northern Ireland, the Rt Hon Margaret Beckett MP before the 61st sission of the UN General Assembly on 22 September 2006; available at https://www.un.org/webcast/ga/61/pdfs/unitedkingdom-e.pdf.

11 François Gemenne, "L'environnement, nouveau facteur de migration?", in *L'enjeu mondial*, ed. François Gemenne (Presses de Sciences Po (PFNSP), 2009); "One good reason to speak of 'climate refugees'", *Forced Migration Review* 49 (2015), p. 137.

Hardin in his piece 'tragedy of the commons': In a system where a given resource is shared, individual users acting independently in their own self-interest behave contrary to the common good of all users by depleting or spoiling that resource through their collective action.[12] The users, in this case mainly the acting States, profit from greenhouse gas (GHG)-producing activities individually and would gain only a fraction of the benefits from unilateral GHG reduction efforts. Moreover, "their sacrifice may be futile if other actors do not exhibit similar restraint".[13] Hence, climate change can rightfully be called "the prototype of the commons issue".[14]

Climate change forces fundamental reconsiderations. In his last and unfinished work, late German sociologist Ulrich Beck cites climate change as a central example for his hypothesis of a 'metamorphosis of the world'.[15] The terminology is an attempt to verbalize the deep structural changes the world is facing. And indeed, climate change seems to be an unerring example – challenging not only the way humankind lives, produces and consumes, but also the ways in which we develop political decisions and societal as well as legal structures. Climate change as a phenomenon, in this vein, could alter the ways in which we conceive of certain political questions, problems and interdependencies. A process of norm creation could unfold that is potentially capable of re-shaping the way in which humankind is assuming responsibility for the effects of the climate change it induced. The question, as Beck points out, is if "that active, sub-political and political metamorphosis is fast enough to counter the galloping process of climate catastrophes that might throw the entire planet into droughts, floods, chaos, starvation and bloody conflicts."[16]

So, what can international climate change *law* do about this and why is it relevant from a research perspective focusing on the development of international law after the Cold War? First, in line with the fundamental challenges outlined above, climate change law is a highly relevant test to international law's ability to allocate legal responsibility and to organize and structure political action in a both complex and highly value-laden field. As this study will elaborate, climate

---

12 Garrett Hardin, "The Tragedy of the Commons", *Science* 162 (1968), p. 1243 et seqq.

13 Kathryn Harrison and Lisa McIntosh Sundstrom, "The Comparative Politics of Climate Change", *Global Environmental Politics* 7, no. 4 (2007), p. 1.

14 Franz Xaver Perrez, *Cooperative sovereignty: From independence to interdependence in the structure of international environmental law* (Kluwer Law International, 2000), p. 317.

15 Ulrich Beck, *The metamorphosis of the world* (Polity Press, 2016), p. 3 et seqq.

16 Ibid., p. 47.

change is one of the issues which international law is struggling to find answers to yet needs to do so if it is to remain the preponderant regulative system of international relations. Second, the field is in many respects a product of the structural developments in the 1990s. In part, that certainly is the case for reasons of pure historical coincidence: When awareness rose for environmental concerns in the 1960s, combined with growing scientific consensus on the effects of global warming in the 1970s and increasing readiness to act politically in the early 1980s, none of this had much to do with the post-Cold War changes which were still a decade ahead. The practical realization of an international, multilateral and legally significant effort to combat global climate change, however, then directly fell into the immediate aftermath of the Cold War's end.

1. Current Signs of International Climate Law Being Under Pressure?

To most observers, discussing international climate law while focusing on possible signs of decline, would have been counter-intuitive at the beginning of 2016. At the 21st Conference of the Parties (COP) to the UNFCCC in Paris, France, an enthusiastic crowd of negotiators, heads of States and governments celebrated the adoption of the 'Paris Agreement' by 195 States and the EU. French President Hollande called the agreement "ambitious", "binding" and "universal" and told negotiators and representatives to be "proud to stand before your children and grandchildren."[17] UN Secretary General Ban-Ki-Moon called the agreement a "resounding success for multilateralism" and hailed the beginning of "a new era of global cooperation on one of the most complex issues ever to confront humanity."[18] In media coverage as well, the agreement was praised with attributes such as "historic"[19] and "the world's greatest diplomatic success".[20] Within month, this enthusiasm suffered a significant blow: The 8th of November 2016 was the second day of COP 22 in Marrakech, Morocco, envisaged to commence the detailed implementation of the Paris Agreement. It was also the day Donald

17 UNFCCC Secretariat, "Historic Paris Agreement on Climate Change: 195 Nations Set Path to Keep Temperature Rise Well Below 2 Degrees Celsius," *News release*, 13 Dec 2015, https://unfccc.int/news/finale-cop21.

18 Ibid.

19 Joby Warrick and Chris Mooney, "196 Countries Approve Historic Climate Agreement", *The Washington Post*, 12 Dec 2015.

20 Fiona Harvey, "Paris Climate Change Agreement: The World's Greatest Diplomatic Success", *The Guardian*, 14 Dec 2015.

Trump was elected US President. The news of Trump's election reached the conference that had otherwise started on the optimistic footing many participants had preserved from the Paris Conference. As a candidate, Trump had repeatedly criticized the Agreement as a 'bad deal' potentially harming American industries and indicated that he would withdraw from the commitments made by the Obama administration if elected. In June 2017, President Trump followed through with his plan and announced the withdrawal of the US from the agreement.[21] The political decision itself was reversed by the following administration, with President Biden re-joining the Paris Agreement as one of his first decisions entering office.[22]

Yet structurally even more relevant than the political setback to the Paris Agreement by the Trump administration was the structural development leading to the Paris Agreement itself: Before the conclusion of the Agreement, there had been an intense debate on the legal form which the envisaged agreement should have. The politically formulated objective was to negotiate a legally binding instrument for the post-2020 period. Opinions ranged from optimism regarding the legal bindingness to more cautious opinions. Yet significantly, there was also a wide range of opinions submitting that the legal form would be less important than widely assumed.[23] To a certain extent in line with this perspective, it was clear from the beginning of the negotiations that the Obama-Administration would need the outcome to be of little enough legal effect that it would be able to conclude it by 'Executive agreement', i.e., without the approval of the US Senate or congress.[24] Regarding international legal scholarship, these arguments

---

21 The White House, Statement by President Trump on the Paris Climate Accord, 1 Jun 2017, available at https://www.whitehouse.gov/briefings-statements/statement-president-trump-paris-climate-accord/ .

22 The White House, Statement on the Paris Climate Agreement, 20 January 2021, available at https://www.whitehouse.gov/briefing-room/statements-releases/2021/01/20/paris-climate-agreement/.

23 Anne-Marie Slaughter, "The Paris Approach to Global Governance," Project Syndicate, http://www.project-syndicate.org/commentary/paris-agreement-model-for-global-governance-by-anne-marie-slaughter-2015-12.2015, who gave a very positive account of the 'Paris Approach' despite of the limited legal effects; See also Joost Pauwelyn and Lilliana Andonova, "A "Legally Binding Treaty" or Not? The Wrong Question for Paris Climate Summit," *EJIL: Talk! Blog of the European Journal of International Law*, https://www.ejiltalk.org/a-legally-binding-treaty-or-not-the-wrong-question-for-paris-climate-summit/.4 December 2015.

24 US constitutional law differentiates between 'Art. II- treaties', i.e., one the one hand, agreements that are concluded by the president with the advice and consent of

connect the issue to the broader debate on whether there is a discernible trend of stagnation in treaty making.[25]

2. Indications of Both Rise and Decline in International Climate Change Law

Current countertrends do exist however. Immediately after the Trump administration's renunciation of the Paris Agreement, a broad range of other actors (re-)emphasized their own commitment to the Agreement and what it stands for. This did not only concern representatives of countries or organizations with a long track record of climate engagement like the EU. For instance, a senior Chinese negotiator was quoted that "It is global society's will that all want to co-operate to combat climate change" ahead of the 2016 COP.[26] The Chinese government seems to intend to deliver on the promises made when ratifying the treaty, even after the US's announcement of withdrawal. In the US, a coalition of cities, States and businesses was formed around the commitment to the Paris Agreement despite the federal government's withdrawal.[27] Former New York City Mayor and billionaire Michael Bloomberg announced that he would pay the share of the federal government's financial contributions to the

---

two-thirds of the Senate, according to a procedure laid out in Art. II of the US Constitution and executive agreements, on the other. The latter are international agreements concluded without the senatorial process. Presidential executive agreements (or *sole* executive agreements) such as the one by which the US accepted the Paris Agreement, are one of three types of executive agreements and the only one requiring neither Senate nor Congress to be involved. Preconditions include the degree of the agreement's influence on existing state law and whether further congressional action would be required to enact the agreement. See Curtis A. Bradley, *International law in the U.S. legal system* (Oxford University Press, 2013), p. 74 et seqq.

25 Joost Pauwelyn, Ramses A. Wessel, and Jan Wouters, "When Structures Become Shackles: Stagnation and Dynamics in International Lawmaking", *EJIL* 25, no. 3 (2014), p. 733 et seqq.

26 Pilita Clark, "China Warns Trump Against Abandoning Climate Change Deal", *Financial Times*, 11 Nov 2016

27 The Climate Group, "US States, Cities and Businesses keep US Climate Action on Track," *News release*, 18 Sep 2017, https://www.theclimategroup.org/news/us-states-cities-and-businesses-keep-us-climate-action-track; Hiroko Tabuchi and Lisa Friedman, "U.S. Cities, States and Businesses Pledge to Measure Emissions", *New York Times*, 11 Jul 2017.

Agreement's institutions.[28] This shift regarding the level on which climate action is taken – from the national State bound by international law-obligations to non-state-actors – is further indicative of deeper changes in the climate regime's structure. With the federal government re-joining the Agreement, the political trend, at least in the US, seems to have revert for the moment. At the same time, with social movements like 'Fridays for Future' or 'Extinction Rebellion', political pressure on governments to tackle climate change more effectively appears to be increasing.

In sum, these examples from recent developments could suggest elements of both rise and decline. In its current state, there seems to be a rather broad international consensus regarding the overarching goal and necessity of the legal regime and its cause. This consensus has been shaped by various (community) values serving as a frame for the arguments made by different actors, which at least partially include non-state-actors. At the same time, there is an apparent trend towards a more flexible legal framework and, in the American case, also of open defiance. The combination of these factors makes international climate change law an intriguing case study for an analysis of how the community-value orientation in international law has changed since the 1990s and whether – in the parlance of the research framework of this study – international law is on the rise and or in decline in the particular field of climate change law and beyond.

III. Approach of This Study

Given the complexities and nature of the envisaged study, some further preliminary remarks on its methodological framework must be made. This concerns both the details of the 'rise or decline' perspective applied in this study as well as the approaches the study takes, specifically, a combination of a system-oriented and historical approach.

1. Rise or Decline?

The perspective of 'rise or decline' deserves further elaboration. How can moments or trends of *rise* or *decline* in international law be assessed in a specific field of law, here international climate law? The answer is the following: First, by specifying the reference points and second, by identifying the core elements of what could be 'on the rise' or 'in decline'.

---

28 Eli Meixler, "Michael Bloomberg Pledged $4.5 Million to Uphold U.S. Commitment to the Paris Agreement", *TIME*, 23 Apr 2018.

The time during and after 1990 as a reference point for analysis is the first important element of the perspective. In the lay(wo)men's observation and media coverage, but also in the work of experts and academics, notions of 'crisis' or 'backlash' are often recklessly mobilized without making the point of comparison explicit. After the end of the Cold War, when the great east-western conflict of political ideologies ceased to determine international politics, the 1990s were shaped by liberal internationalist optimism. International politics made what some international relations scholars called a 'move to law', meaning an increasing emphasis on the use of legal language, institutions and mechanisms in finding solutions to major political challenges.[29] In political science, especially the increasing juridification of human rights led to a perceived trend towards a more value-oriented international order.[30] The debate in international law scholarship increasingly featured the 'community' aspects of international law and the necessary normative grounding of that community in shared 'values'.[31] The step from an order of 'co-existence' to an order of 'co-operation', famously predicted and analyzed in its early stages by Wolfgang Friedmann in the 1960s[32], appeared to be in reach after all. These trends could be discerned in various and structurally different fields of international law, such as international environmental law, cultural heritage protection, human rights law or even state sovereignty.

Second and in more general terms, there is increasing institutionalization at the international level in the period after 1990. This can be seen in the further proliferation of rules in many areas, the recognition of 'thicker' human rights standards, including in areas where the applicability of human rights had been contested, and in certain aspects of the extraterritorial application of human

29 Kenneth W. Abbott et al., "The Concept of Legalization", *International Organization* 54, no. 03 (2000).

30 Cf. Thomas Risse, Steve C. Ropp, and Kathryn Sikkink, *The persistent power of human rights: From commitment to compliance* (Cambridge University Press, 2013).

31 Andreas L. Paulus, *Die internationale Gemeinschaft im Völkerrecht: eine Untersuchung zur Entwicklung des Völkerrechts im Zeitalter der Globalisierung; The "International Community" in Public International Law: english summary* (Beck, 2001), p. 250 et. seqq.; Mehrdad Payandeh, *Internationales Gemeinschaftsrecht: zur Herausbildung gemeinschaftsrechtlicher Strukturen im Völkerrecht der Globalisierung = International community law: The evolution of community structures in the international legal order in the era of globalization; (English Summary)* (Springer, 2010).

32 Wolfgang Friedmann, *The changing structure of international law* (Columbia University Press, 1964).

rights.[33] For a certain period, it seemed as if those advocating theoretical concepts featuring an ever deeper legal integration and a steadily declining role for sovereign national States were going to win the argument about the future of the international legal order.[34] The concept of 'global constitutionalism' is one important example.[35] Also in more cautious accounts, the question arose whether international law was in the process of fundamentally changing its character. Apart from the discourses in international law scholarship itself, these questions also occupied political scientists and (legal) philosophers.[36] Some 25 years later, the situation has significantly changed, and the many initiatives to reshape international law have taken different courses.[37] The progressive development of international law after 1990 has, in many regards, met intensive criticism and other scholars call for a return to a rather positivist or pragmatic[38] international legal order. It is questionable if one, under these circumstances, can still speak of a juridification of international relations based on a universal understanding of values, or if there is rather a tendency towards informalisation. The elements of structural change were at the time, albeit to different extents, widely acclaimed as constituting progress in comparison to the classical international law established and developed under the UN Charter after World War II. The very same

---

33 Krieger and Nolte, "The International Rule of Law – Rise or Decline? Points of Departure ", p. 8.

34 Cf. Heike Krieger, "Verfassung im Völkerrecht – Konstitutionelle Elemente jenseits des Staates? The Constitutionalization of Public International Law – Constitutional Elements Beyond the State?", in *Verfassung als Ordnungskonzept. Referate und Diskussionen auf der Tagung der Vereinigung der Deutschen Staatsrechtslehrer in Speyer vom 7. bis zum 10. Oktober 2015*, ed. Franz Mayer, et al. (De Gruyter, 2016), p. 439 et seqq.

35 Cf. Jochen Frowein, "Konstitutionalisierung des Völkerrechts", *Völkerrecht—Menschenrechte—Verfassungsfragen Deutschlands und Europas* (2004); for a theoretical overview, see Anne Peters, "Fragmentation and Constitutionalization", in *The Oxford handbook of the theory of international law*, ed. Anne Orford, Florian Hoffmann, and Martin Clark (Oxford University Press, 2016), p. 1011, especially p. 1015 et seqq.

36 Ronald Dworkin, "A New Philosophy for International Law", *Philosophy & Public Affairs* 41, no. 1 (2013), p. 2 et seqq.

37 A prominent example for an initiative that nowadays is widely perceived as one that failed the expectations it raised is the Responsibility to Protect; instead of many, see Charles E. Ziegler, "Critical Perspectives on the Responsibility to Protect: BRICS and Beyond", *International Relations* 30, no. 3 (2016), p. 262 et seqq.

38 Krieger, "Verfassung im Völkerrecht – Konstitutionelle Elemente jenseits des Staates? The Constitutionalization of Public International Law – Constitutional Elements Beyond the State?", p. 460 et seqq.

elements were criticized by others – at the time for being over-idealistic or pushing the boundaries of positivist international law or today as having contributed to the perceived crisis of acceptance of international law as a regulatory framework for international relations.

In an analysis like in this study, certain initial caveats need to be made. First, the diagnosis of a crisis or possible decline must be treated with caution. It can be misleading or even misused to further certain political causes. On the other hand – the present author submits – international lawyers should also not retreat to a limited area of purely technical craft(wo)manship and exclude current developments from their perspective. Connected to this is the second caveat concerning the pitfall of overestimating the significance of one's own time.

A third caveat concerns the choice of 1990 or the end of the Cold War as a reference point. Here, objections could be made that such a choice is euro- or even germanocentric given the meaning largely ascribed to the fall of the Berlin wall for the history of Germany and Europe. Furthermore, many of the changes after 1990 have their root causes in earlier historical phases. Yet some reference point must be picked and 1990 is arguably the relatively best one available.[39] And these caveats – in the author's view – are rather a reminder to remain self-critical than a reason not to undertake an analysis such as this.

2. Applying 'Rise or Decline?' on International Climate Change Law

When looking specifically at the evolution of international climate change law and its moments of rise and decline, which period can be considered as a suitable point for comparison? In line with observations of the broader developments of international law[40] outlined above, this reference point can reasonably be situated in the 1990s. For international climate change law, the most promising reference point is the period between the adoption of the UNFCCC 1992 and the Kyoto Protocol 1997. Historically, these years right after the inception of the modern climate change regime are the clearest embodiment of the overlap between community value-orientation in international law generally and in climate change law in particular.

39 Krieger and Nolte, "The International Rule of Law – Rise or Decline? Points of Departure ", p. 9.

40 Ibid.

Three key components arguably marked this period: An endeavor to create legal bindingness, the emphasis on multilateralism and the combination of the two former components with an underpinning of acclaimed universal values driving the process. These components are directly linked to the way in which this study will classify and assign its observations to the seemingly dichotomous categories of 'rise' and 'decline'. Where they are, respectively, more (or less) emphasized and where the legalization discernibly becomes more (or less) central for the most significant actors – first and foremost States – they will be understood as being on the rise (or in decline).

It is important to note that taking this phase of international (climate) law as a point of reference serves first and foremost an analytical purpose. It delivers a clearly delineated comparative point that allows one to trace changes and assess where and in how far we can speak of 'rise' or 'decline' of international law or components of it. It must be stressed that this, in a first step, is independent of a normative assessment of what international law *should* or *should not* be. It starts from the assumption that "rise or decline are not synonymous with desirable or undesirable".[41] While this still leaves space for normative reflections, of which the present author will offer in the concluding part of this thesis, analytically this research is primarily concerned with the changes of the role international legal structures play and what contribution they make in international relations, also in comparison to other normative orders.[42]

3. Combination of a System-Oriented and a Historical Approach

In its analysis, this study will follow two interlinked lines of inquiry.

First and foremost, the study is based on a system-oriented approach. Such approaches analyze possible causes for structural changes of the international legal order beyond classical legal indicators such as the compliance with legal rules. As understood here, it means to focus on the role legal form plays both in the overall regime and especially regarding norms embodying community values. This includes phenomena and trends such as making a legal regime more flexible and the extent to which 'soft law' provisions are preferred over legally binding norms. Taking a system-oriented approach is particularly useful dealing with a field of law heavily rooted in the environmental field. Here, various scholars have pointed out the regulatory challenges which at times may be so complex

41 Ibid., p. 17.

42 Ibid., p. 10, one of whose main points of interest in this context is "intrinsic value of international law" (German *Eigenwert des Rechts*).

that traditionally known forms of law may not be sufficient to provide effective regulation. This has sometimes been cited to explain why in the field of environmental law many existing instruments are characterized by the recurrence to soft law and informal standard setting instead of binding obligations. Herein lies the reason why the system-oriented approach in this study makes supplemental use of norm-focused perspectives from international relations scholarship.[43] This especially concerns perspectives on how norms are influenced by different actors on different levels. Likewise, it concerns perspectives emphasizing that legal norms are necessarily grounded in the social interactions either first producing non-legal norms or on which a legal norm then can be based.[44] The inception, change or stability of such norms below the threshold to legal norms therefore must be taken into account when analyzing a field of law heavily influenced by such norms, albeit without blurring the lines between the two.

Historical elements of the present analysis are twofold: First, it contains the historical evolution of the climate regime itself and that of the normative concepts identified as embodying community values. Second, it contextualizes the relevant discourses on the structural developments and points out where they are related to or rooted in earlier debates. This is especially important to account for the possibility of the 1990s being in fact a historical exception in the long-term development of international law and relations.[45] The shifts between different fora or structural approaches often attributed to an increased use of value-laden and/or non-legal norms will be evaluated through a historical approach. In this vein, the first perspective will be complemented with a second, namely an analysis of the structure of the climate change regime, the regulatory approaches taken and the pivotal changes therein. A historical overview will be combined with the identification of important shifts in the regulatory approach. The most notable of them being an incremental one

---

43 On norm erosion through systematically relevant contestation, see Nicole Deitelhoff and Lisbeth Zimmermann, "Things we lost in the fire: how different types of contestation affect the validity of international norms" (Frankfurt am Main: Hessische Stiftung Friedens- und Konfliktforschung (Ed.), 2013); http://nbn-resolving.de/urn:nbn:de:0168-ssoar-455201); for a constructivist perspective, see Martha Finnemore and Kathryn Sikkink, "International Norm Dynamics and Political Change", *International Organization* 52, no. 04 (1998), p. 887 et seqq.

44 Jutta Brunnée and Stephen J. Toope, *Legitimacy and legality in international law: An interactional account* (Cambridge University Press, 2010), p. 56 et seqq., p. 65 et seqq.

45 Krieger and Nolte, "The International Rule of Law – Rise or Decline? Points of Departure ", p. 19.

from ambitions of largely centralized regulation on the international level in the second half of the 1990s to the re-emphasis of national sovereignty and flexibility in recent years.

In line with the move towards (community) values in international law, value-laden norm concepts and provisions played a pivotal role in the inception of the United Nations Framework Convention on Climate Change (UNFCCC) and have continued to do so in the practice of the climate regime since then. For the purpose of this study, the core principles of the UNFCCC ('Common but Differentiated Responsibilities', inter- and intragenerational 'equity', 'Sustainable Development', 'Precaution' and 'Prevention'), as well as the 'common concern' concept will be the primary examples for this community value orientation in modern climate law. Finally, the no-harm rule is included in the analysis, presenting the oldest and most basic notion of obligations to other States in IEL and remaining the cornerstone of legal thinking in connection to the environment.

To understand how a trend towards *community* value orientation shapes the development of international climate change law, the different norm concepts in the field need to be scrutinized, which are (1) related to community values as defined here and (2) have come to play a noteworthy role in the legal provisions of the regime. The present study will do so by tracing their conceptualization from their inception to their development and reception in legal practice, most notably by States. How (and by which actors) norm concepts are introduced and shaped will often be an important explanatory factor for the gaps between normative ambition and legal practice.

Complementing the systemic analysis, recent trends in climate change related adjudication practice are considered as a further potential source for the advancement of community value norms and their legal implementation.

4. Overview of This Study's Structure

The thesis consists of four main parts – broadly speaking a conceptual, two empirical and a concluding part.

Part B ("Community Values and Legality in International Law") provides the conceptual framing of the analysis. It analyzes the relationship and conceptual tensions between the notion of community values and the existing structures of international law. First, the role of values in international law is discussed, with a special focus on the alleged turn to a more value-based or value-oriented legal order after 1990. Second, the specific influence of ideas surrounding the notion of an 'international community' is discussed, sketching the evolution from classical structures of post-Westphalian international law to the emergence of community thinking and value-orientation in international law in the second half of the 20th century, especially after 1990. Subsequently, the relationship between community values and the sources of international law is scrutinized. This analysis shows which of the existing sources are capable of accommodating community value-related provisions and point to their limits in doing so.

These broader themes are contextualized within the relevant discourses in legal scholarship and supplemented with insights from political science. The study takes into consideration both the arguments of proponents of international law including community values as well as fundamental objections others have, e.g., that there is a structural paradox in bringing self-interested States to acting in the interest of the entire community or some form of international public good. From the points of tensions between international law and community values, the chapter deduces the core elements or criteria that will guide the case study and provides the basis for assessing rise or decline: The emphasis on multilateralism by States, the role of legal bindingness and the underpinning with (allegedly) universalized values are identified as the main markers in analyzing 'rise' and 'decline'. Part B concludes with outlining the authors own starting position and clarifying necessary definitions.

Part C ("Historical Background of Climate Change as a Matter of Community Values and International Law") bridges the conceptual and the empirical part of the study. In its historical sections, it points to the strong interlinkages between the general development of community value orientation in international law and the historical antecedents of what later became the climate change regime. Moreover, it establishes the background of climate change as a matter of (community) values.

Part D ("Structural and Conceptual Analysis of the International Climate Regime Since 1992") is the largest part of the thesis and entails its main analysis. It first analyzes the overall structure of modern international climate change law and the overall shift indicating a 'decline' of international law through a trend of informalisation, compared to the 1990s strong and combined emphasis on multilateralism, legal bindingness and value-underpinning. Then, Part D analyzes concrete community value-related norm concepts of the climate regime. As this section will show, the legal status and role of such norm concepts in the political and legal process remains contentious. Finally, the structural and conceptual perspectives will be complemented by an analysis of the prospects of adjudication fostering the implementation of community values by legal means.

This includes both recent trends in climate litigation on the national and regional level as well the internationally.

Part E ("Conclusion") draws the previous results together. Having established in how far different elements of community values and international law are 'on the rise' or 'in decline', possible conceptual and practical responses are outlined.

Part B: Community Values and Legality in International Law

"The rise and recognition of community interests is one thing,
their impact on the real world quite another."
Bruno Simma[46]

I. From State Interests to Community Values?

Concepts like the 'international community' and how its interests or values evolve, as well as theoretical reflections on their role in and influence on international law, have occupied legal scholars for many years. Their debates and disagreements have not only been reflections of international law's actual developments during the respective periods, but also important reference points for what further progress of the international legal system could resemble.

Whether values or any kind of moral or ethical considerations beyond the realm of positive legal rules have any role to play in the international legal order has been a contentious matter for decades. In many of the recent scholarly debates, however, those arguing in favor of value orientation and community thinking give the impression that the idea of value promotion through law is specific or even exclusive to post-Cold War international legal thinking and the 'progressive' developments in legal scholarship.[47] In reaction to that, scholars defending the 'classical' perspectives on international law fall into the same trap, making the argument about whether values should play a role in international law or not.[48]

In opposition to both perspectives, the present author shares the assumption, with authors like Henkin, that basically every legal system, be it national,

46 Bruno Simma, "From Bilateralism to Community Interest in International Law", in *Recueil des Cours*, ed. Académie de Droit International (Martinus Nijhoff, 1994)p. 247.

47 Dire Tladi, "South African Lawyers, Values and New Vision of International Law: The Road to Perdition Is Paved with the Pursuit of Laudable Goals", *S. Afr. YB Int'l L.* 33 (2008), p. 167.

48 d'Aspremont, "The foundations of the international legal order", p. 219 et seqq.

regional or international, rests on some basic values which are promoted by legal rules and, furthermore, that no legal system can ever be entirely value agnostic.[49] Moreover, the 'classical' or bilateralist inter-state system can and does already serve many common interests of all States. For instance, by providing peaceful dispute settlement mechanisms and thus helping avoid widespread conflicts. It has also legitimately been suggested that 'classical' international law can serve the common good without explicit community or value orientation.[50] These presumptions are not contradicted by this study. Hence, the debate about community values is not about the presence or absence of values *per se*. It is rather a question about the changing prioritization of different sets of values and in how far such changes materialize in legal norms.

This section will delineate the theoretical and practical challenges connected to the role values play in international law (1.) as well as the notion of an international community (2.). The focus will be on the inherent tensions of both values and community-thinking with the classical or bilateralist structures of international law. An interim conclusion (3.) will bring both together and clarify the author's position on community values in international law for the subsequent analysis.

1. The Notion and Role of Values in International Law

(a) Values and Interests: A Distinction

First, it is important to illustrate how the terms *values* and *interests* are interpreted in this study. The 'Oxford dictionary' defines values as "Principles or standards of behaviour" as well as "one's judgement of what is important in life".[51] The Cambridge dictionary suggests defining values as "the principles that help you to

49 As in, for instance, Louis Henkin, *International law: Politics and values* (Nijhoff, 1995) p. 102 et seq. naming the maintenance of peace as the principle purpose of international law and discussing similarities between the values promoted by international and national laws, such as the protection of persons and property and, to a limited extent, the promotion of justice.

50 Interesting in this regard is the critique of a value oriented legal order by d'Aspremont, "The foundations of the international legal order", although his dichotomous notions of 'objective' values and 'subjective' interests are not shared by the present author, given the inter-subjective nature of values.

51 'Value' in *Oxford English dictionary*, available at: https://en.oxforddictionaries.com/definition/value .

decide what is right and wrong, and how to act in various situations".[52] In opposition, interests are defined as "the advantage or benefit of a person or group"[53] (Oxford) and as "something that brings advantages to or affects someone or something"[54] (Cambridge). In contemporary philosophy, a concise definition of values describes them as "highly emotional ideas about what is really worth wishing for."[55] In social science, values are often understood as "deeply rooted motivations or orientations guiding or explaining certain attitudes, norms, and opinions which, in turn, direct human action or at least part of it".[56] Political values, in this vain, are understood as perceptions of a desirable order and determining of how a political situation or event should be evaluated.[57]

While not authoritative in defining either interests or values when used in any legal source, the definitions offered point to a conceptual difference that informs their understanding in this study: The key difference between values and interests, as understood here, is both the normative substance of the concepts as well as the conceptual scope regarding their validity. The notion of interest includes an understanding that they are inherently different among different actors. They can be objectified and, on the whole, be measured materially. Values, on the other hand, have at least a universal ambition in their validity. They are rather (inter-) subjective in nature and the result of either ethical or moral considerations. For the matter at hand, this differentiation is key as it points to the underlying structure of the phenomena this study is dealing with. Rather than the *balancing* of interests, discussing values in international law means to engage with normatively charged extra-legal considerations. The complicated relationship between values and positive law is what this study focusses on in analysing the field of climate change law.

---

52 'Values' in *Cambridge English dictionary*, available at https://dictionary.cambridge.org/dictionary/english/values.

53 'Interest' in *Oxford English dictionary*, available at https://en.oxforddictionaries.com/definition/interest.

54 'Interests' in *Cambridge English Dictionary*, available at https://dictionary.cambridge.org/dictionary/english/interest?q=interests.

55 Hans Joas, "Die kulturellen Werte Europas – Eine Einleitung", in *Die kulturellen Werte Europas*, ed. Hans Joas and Klaus Wiegandt (Fischer Taschenbuch Verlag, 2005) p. 24 et seq. (translation by the author).

56 Loek Halman, "Political Values", in *The Oxford handbook of political behavior*, ed. Russell J. Dalton and Hans-Dieter Klingemann (Oxford University Press, 2007), p. 309.

57 Ibid., p. 309 et seq.

(b) *Classical or 'Bilateralist' International Law and Its Relation to Values*

Any inquiry about the influence of values in international law after 1990 should start against the backdrop of how the 'classical' structures of international law came into being and what their relationship to values is. The question about the relationship between legal rules and their underlying values has been a subject of discussion in international law as a legal system throughout its development. In the pre-Westphalian era, scholars like Thomas of Aquin, with his concept of a just war[58], Francisco de Vitoria[59] and, later, Hugo Grotius[60], wrote on the moral principles and values that would need to underlie any substantial international order.[61] Most of these early writings were based on the idea of a natural, God-given law, which would make it possible to derive universal rules of general validity.[62]

A key element of the post-Westphalian order was a fundamental shift in the organization of international relations from a hierarchical order based on the recognition of (primarily Christian European) authorities above the States to a "horizontal system characterized by the coexistence of a multiplicity of territorially defined autonomous entities and sustained by a new type of law operating between rather than above the members of the system."[63]

With this shift towards a more horizontal and diverse order, the question whether there is, or should be, any definitive value system faded into the

58 St. Thomas Aquinas, *St. Thomas Aquinas: Political writings*, ed. R.W. Dyson, Cambridge Texts in the History of Political Thought ed. (Cambridge University Press, 2002), p. 239 et seqq.

59 Francisco De Vitoria, *Vitoria: Political writings* ed. Anthony Pagden and Jeremy Lawrence, Cambridge Texts in the History of Political Thought ed. (Cambridge University Press, 1991), especially p. 163 et seqq. with a translation of Vitoria's *Scripta Teologica* I.-II.91 on the varieties of law; See also p. 10 et seqq. with a translation of Vitoria's *On civil power, § 6–7.*

60 Hugo Grotius, *De Jure Belli Ac Pacis Libri Tres*, ed. James Brown Scott, trans. Francis W. Kelsey, The Classics of International Law: Grotius, Vol. 2 ed. (William S. Hein & Co., 1995), especially Book I, chapter II on the lawful reasons for war (pp. 51–90) and chapter XXV on causes of undertaking war on behalf of others (pp. 578–586).

61 Alexander Orakhelashvili, "Natural Law and Justice", in *MPEPIL*, ed. Rüdiger Wolfrum (Oxford University Press, 2007), para. 7 et seq.

62 Ibid., para. 5.

63 Rainer Grote, "Westphalian System", in *Max Planck Encyclopedia of Public International Law [MPEPIL]*, ed. Rüdiger Wolfrum (Oxford University Press, 2006), para. 1.

background of scholarly debates. The emerging order was demarcated for being rather value-free and driven by the economic interests of influential actors.[64] It was not until the late 19th and early 20th century, that a wide range of views were put forward as to how the relationship between international law and values should be conceived.

One view, prominent in the first half of the 20th century, proposed a rationalist naturalism and understood morality as natural justice that always remains in the background of the positive legal order. Morality's importance remained central even if only subconsciously filling gaps and directing legal development towards an enlightened individualism.[65]

Further scholars have dismissed the understanding that there is any role for values or morality to play in modern international law. Legal positivist's focused on the Kantian differentiation between obligations deriving from the realm of *moral* 'ought' and those obligations stemming from the realm of *legal* 'ought'. With this separation of morality and law, Kant aimed to avoid an understanding of law where individual moral intuitions could replace a formal approach to legality.[66] Insisting on the categorical separation of the two, the legal positivist view holds that the diverging values advocated in international relations can only be of a relative, subjective nature, hence, excluding any possibility for universalized and objective notions of values or justice.[67] Other scholars dismissed the idea that an international legal order could effectively constrain national sovereigns. They dismissed this notion as fictious and unrealistic, thereby also excluding any role for values in such a legal order.[68]

---

64 Andreas L. Paulus, "International Community", in *Max Planck Encyclopedia of Public International Law [MPEPIL]*, ed. Rüdiger Wolfrum (Oxford University Press, 2013), para. 9 et seqq.

65 Hersch Lauterpacht, *International law: Being the collected papers of Hersch Lauterpacht. International law in general*, ed. Elihu Lauterpacht, vol. 2 (Cambridge University Press, 1975), p. 425 et seqq., developing a critique of Kelsen's rejection of natural law.

66 Jochen von Bernstorff and Ingo Venzke, "Ethos, Ethics, and Morality in International Relations", in *Max Planck Encyclopedia of Public International Law [MPEPIL]*, ed. Rüdiger Wolfrum (Oxford University Press, 2011), para. 5.

67 Hans Kelsen and John H. Herz, "Essential Conditions of International Justice ", *Proceedings of the American Society of International Law at Its Annual Meeting (1921–1969)* 35 (1941), p. 71 et seq.

68 Martti Koskenniemi, *The gentle civilizer of nations: The rise and fall of international law; 1870–1960* (Cambridge University Press, 2007) p. 249 et seqq. and 432 et seqq. on early perspectives related to later 'realist' perspectives.

In the UN Charter-era, policy-oriented perspectives on international law suggested that the law's function on the international level is to identify and ensure the realization of certain values, rather than the restraint of behavior.[69] According human dignity as a core value, this perspective sees as a key task for international lawyers "to invent and recommend the authority structures and functions (principles and procedures) necessary to a world public order that harmonizes with the growing aspirations of the over-whelming numbers of the peoples of the globe and is in accord with the pro-claimed values of human dignity enunciated by the moral leaders of mankind."[70]

An intermediary view put forward in the late 20th century suggests that the inter-state system of international law is already far from being value agnostic. As promoted by the classical international law of the inter-state system, the basic "state values"[71] are state *independence*, state *equality* and state *autonomy*, the latter comprising state *impermeability* and a state's commitment to its *national interest.* State equality, understood as the equality of status as well as of rights and duties, is indeed an axiom of the inter-state system of international law. Understood this way, international law promotes the interests that all States have in common and accommodates competing interests even-handedly.[72] State autonomy means here that international law recognizes and promotes the States' authority to make their decisions without constraints or limitations by others. The exception to this is international law itself as it is a system of constraint that States have consented to.[73]

---

69 Richard A. Falk, *Status of law in international society* (Princeton University Press, 1970), p. 14.

70 Myres S. McDougal and Harold D. Lasswell, "The Identification and Appraisal of Diverse Systems of Public Order", *American Journal of International Law* 53, no. 1 (1959), p. 28.

71 Henkin discusses the idea of "state values" in juxtaposition with "human values". The two, he holds, are not necessarily in opposition. Rather they are different, calling for differentiated analysis, emphasis and priorities. See Henkin, *International law: Politics and values*, p. 99.

72 Ibid., p. 100.

73 Ibid.; see also section III. on the state consent-based structures of the sources and law-making of international law.

(c) A Turn to a Value-Based International Order in the Post-Cold War Era?

As alluded to in Part A, many scholars in 'globalist', 'internationalist' or 'progressive' traditions evaluate the time shortly after the Cold War and the developments in the international legal system as a move towards a more value-based and value-oriented legal order.[74] Even views sceptical of such developments, where concern is directed towards a broad reading of the 'new international law', recognized a turn towards "value-based international law".[75]

A concise account from such a value-oriented perspective has recently been given by a member of the International Court of Justice. Looking back on the developments during the 1990s and early 2000s, Judge Cançado Trindade expressed that, "the growing consciousness of the need to bear in mind common values in pursuance of common interests has brought about a fundamental change in the outlook of international law in the last decade."[76] This fundamental change he sees evidenced in "the growth of entire areas of International Law wholly devoted to the safeguard of human beings" and "by the invocation of humankind in multiple international treaties and instruments in distinct areas of International Law". Among the fields of international law most prominently cited as reference points for such a value-based or value-oriented order are international environmental and climate law. For instance, when Judge Trindade describes the value-oriented 'International Law of Humankind"[77] he aspires towards, two of the main examples for its "Conceptual Constructions" have a strong linkage to international climate change law: These are namely, the concept of "common heritage of mankind" and secondly, that of "common concern of mankind".[78]

Further examples quoted in this perspective are international tribunals considering the concerns of individual human beings and humankind as well as the practice of States and international organizations "bearing witness of the needs

74 See already Part A, III.

75 Tladi, "South African lawyers, values and new vision of international law: The road to perdition is paved with the pursuit of laudable goals", p. 167.

76 Antônio Augusto Cançado Trindade, *International law for humankind – Towards a new Jus Gentium*, ed. The Hague Academy of International Law (Martinus Nijhoff Publishers, 2010), p. 4.

77 Ibid., p. 289 et seqq.

78 Ibid., p. 327 et seqq.; The connection of international climate change law to value-considerations will be discussed more extensively in Part C.

and aspirations of human beings, of peoples, and of humankind as a whole". The status quo of international law, which allows injustices and is "unable to provide answers to the pressing needs of protection to whole segments of the world population", Judge Trindade argues, is "incompatible with the very conception of an international community, which assumes the existence of common and superior interests, and of duties incumbent up-on all, – States, international organizations, peoples, and human beings".[79]

As far as the view put forward by scholars like Judge Trindade suggested fundamental changes in the international legal order, so too did it attract fundamental criticism. A saying accorded to 19th century French sociologist and anarchist politician Pierre-Joseph Proudhon, says "whoever invokes humanity wants to cheat".[80] This saying became much-cited by early 'realists' to modern critical scholars of international law. Internationalist ambitions in international politics and law in the early 20th century, especially in the inter-war period, have attracted far reaching criticisms. Likewise, so too did the enthusiasm for a supposed juridification of values in the 1990s. These criticisms of the notion of an international legal system being underpinned by universalized values can be differentiated between three main aspects.

One view challenges the definition of universalized values including the question of *who* can define them. This critique has two focal points: The first is the argument of values being necessarily culturally contingent. It suggests that the idea itself of analyzing international law through a lens of values is an inherently western concept incompatible with traditions from other cultural backgrounds.[81] In this vein, some authors reject any notion of community values, criticizing hegemonic or imperialistic behavior of mostly western States in international law and international relations.[82] This concerns both the theory and practice of international law.[83] The second and related, but slightly different focal

79 Ibid.

80 M. Koskenniemi, "International Law in Europe: Between Tradition and Renewal", *European Journal of International Law* 16, no. 1 (2005), p. 116 and 117 et seq. on the different application of the thought expressed by Proudhon in the respective scholarly traditions.

81 Jean d'Aspremont, "International Law in Asia: The Limits to the Western Constitutionalist and Liberal Doctrines", *Asian Yearbook of International Law* 13 (2007), p. 28.

82 Exemplarily, see B.S. Chimni, "International Institutions Today: An Imperial Global State in the Making", *EJIL* 15, no. 1 (2004), p. 1 et seqq.

83 d'Aspremont, "International Law in Asia: The Limits to the Western Constitutionalist and Liberal Doctrines", p. 27 et seqq.

point is the critique of which values are being implemented in international legal norms and the asserted western dominance in determining them.[84]

The second view focusses its criticism more on the contentious question of who is entitled to and responsible for the implementation and realization of universalized values. This includes the controversial relationship between values and, mostly western, unilateralism in international law and relations.[85] Located at the conjunction between the idea of universal values and unilateralizm is another notable line of criticism towards universal values. If an aspired universalism of values is to coincide with the unilateralisation of their realization, many scholars have criticized the potentially destabilizing effect for the legal order.[86] Others have focused their criticism on the arbitrariness in the selection of situations where values are protected or not. For instance, where the interests of great powers are concerned or not.[87]

A third angle of criticism, which is related to both views previously discussed, is rather legalistic. It criticizes the overdue influence of extra-legal considerations on what should, in this view, be a more technical and positivist international legal system.[88]

(d) Values' Need for Compatibility with Existing Legal Structures

The role of values in international law remains a controversial issue. The aforementioned perspectives have all contributed to establishing the essential components for a suitable understanding of this field. According to the view put forward here, their arguments can be assessed as follows.

---

84 See for instance, on the 'traditional values debate' in the Human Rights Council, Christopher McCrudden, "Human Rights and Traditional Values", in *Law's ethical, global and theoretical contexts: Essays in honour of William Twining*, ed. Abdul Paliwala, Christopher McCrudden, and Upendra Baxi (Cambridge University Press, 2015), p. 40 et seqq.

85 Charles E. Ziegler, "Contesting the Responsibility to Protect", *International Studies Perspectives* 17, no. 1 (2016), p. 83 et seqq. with a concise description of criticism towards the implementation of value-laden concepts like the R to P from sovereignty-oriented and non-western countries like Russia.

86 On this conflict in scholarship and practice, see Emmanuelle Jouannet, "Universalism and Imperialism: The True-False Paradox of International Law?", *European Journal of International Law* 18, no. 3 (2007), especially p. 385 et seq. with further reference.

87 Again, the debates surrounding the Responsibility to Protect are a case in point, see Ziegler, "Contesting the Responsibility to Protect", p. 93 et seqq.

88 E.g. d'Aspremont, "The foundations of the international legal order", p. 36 et seq.

Realist perspectives raise important and legitimate concerns regarding the role of power and interests in international politics. Yet, the perspective contesting the very idea of values in law is not compatible with the understandings put forward here. Realists tend to overstate the dimension of conflict between different entities in international law and international relations.[89] Moreover, they have little to contribute in offering solutions for the underlying moral dimension that is connected to any legal system.

Legal positivist perspectives insisting that there be no value considerations have difficulties in responding to the embeddedness of legal practices in social ones, a concept that constructivist perspectives have insisted on. Moreover, for the question at hand, they do not sufficiently account for the dependency of legal systems on their key actor's continuing acceptance, and thus, the influence of power and conflict which realists insist on.

Views emphasizing that (international) law never operates in a vacuum free from moral or ethical considerations make an important point. To be explicit, moral and ethical considerations are always in the background of legal practices, influencing the acceptance of legal norms and informing their implementation. On the other hand, the 'globalist', 'cosmopolitan' or 'progressive' spectrum underestimates the conflict potential connected to the notion of values. This was especially noteworthy after 1990. They downplay the challenges connected to an increased role of values in the international legal order in relying too much on the validity of the proposed values by virtue of their inherent quality.

Modern critical scholarship offers an interesting contribution. Namely, how to cope with the potential dominance of one cultural perspective in norm-setting processes. This contribution is especially seen in the branch of scholarship criticizing the dominance of western-liberal ideas after 1990 in both defining and the implementation of values.

Mirroring this problem of subjectivity in the definition of values, further tensions surround the question of who is allowed and supposed to ensure the realization of values. Herein lies a contentious connection between universalism and unilateralism: If any given value is understood as universal or even non-derogable, it appears inherently logical that their protection or realization cannot be left to actors who might object them, nor to procedures that may grant the right to object or halt any action. The most salient is blatant human rights violations (i.e., genocide) and the question whether the UN Security Council takes action or not. The position that it is unjustifiable for the international community *not* to act to prevent blatant human

89 Similarly, Andrew Hurrell, *On global order: Power, values, and the constitution of international society* (Oxford University Press, 2007), p. 39.

rights violations, irrespective of the decision of the Council or the positions leading to it, is at the root of concepts like 'humanitarian intervention'. This position also relates in part to the 'Responsibility to Protect': If a certain threshold of human suffering is reached, the procedures that aim to balance conflicting values and interests can be abandoned in favor of the supposed realization of human rights. The problem with this ambition – however well-intentioned it may be – is its conflict with existing law which also protects important values like legal certainty and the reliability of legal procedures. As Andrew Hurrell has put it, "*in an international society characterized by deep and fundamental value conflict and by the constant difficulty of managing unequal power, a viable and stable international legal order must be built around shared processes and procedures, accepted understandings of legal sources, and a commitment to diplomatic negotiation and dialogue.*"[90] This argument points to a necessary caution in including value considerations into international legal processes.

Relatedly, the systemic argument warning against the danger of destabilizing international law through universalist aspiration of values and the unilateralisation of their realization deserves special notice. It points to the arguably central problem of the notion of universal values taken seriously. Where any universal value is taken absolute, it is rendered incommensurable with a legal order balancing different values.

Summarizing these arguments, it becomes apparent that if any notion of values has potential to be accepted in international relations and international law, it must be one that is rooted in a differentiated, deliberative process that refrains from unilateralising their realization. For such a notion of values, it is key to ensure a sufficient level of differentiation and state consent. At a political level, various non-state actors can conceivably contribute to the definition of the values to be protected by international law. But their entry into the legal realm needs to be compatible with existing legal structures, including the key role of State consent in providing legitimacy. Values as such are, and can be, guiding in setting and applying legal norms. Where they are implemented into law, they need to be appropriately translated into legal language to ensure the functioning and applicability of the resulting legal norms.

2. An 'International Community'?

The 'international community', and the function of international law within it, have been key elements of international law scholarship since the late 1920s and early

90 Ibid., p. 312 et seq.

1930s.[91] Yet, the notion of the 'international community' gained particular traction in the 1990s. Fueled by the historical situation after the end of the Cold War, there was a notable increase in the attention and political influence given to lines of reasoning which advocated for the advancement of an international community. Much of this attention and influence has come under pressure and has since been relativized. Nevertheless, the conceptual significance for the matter at hand remains, namely, informing the way community values can be conceived.

Every concept and theory of international law is grounded in a certain understanding of the social structure international law applies to. Hence, and decisively for the matter at hand, every theory of international law involves an understanding of what an international 'community' or 'society' looks like and what actors it consists of. At the same time – and as indicated by the discussion of the notion of values in international law – these foundational understandings are not of an exclusively legal character.[92]

(a) Conceptual Arguments for the Existence of an International Community: Liberal Cosmopolitanism, Institutionalism, Constitutionalism

> *"The international community does exist. It has an address. It has achievements to its credit. And it is the only way forward."*
>
> *UN Secretary General Kofi Annan*[93]

International law, as traditionally conceived, was primarily an instrument for States to settle inter-state disputes. The peace of Westphalia in 1648 historically accounts for the starting point of modern international law in spite of rightfully made reservations about the euro-centricity of this description.[94] Throughout the

---

91 See Lauterpacht, *Collected Papers of Hersch Lauterpacht*, 2, p. 26 et seq.; For an historical account of the perspectives dominant at the time, see Martti Koskenniemi, "Lauterpacht: The Victorian Tradition in International Law", *European Journal of International Law* 8, no. 2 (1997), p. 224 et seqq.

92 Paulus, "International Community", para. 16.

93 Secretary- General examines 'Meaning of International Community' in address to DPI/NGO Conference," Press Release SG/SM/7133, PI/1176 (15 September 1999), available at https://www.un.org/press/en/1999/19990915.sgsm7133.doc.html.

94 See e.g. Martti Koskenniemi, "Histories of International Law: Dealing with Eurocentrism", *Rechtsgeschichte Legal History – Zeitschrift des Max-Planck-Instituts für europäische Rechtsgeschichte*, no. 19 (2011), especially at 174 et seq., suggesting to

post-World War II legal system based on the Charter of the United Nations, the founding pillars of the international order have largely remained the same: The sovereignty and independence of States, the principle of non-intervention – later the prohibition of the use of force – flanked by some rules implementing these principles.[95] This framework was intended to fulfill multiple objectives including, building an order based on the freedom of States to pursue their interests, regulating their interaction with each other and offering mechanisms of *peaceful* settlement, when possible, where disputes arose. When the UN was founded, a much more intricate system of cooperation was developed, but its foundations and basic principles remained the same. The central feature of this order was – and remains until today – the state itself. Despite being more a matter of historic fact than of normative conception, the state proved to be the most stable entity available in international relations.

A significant strand in international relations scholarship conceived this international system under the UN Charter as an 'international society'. For them, this international society consisted of States forming their interests and interacting in societal structures without necessarily forming significant subjective cohesion.[96] Important for the matter at hand is that this scholarship recognizes the material interests of States as their main driving force while holding that societal structures between States are nonetheless possible. In such an international society, States organize their coexistence and sometimes cooperation, form norm-governed relationships and accept that they have at least limited responsibilities towards one another and society as a whole.[97] States thus follow their interests, but not at all costs. The accommodation of diversity and pluralism among States remains key in more recent variations to this line of thinking.[98] The role of international law, in this view, is to organize these processes.

During the second half of the 20th century, community-oriented perspectives gained significant traction in international law scholarship. One strand of research aimed at identifying structures that transcend the classical realm of

---

'provincialize' international law, i.e. to contextualize it regarding its anthropological roots without any ambition to de-legitimize it.

95 Wolfgang Preiser, "History of International Law, Basic Questions and Principles", in *MPEPIL*, ed. Rüdiger Wolfrum (Oxford University Press, 2007), para. 3 et seqq.

96 Barry Buzan, *An introduction to the English school of international relations: The societal approach* (Polity, 2014); Timothy Dunne, "The Social Construction of International Society", *European Journal of International Relations* 1, no. 3 (1995).

97 Chris Brown, Kirsten Ainley, and Chris Brown, *Understanding international relations* (Palgrave Macmillan, 2009), pp. 48–52.

98 Hurrell, *On global order*, p. 28 et seq.

(nation-) States. Influenced by scholars like R.-J. Dupuy[99], the concept of the 'international community' became a main object of focus. Drawing on sociologists like Ferdinand Tönnies or Max Weber, some suggested a possible distinction between a 'society' and a 'community': While the former is based on a rather formal set of rules and procedures, the latter typically is founded in a broader set of norms and values and has higher group cohesion than a 'mere' society.[100] Distinct from the largely functional understanding of the international *society* theories, interpretations were now put forward that added a certain level of cohesion, solidarity and a pursuit of common interest to the concept of the 'international community'.[101] Similarly, suggestions were put forward to include a broader notion of which actors should be comprised by the term 'international community'. It was suggested that international law has "entered a stage at which it does not exhaust itself in correlative rights and obligations running between States, but also incorporates common interests of the international community as a whole, including not only States but all human beings."[102]

One of the original ideas was that of an international *legal* community.[103] This view was promoted especially by those who subscribed early to the idea that international law contains a community aspect. Foreshadowing some aspects of the aforementioned perspectives on an international *society*, this view assumes that it is international law itself that binds parts of the community together, confirms the existence of a community of States and serves as its normative grounding. In this concept, the community exists only under international law and only comprises the States.[104]

---

99 René-Jean Dupuy, *La Communauté internationale entre le mythe et l'histoire* (Economica, 1986).

100 Paulus, *Die internationale Gemeinschaft im Völkerrecht*, p. 10 et seqq. with further reference.

101 Gleider I. Hernández, "A Reluctant Guardian: The International Court of Justice and the Concept of 'international community'", *British yearbook of international law.* 83, no. 1 (2013) p. 8 et seq.

102 Simma, "Universality of International Law from the Perspective of a Practitioner", p. 268.

103 Hermann Mosler, "The International Society as a Legal Community", in *Recueil des Cours*, ed. Académie de Droit International (A. W. Sijthoff, Leyde 1974)p. 1 et seqq.

104 Ibid., p. 32; Alfred Verdross, *Die Verfassung der Völkerrechtsgemeinschaft* (J. Springer, 1926), preface p. V.; criticising this definition as circular: Simma, "From bilateralism to community interest ", p. 245.

The use of the very term 'international community', however, was not new when scholars picked up on it in the late 1970s and 1990s. It entered the sphere of positive international law when the 1969 Vienna Convention on the Law of Treaties[105], in its Art. 53 on *jus cogens*, mentions the 'international community *of* States'.[106] This traditional use of the term 'community' at the international level was understood to describe the sum of sovereign States that constitute it.[107] The use of this terminology by important international actors shifted towards the term 'international community as a whole', yet this shift in terminology was done without the provision of transparent motivations. This wording has been used by the International Court of Justice (ICJ) since its *Barcelona Traction* Judgment in 1970.[108] Later, the International Law Commission's Articles on state responsibility also used the same terminology.[109] In lack of any authoritative definition of what the international community is, along the lines of the two formulations would run an important division between a States-only notion of the international community and one that would include also non-state actors.

Views as to how an international *community* comes into being and forms its interests and values vary significantly. Moreover, the shift towards community thinking during the last twenty years of the 20th century, especially after the end of the Cold War, is based in different lines of reasoning. The boundaries between them are often blurred. But for better legibility, they can be grouped in institutionalist or functionalist perspectives on the one hand, and liberal cosmopolitan perspectives on the other. At their intersection, constitutionalist

105 United Nations Treaty Series, vol. 1155, p. 331.

106 Emphasis added.

107 Cf. Hernández, "A reluctant guardian", p. 7 et seq.

108 *Barcelona Traction, Light and Power Company Limited* (Belgium v. Spain) (New Application, 1962), Judgment, Merits, Second Phase, I.C.J. Rep. 1970, p. 3 [hereinafter *Barcelona Traction*], para. 31.

109 The ILC commented on this difference, stating: "As a matter of terminology, it is sufficient to use the phrase 'international community as a whole' rather than 'international community of States as a whole', which is used in the specific context of article 53 of the 1969 Vienna Convention. The insertion of the words "of States" in article 53 of the Convention was intended to stress the paramountcy that States have over the making of international law, including especially the establishment of norms of a peremptory character. On the other hand, the ICJ used the phrase "international community as a whole" in the Barcelona Traction case, and it is frequently used in treaties and other international instruments in the same sense as in paragraph 1(b)", see International Law Commission, "Draft Articles on State Responsibilities – with commentaries", *Yearbook of the International Law Commission* 2, no. 2 (2001), p. 84 (Art. 25, para. 18).

perspectives on international law and relations draw on the theme of the international community.

(aa) Institutionalist Reasoning

One view of institutionalist reasoning holds that the establishment of international organizations and institutions during the second half of the 20th century is the most tangible sign that there was a shift away from an international society towards an international community dealing with matters exceeding the limits of national borders.[110] This is often connected to the insight that decisions made by international bodies have an increasingly direct influence on individuals, companies and domestic societies in general.[111] With substantial decision-making powers shifting from the national to the international level in areas like international economic law, international environmental law and international human rights law, scholars have argued for an understanding of international relations and law that would include these different actors and the implications international law had on them to enhance the legitimacy of their decisions.[112]

Other scholars took this notion of a community beyond the Stats further and argued for making humanity itself the point of reference for international law.[113] Others saw the international society at a point of "recognizing itself as a society in which the state-societies are agents and instruments of the survival and prospering of the human race".[114] In a further variation of this view, it is held that moral as well as legal progress can be made through the extension of law, and thus further institutionalization and legalization of the international community.[115]

---

110 Inis L. Claude, *Swords into plowshares: The problems and progress of international organization*, 4th ed. (Random House, 1971), p. 447 et seq.

111 Tetsuo Sato, "Legitimacy of International Organizations and their Decisions: Challenges that International Organizations Face in the 21st Century", *Hitotsubashi journal of law and politics* 37 (2010), p. 16.

112 See for example Ruti G. Teitel, *Humanity's law* (Oxford University Press, 2011), See also Sato, "Legitimacy of International Organizations and their Decisions", who draws the line from here to the legitimacy, transparency and accountability discourses in international law.

113 Dupuy, *La Communauté internationale entre le mythe et l'histoire*, p. 180.

114 Philip Allott, *Eunomia: New order for a new world* (Oxford University Press, 1990), p. 328.

115 Robert O. Keohane, "Twenty Years of Institutional Liberalism", *International Relations* 26, no. 2 (2012), p. 128 et seq.

Related perspectives from international relations scholarship emphasize the interdependence between institution-building and the self-understanding of the participating actors, suggesting that "[t]he process of creating institutions is one of internalizing new understandings of self and other, of acquiring new role identities, not just of creating external constraints on the behaviour of exogenously constituted actors."[116] This would potentially transform an interdependence of outcomes into a interdependence of collective interest organized around norms. These norms are tied to actors' commitments to their identities and interests, which would therefore be more resistant to change.[117]

A comprehensive analysis done in the mid-1990s noted that "the quest to realize community interests' has led to an ever-stronger 'institutionalization, or organization, of international society".[118] This view also advocates a move from a rather 'minimal law' to a more substantial framework. Nevertheless, it holds that the classical bilateral international law remains the conceptual basis of the international order.[119] Starting from a supposed 'value poverty' of 'bilateralist' international law, it delivers a first 'tentative definition of community interests', which

> *"could perceive it [community interest(s)] as a consensus according to which respect for certain fundamental values is not to be left to the free disposition of States individually or inter se but is recognized and sanctioned by international law as a matter of concern to all States."*[120]

In this view, the "identification of community interests does not derive from scientific abstraction but rather flows from the recognition of concrete problems".[121] This means a demarcation from the idea that community interests would be identified through broad meta theories and then merely transferred to practice. While this conception still seems to highlight a certain objective dimension in the identification of community interests, it is important to note a related, but slightly different perspective.

This perspective, while aligned with Simma's assumptions and research perspective, has emphasized the subjective-normative dimension of the phenomenon at hand, preferring therefore the term 'community *values*' over 'community

---

116 Alexander Wendt, "Anarchy Is What States Make of It: The Social Construction of Power Politics", *International Organization* 46, no. 02 (1992), p. 417.

117 Ibid.

118 , p. 235.

119 Ibid., p. 229.

120 Ibid., p. 233.

121 Ibid., p. 235.

interests'.[122] This new terminology was intended to highlight the deliberative process behind the normative visions in question. This subjective-normative dimension is distinguished from objective or objectifiable material interests that are separate from any normative notion. This view also maintains that there is a distinction between an international 'society' and an international 'community' along the lines of the idea of 'subjective cohesion'.[123] This increased level of subjective cohesion further defines the international community as separate from a society. It is important to note that in this perspective, the notion of community values does not mean to introduce a set of "pre-ordained values".[124] Additionally, the law of the international 'community' is not meant to replace the consent-based law of the international 'society', but to reasonably supplement it.[125]

(bb) Liberal-Cosmopolitan Reasoning

Another conceptual angle is that of liberal-cosmopolitan reasoning. This view is rather normative and often connected to ethical reasoning. Based on the idea that all human beings share certain basic aspects of human nature (i.e., mortality or rationality)[126] or on other ethical concepts[127], it has been argued that a global, universalist ethic is possible. In this logic, international law would often assume the function of ensuring that such universal ethical principles are not endangered by political ends other than those desired such as the interests of humanity and its representation on the international level. In this line of reasoning resonates a long-standing tradition in (European) international legal thinking, specifically, the ambition to pursue a "human world order" as argued by 19th century scholars like J.C. Bluntschili.[128] This line of reason also encapsulated the

---

122 Paulus, *Die internationale Gemeinschaft im Völkerrecht*, p. 250.

123 Paulus relates this distinction to the work of German sociologist Ferdinand Tönnies' *Gemeinschaft und Gesellschaft* (1887) (8th edn Buske, Leipzig, 1935), see ibid. p. 10 et seqq., p. 439 et seq. for an English summary.

124 "Reciprocity revisited", in *From bilateralism to community interest essays in honour of Bruno Simma*, ed. Ulrich Fastenrath and Bruno Simma (Oxford University Press, 2011)p. 125.

125 *Die internationale Gemeinschaft im Völkerrecht*, p. 431.

126 Michael J. Perry, "Are Human Rights Universal? The Relativist Challenge and Related Matters", *Human Rights Quarterly* 19, no. 3 (1997), p. 481; cf. also Payandeh, *Internationales Gemeinschaftsrecht*, p. 87, discussing related perspectives with further references.

127 Seyla Benhabib, "In Defense of Universalism: Yet Again! A Response to Critics of Situating the Self", *New German Critique* 62 (1994).

128 See Koskenniemi, *The gentle civilizer of nations*, p. 53.

desire to eliminate any arbitrariness of the state in following or rejecting international law.[129] Modern variations of these approaches argue for internationalized or globalized versions of justice[130], the distribution of resources and goods[131] and/or the protection of human rights independent from the will of States.[132]

Still others take liberal-cosmopolitan perspectives and the focus on the international community and international law as a guardian of individual rights even further, developing a strong "anti-étatist impulse".[133] Here, the State is – at least partially – perceived as an obstacle to the fulfillment of individual rights and the concerns of the international community. With concepts reducing or redefining state sovereignty, the solution for overcoming this obstacle is by giving the international community more influence in protecting the individual against the will of the State.

Liberal conceptions see any community based on some sort of contract (either factual or imaginary)[134] or on social practice[135] respectively. A common denominator between many of the theoretical approaches focusing on the international community is that the community has its own existence. This existence is based on the community's goals and functions[136] and plays a key role in the self-conception of its members. Essentially, the assumed "community" then in turn shapes how the members, both State and non-State actors, develop their own self-conception vis-à-vis both the community and the other members individually. Also transferred to the international realm, liberal conceptions differ in the emphasis they place on the significance of the 'community'.

---

129 Ibid., p. 50.

130 Thomas Pogge, *Realizing rawls* (Cornell University Press, 1989).

131 Brian Barry, "Statism and Nationalism: A Cosmopolitan Critique", *Global Justice* 41 (1999).

132 Teitel, *Humanity's law*, see also the discussion regarding the Responsibility to Protect, cf. Carsten Stahn, "Responsibility to Protect: Political Rhetoric or Emerging Legal Norm?", *AJIL* 101, no. 1 (2007).

133 Christian Tams, "The 'International Community' as a Legal Concept", in *Fundamental concepts of international law*, ed. Jean D'Aspremont and Sahib Singh (Edward Elgar, Forthcoming (Available at SSRN: https://ssrn.com/abstract=3086270)), p. 6.

134 John Rawls, *The law of peoples: With 'the idea of public reason' revisited* (Harvard University Press, 2001), p. 12 et seqq., p. 30 et seqq.

135 Richard H. Fallon Jr., "Reflections on Dworkin and the Two Faces of Law", *Notre Dame L. Rev.* 67, no. 3 (1991), p. 557 et seqq. with further reference.

136 Not any 'organic' entity like in the writings of Tönnies.

(cc) Overlap: Constitutionalist Perspectives

Constitutionalisation of international law is a view which further advances the concept of the international community. This is situated at the intersection between institutionalist and cosmopolitan reasoning. What unites constitutionalist perspectives is their reasoning that public international law occupies a role for the international community comparable to a constitution on the national level. International law is to be "reconstructed"[137] as a "constitutional law of the international community".[138] Views vary between schools of thought as to how such constitutionalisation processes develop and what their purposes should be.

Certain conceptions have held that the UN system has developed to a degree where the UN Charter can be regarded as the constitution of the international community.[139] Likewise, these conceptions maintain that the international community is normatively grounded in the universal acceptance of the UN and other foundations of the international order.[140]

International legal norms are generally of equal status, being grounded in State consent. Some constitutionalists argue that there are developments which indicate that particular sets of norms might take the role that constitutional law holds in domestic legal systems, i.e., take a superior position in the hierarchy of norms. Fundamental normative decisions are, in this vein, understood as a step towards the protection of common values through law. One such example is the development of the international protection of human rights. The assumption that this tendency of hierarchy-building is exemplified by basic human rights norms (like the prohibition of torture or genocide) entering the canon of *jus cogens* norms.[141] This commitment of States to higher values is also an important

137 Thomas Kleinlein, "Konstitutionalisierung im Völkerrecht", *Konstruktion und Elemente einer idealistischen Völkerrechtslehre* (2012), p. 5.

138 Jonathan Bauerschmidt et al., *Konstitutionalisierung in Zeiten globaler Krisen*, vol. 1 (Nomos, 2015), p. 8.

139 Bardo Fassbender, "The United Nations Charter as Constitution of the International Community", *Colum. J. Transnat'l L.* 36 (1998), p. 569 et seqq.

140 Christian Tomuschat, "Obligations Arising for States without or against Their Will", in *Recueil des Cours*, ed. Académie de Droit International (Martinus Nijhoff, 1993), p. 236. Elsewhere in the same work, the author held that there is an "interdependence that exists between the two concepts of international community and its constitution", see p. 219.

141 Cf. Erika de Wet, "The Emergence of International and Regional Value Systems as a Manifestation of the Emerging International Constitutional Order", *Leiden Journal of International Law* 19, no. 3 (2006), p. 614 et seq.

differentiation between the often normative and politically colored constitutionalisation theories and other analytical perspectives on legalization or juridification tendencies in international relations.

(b) Reservations About the Notion of an International Community

> *"The world is not a 'global community' but an arena where nations, nongovernmental actors, and businesses engage and compete for advantage."*
> *H.R. McMaster and Gary D. Cohn*[142]

The developments of international law since the 1990s, of which community thinking and value orientation are an important part, have led scholars in international law and international relations to analyze a tendency of contestation against these developments.[143] Indeed, there are various perspectives on international law and international relations that are difficult to reconcile with the idea of an international community in which international law fulfills an organizational role. To conceive of international relations as being conducted in the framework of an international community based on values protected and promoted through law necessarily creates tensions with other perspectives on world politics and the role of international law in it. The opening quote in this section by current US administrations is but one recently influential example of such perspectives. This new perspective develops the broader argument that

---

142 H.R. McMaster and Gary D. Cohn, "America First Doesn't Mean America Alone", *Wall Street Journal*, 30 May 2017; At the time of the article's publication, the authors were both senior advisors to US President Trump, Mr McMaster as US National Security Advisor and Mr Cohn as Director of the National Economic Council.

143 On contestation in international law, see Karen J. Alter, "The Contested Authority and Legitimacy of International Law: The State Strikes Back", *iCourts Working Paper Series* 134 (2018); on contestation and sources of international law, see Samantha Besson and Jean d'Aspremont, "The Sources of International Law: An Introduction", in *The Oxford handbook on the sources of international law*, ed. Samantha Besson, Jean d'Aspremont, and Sévrine Knuchel (Oxford University Press, 2017), p. 13 et seqq.; in IR scholarship, see e.g. Antje Wiener, *Contestation and constitution of norms in global international relations* (Cambridge University Press, 2018). The 'rise or decline' perspective on international law taken in this study is to some extent informed by these tendencies, see Krieger and Nolte, "The International Rule of Law – Rise or Decline? Points of Departure ", p. 10 et seq.

the world is best understood as both a marketplace and an arena, where actors pursue their (largely) rational, economic interests and compete in the quest for their realization. In their understanding, this does not exclude collaboration, but does exclude any form of 'global community', and with it any further legal integration that would only impede the actors in their pursuits.

And indeed, there are tensions resulting from a turn towards community thinking in a legal system that is based on sovereign States with often conflicting interests.

The most fundamental objection against the idea of an 'international community', can be situated with the so-called 'realist' perspective in both international relations and international law scholarship. During the 20th century, the 'realist school' became the most influential school of thought in the still emerging discipline of international relations. What started as a reaction to the idealist thinking in American international politics of the 1930s and 1940s, eventually developed into a theory of international law of remarkable influence. Hans J. Morgenthau became the most important representative of this emerging view. He took as a starting point the anthropological premise of individuals being primarily determined by an instinct of power and self-preservation. Applied to the sphere of international relations, he claimed the centrality of the States' "struggle for power" and material advantages in any valuable explanation of international politics.[144]

A variation of this view, often classified as 'neo-realism', shifted the emphasis to rational individuals and rationally acting States pursuing their own interests.[145] Still others modified the theory by pointing to the difference between state power and interests. Allowing for the possibility of interests being shaped by influences other than the sheer materialistic features of power.[146]

A recent view takes international law realism further, challenging international law in its very existence as a legal system.[147] Introducing economic rational choice theory, this view claims to deviate from classical realism in so far

---

144 Hans J. Morgenthau, Kenneth W. Thompson, and David Clinton, *Politics among nations: The struggle for power and peace* (McGraw-Hill Education – Europe, 2005).

145 Kenneth Waltz, *Theory of international politics* (Waveland Press, 1979, reissued 2010), p. 62 et seqq.

146 Martha Finnemore and Judith Goldstein, "Power Politics in the Contemporary World – Lessons from the Scholarship of Stephen Krasner", in *Back to basics: State power in a contemporary world*, ed. Martha Finnemore and Judith Goldstein (Oxford University Press, 2013), p. 19 et seq.

147 Jack L. Goldsmith and Eric Posner, *The limits of international law* (Oxford University Press, 2007).

as they claim to assume less about the content of state interests.[148] This view still fundamentally questions several basic assumptions about international law as a normative order: It claims that the causal link in the relationship between state interests and international law is not that the former are contained and influenced by the latter, but exactly the opposite. International law emerges from States' pursuits of self-interested policies on the international stage. International law is, in this sense, endogenous to state interests.[149] Hence, it suggests that a central problem in the analysis of international law is the confusion of strategic versus moral behavior of States. In this view, when States follow the rules of international law this is because the prescribed behaviour is congruent with their own interests and not because States follow any form of *moral* obligation to abide by the legal rules. [150]

The common denominator of 'realist school' theories is the assumption of anarchy as the fundamental pre-condition of international relations. From this pre-condition a system develops in which States must compete for their interests and their place within said system. The consequence is often to treat States like 'black boxes' in the analysis of these power struggles, meaning to largely ignore factors like their internal organisation, history or social traditions, and assume their pursuit of material interests independent from such internal factors.[151] The same is true for adaptations of these theories in international law scholarship.

The assumption of an international community has been further challenged by research focusing on the mechanisms of in- and exclusion of actors. In this view, both the emphasis on institution-building as well as the emphasis on liberal values and individual rights are overly culture-dependent, exclusive in character and ultimately instruments of hegemonial ambitions.[152]

---

148 Ibid., p. 6.

149 Ibid., p. 13.

150 Ibid., p. 183 et seq.

151 John J. Mearsheimer, "Structural Realism", in *International relations theories: Discipline and diversity*, ed. Tim Dunne, Milja Kurki, and Steve Smith (Oxford University Press, 2007), p. 78.

152 Chimni, "International Institutions Today: An Imperial Global State in the Making", p. 4 et seqq. For an overview of postmodernist criticism of bureaucracy, see Ralph P. Hummel and Camilla Stivers, "Postmodernism, Bureaucracy, and Democracy", in *The Oxford handbook of American bureaucracy*, ed. Robert F. Durant (Oxford University Press, 2010), p. 329 et seq.

(c) The 'International Community' as an Analytical Tool to Identify Structural Developments in International Law

Perspectives emphasizing and criticizing the notion of an international community have significantly contributed to the research of the international legal order today. They have informed the present author's perspective in different ways.

Proponents of an international community raise important points for coping with the deficiencies and shortcomings of the 'classical' or 'bilateralist' international legal system: A purely state-centered system of international law has difficulties allocating legal responsibilities for problems that States cause together and can only jointly solve – a problem that is most visible in the field of climate change.[153] Here, it is nearly impossible to assign responsibility for particular effects of climate change to a single state. Joint action by all States is needed, in some cases in opposition to their short-term material interests. Moreover, a completely state-centered system treating States like sovereign proverbial 'black-boxes'[154] creates inconsistencies if it introduces legal mechanisms to protect certain goods beyond the disposition of States. One prominent example of this is *jus cogens*, creating an apparently strict regime which conceptually and normatively points beyond the sphere of 'bilateralist' law balancing sovereign interests, but at the same time, leaving the initiative to invoke the invalidity of legal norms to those who created them.[155]

One important argument made by institutionalist reasoning is the necessity to cope with the growing influence of international institutions, and the implications of this development for legal structures. At the same time, international institutions remain grounded in bilateralist law, receiving their competencies by means of States consenting to them. Hence, the sheer existence of a larger number of international institutions does not conclusively answer whether there is a need to conceive of international affairs as an international community.

The perspectives emphasizing a growing level of inter-subjective cohesion on the international level have made important points. The development of the meta-phenomenon 'globalization', the large increase in transnational political processes, and the growing exchanges of goods, persons and ideas must all be taken into account when conceiving of international legal and political processes.

---

153 On climate change as a collective action problem, see also part C, section II.

154 John J Mearsheimer, *The tragedy of great power politics* (WW Norton & Company, 2001).

155 cf. Villalpando, "The legal dimension of the international community", p. 411 et seq., see also section III. on sources and law-making below.

Those views that are *per se* negating the possibility of community structures on the international level, especially in the 'realist' tradition, cannot account for influence of constant exchange between actors on the international level. Moreover, it cannot account for the influence the regard of others and their behavior necessarily has on actors' behavior. To assume that States develop their interests independently from other actors' behavior towards them, while simultaneously disregarding the normative environment States participated in building, does not do justice to the complex interactions of international politics and the dense net of normative commitments that States have entered into.[156] The assumption of anarchy and constant threat or struggle being a central feature in these concepts makes realist perspectives on international law and international relations largely irreconcilable with the understanding presented here.

Notwithstanding, 'realist' scholarship has made important contributions by carving out the central role of States, their power and their material interest in international politics, influencing the social realities that international law must accommodate. It teaches us that we "cannot and should not ignore power relations".[157]

This observation shows the merits of liberal cosmopolitan perspectives. Where 'realist' perspectives overemphasize the struggle for power in hindering the emergence of community structures, cosmopolitan perspectives seem to underestimate this phenomenon. Conceptions of an international community founded on ideas of universally valid ethical considerations are too heavily depending on presuppositions they cannot themselves ensure. These perspectives are thus unsuitable to account for the plurality of interests, values and backgrounds of actors that exist on the international level. A thicker community understanding, extending towards the idea of a substantive, and ultimately legal personality of this community, is to be rejected for the same reason.

Similar reservations are held here regarding views advocating a 'constitutionalisation' of international law. This especially concerns the tendency of normatively overcharged perspectives which no longer want to describe and analyze

156 Ultimately, the basic assumptions of constructivist reasoning – which the argument made here is connected to – and those of realist perspectives are hard to reconcile. Not even those taking legal realism to an extreme position claim the ability to prove constructivist assumptions about international law influencing state interests wrong. See Goldsmith and Posner, *The limits of international law*, p. 8 et. seq.

157 Finnemore and Goldstein, "Power Politics in the Contemporary World – Lessons from the Scholarship of Stephen Krasner", p. 12.

changing structures, but have shifted to a rather normative program of criticizing existing international law for its weaknesses in comparison to the analogy of a national constitution.[158] As well, the idea of a constitutionalisation is too heavily reliant on claims of the general validity of conceptions which are working and accepted in states with a constitutionalist and mostly democratic tradition. Thus, these views do not offer a suitable understanding of what the international community is or should be.

An intermediary position appropriate for conceiving of the international community becomes apparent when considering both the warning of realists not to ignore power relations and the emphasis on interaction and collective norm-building processes advanced in constructivist scholarship. In this vein, the international community is primarily a useful analytical lens to look at the changes in the international legal and political system. The ever-increasing extent of political and legal interaction necessarily impacted the parameters of international law. The notion of an 'international community' is useful for analyzing if and where there are elements in international law that are institutionally, conceptually and normatively implicating dimensions beyond the States and their bilateral relationships. Here, the notion helps to distinguish such developments from the purely State-centered and interest-balancing understanding of 'classical' or 'bilateralist' international law. It is thus useful to verbalise the structural changes in international law, especially after 1990.

II. Community Values, Law-Making and the Sources of International Law

When different values conflict, these conflicts cannot be solved on an abstract level. For the matter at hand, the conflict between community values with other interests or values in particularly relevant. It follows that a balance often needs to be found in positive law.[159] An important practical influence of the theoretical debate on community thinking and value orientation has been on law-making. Any substantial notion of the international community and its values involves many aspects, including, the interpretation of sources, the role and relative

---

158 For an in-depth critical analysis of the constitutionalisation hypothesis, see Krieger, "Verfassung im Völkerrecht – Konstitutionelle Elemente jenseits des Staates? The Constitutionalization of Public International Law – Constitutional Elements Beyond the State?", p. 439 et seqq.

159 Paulus, *Die internationale Gemeinschaft im Völkerrecht*, p. 283.

importance of different sources as well as the question whether there is a hierarchy between different sources. Moreover, this notion concerns the actors involved in international law-making processes. This section will outline some implications of the theoretical approaches outlined above for different forms of law-making and how they reflect the implementation of community thinking and value orientation. The key areas of tension between community value approaches – constituency, objectivity/subjectivity and degree of substitution of bilateralist foundations – are reflected in questions concerning the law-making in international law.

The existent principles of law making are rooted in a system based on what Henkin called 'state values'. By attributing a central role to state consent, they reflect the inter-state system's commitment to state autonomy and state equality. This commitment shapes the content of the law.[160] Non-regulation, in turn, can be a form of law making in the form of an "affirmative commitment to non-regulation" or – in other words – a commitment to laissez-faire as a dominant value of the state system.[161] The question is whether the present forms of international law are in fact capable of effectively protecting community values where they emerge. It has been rightfully noted that "international law […] has been very conservative of its traditional institutions, which have not been challenged by the new developments towards the protection of community interests […]".[162] This section focuses on those areas where tensions arise between the notion of community values, as outlined above, and the system of sources and law-making in international law. Hence, this section is limited to observations concerning treaties, customary international law, the concepts of *jus cogens* and obligations *erga omnes* and the role of soft law provisions.

As will be outlined below, the system of international law-making and its sources have undergone several changes. The debate about community thinking and value orientation has influenced scholarship and policies concerning the sources of international law and their interpretation. This is most tangibly seen in the increasing emphasis on human rights, on protection of common goods (i.e., the environment) or the (limited) acceptance of concepts like *jus cogens* or obligations *erga omnes*. These developments have not led to a fundamental redefinition of the entire system, as suggested by some, as they concern only certain fields of international law and as 'bilateralism'[163] continues to be the rule.[164]

---

160 Henkin, *International law: Politics and values*, p. 100.

161 Ibid., p. 101.

162 Villalpando, "The legal dimension of the international community", p. 410.

163 Simma, "From bilateralism to community interest ", p. 230 et seqq.

164 Villalpando, "The legal dimension of the international community", p. 411.

1. Treaties

Treaties are by far the most important instruments of international law. For centuries, they have been used to organize inter-state relationships, deliberate compromises between conflicting state interests and create legal security. Although there is a decrease in the growth of treaties numbers in recent years[165], they remain the centerpieces of the international legal order. Their continuing importance and pivotal role are because they are the least controversial source of international law, especially in comparison to customary law and the controversies about its making.[166] For the promotion of community values, multilateral treaties are of particular interest. As a relatively new phenomenon in the history of international law, they "consolidate unwritten international law like iron bonds reinforcing a cracking building, and add layer upon layer to the general international law of mere co-existence in order to satisfy the need for norms in an increasingly more complex world."[167]

There are also limits to the function of treaties in promoting community values. There is "a […] dilemma inherent in the international society, where there is no alternative but to act by means of treaties which can, based on the principle of contract, bind only consenting States in order even to realize the public interest and organization despite the fact that the public interest of the whole of international society has become apparent."[168] This dilemma is especially apparent in cases of multilateral treaties that would require concerted action and (almost) universal participation to effectively protect the community values in question. One a key example of this being the climate change regime. Other examples are the participation of non-state actors and the possibility of reservations towards human rights treaties which are sometimes, especially from a constitutionalist point of view, understood as efforts to establish an objective order.[169] Concerning human rights treaties, it is argued that they often entail non-reciprocal forms of normativity.[170]

---

165 Pauwelyn, Wessel, and Wouters, "When structures become shackles", p. 733 et seqq.

166 See III. 2.

167 Simma, "From bilateralism to community interest ", p. 323.

168 Sato, "Legitimacy of International Organizations and their Decisions", p. 15, naming the establishment of an international criminal tribunal as an example where only a universal system can ensure effectiveness in the protection of the public good concerned.

169 Tomuschat, "Obligations arising for states without or against their will", p. 248.

170 Ibid., p. 114 et seq.

Moreover, multilateral treaties also serve community values by institutionalizing them. Over time, increased interaction based on mutually accepted procedural rules can cause 'communities of practice' to become more interconnected and value based. This eventually allows for richer substantive rules to emerge.[171] Here again, the climate change regime is an important example of a multilateral system based on a treaty. It also exemplifies a framework in which States are bound to legally interact on a regular basis. The still developing system is a combination of many non-binding and some binding instruments. It arguably promotes international efforts regarding climate change more effectively than any single treaty or conference could.

2. Customary International Law

In customary international law, modern developments have led to suggestions from both scholars and practitioners that the methodology of its formation and interpretation is, and needs to be, changing.[172] The traditional understandings of its two elements, state practice and *opinio iuris*, were no longer capable of accommodating the realities of modern international law. From a community value perspective, two aspects of the attempts to modernize the methodology of customary international law are interesting. First, the broader inclusion of non-state actors as contributing to the elements of custom has been a controversial feature of the debate. The actors which were under consideration for inclusion were primarily international organization and to a lesser extent other non-state actors.[173] Second, more emphasis was put on the element of *opinio iuris*, even in the absence of state practice. It was famously found by the prosecutor of the International Criminal Tribunal for the former Yugoslavia (ICTY) in the "requirements of humanity and the dictates of public conscience".[174] Following approaches like this, and hence lowering the threshold for the identification of customary international legal norms, would improve the integration of non-legal, value-oriented

171 Brunnée and Toope, *Legitimacy and legality in international law*, p. 70 et seqq. with what they call the 'long-term interaction framework approach'.

172 For a broader discussion of the issue, see Noora Arajärvi, "The Requisite Rigour in the Identification of Customary International Law – A Look at the Reports of the Special Rapporteur of the International Law Commission", *International Community Law Review* 19, no. 1 (2017), p. 9 et seq.

173 Lung-chu Chen, *An introduction to contemporary international law: A policy-oriented perspective*, 3rd ed. (Oxford University Press, 2015), p. 429.

174 Prosecutor v. Kupreškić, 14 January 2000, IT-95-16-T, para. 527.

normative concepts. These suggestions and developments have been met with resistance. The ILC has recently been working on the item of formation and evidence of customary international law[175] and rejected many of the 'progressive' ambitions of broadening the scope of actors and lowering the threshold for the identification of customary international legal norms.[176] As these examples show, customary norms can also play a role in the promotion and protection of community values. Although, it has been rightly noted that this role, like the one of treaties, is limited by the necessity of state consent.[177] Given the ambiguities of customary norms and their often-contested identification, this limitation is even more restrictive.

In international environmental and climate law, customary international legal norms are "both omnipresent and of paramount importance."[178] However, there are also field-specific difficulties related to the role of customary norms. As alluded to previously in the discussion about the role of legal bindingness in the implementation of community values, it is often difficult to determine whether a given norm has developed a compulsory character and found entry into general international law. This is in sharp demarcation from the vast amount of soft law norms found in this field. This problem is exacerbated by the fact that questions about the state of the law are authoritatively answered by international courts only on rare occasions. In particular, the ICJ does not often have the opportunity to further develop its jurisprudence in this regard.[179] The resulting uncertainty about the legal status of many norms promotes broad scholarly debates attempting to fill such gaps. Consequentially, a central challenge in this regard is to refrain from reading too far into state action surrounding customary norms, both in climate law and in general. Seen in conjunction with the recent ILC report

175 International Law Commission, First report on formation and evidence of customary international law by Michael Wood, UN Doc. A/CN.4/663 (2013); Second report on formation and evidence of customary international law by Michael Wood, UN Doc. A/CN.4/672 (2014); Third report on formation and evidence of customary international law by Michael Wood, UN Doc. A/CN.4/682 (2015).

176 Arajärvi, "The Requisite Rigour in the Identification of Customary International Law", p. 44 et seq.

177 Simma, "From bilateralism to community interest ", p. 324.

178 Pierre-Marie Dupuy, "Formation of Customary International Law and General Principles", in *The Oxford handbook of international environmental law*, ed. Daniel Bodansky, Jutta Brunnée, and Ellen Hey (Oxford University Press, 2008), p. 452.

179 Ibid.

series on customary international law, it remains critical that the assessment of what can be regarded as customary law and what cannot be conducted carefully.

Given the theoretically and practically controversial nature of customary law and its firm grounding in the bilateralist structures of the international legal system, Simma concluded "that law-making by way of custom is hardly capable of accommodating community interest in a genuine sense."[180] Even without sharing such far-reaching assessments, the difficulties in the relationship of customary international law and community values must be granted. It needs to be considered when analyzing the legal nature and status of any given norm in the climate change regime that could potentially develop to bear legal force.

3. Jus Cogens and Obligations Erga Omnes

In response to the dilemmas and limitation of treaties and custom, both concepts of *jus cogens* and obligations *erga omnes* have been explored as possible mechanisms for the protection of community values in international law. Peremptory norms have been suggested to represent the core values of the international community.[181] This and other issues surrounding *jus cogens* have recently been the subject of intensified discussion after being included in the ILC's working program in 2015.[182] In the words of the current ILC special rapporteur on *jus cogens*, "the idea of "community" or "common interest" is an important element of any understanding of non-derogability – whether based on natural or positive law ideas."[183]

In the context of climate change, both concepts have been discussed as potential vehicles for transporting the normative ambitions underlying the climate regime and its core concepts into positive international law.[184]

---

180 Simma, "From bilateralism to community interest ", p. 324.

181 Pierre-Marie Dupuy, "Some Reflections on Contemporary International Law and the Appeal to Universal Values: A Response to Martti Koskenniemi", *European Journal of International Law* 16, no. 1 (2005), p. 133 et seq.; Erika De Wet, "Entrenching International Values Through Positive Law: The (Limited) Effect of Peremptory Norms", in *A Metamorphosis of International Law – Tracing Value Changes in the International Legal Order From the Perspectives of Legal and Political Science (Forthcoming)*, ed. Heike Krieger and Andrea Liese (KFG Working Paper Series, No. 25, Berlin Potsdam Research Group "The International Rule of Law – Rise or Decline?", 2019), p. 6 et seq.

182 See UN Doc. A/Res/70/236 of 23 December 2015, para. 7.

183 International Law Commission, First report on jus cogens by Dire Tladi, UN Doc. A/CN.4/693 (2016) para. 24.

184 See Lavanya Rajamani, "The Reach and Limits of the Principle of Common but Differentiated Responsibilities and Respective Capabilities in the Climate Change Regime",

Jus cogens, as a concept, is as audacious as it is ambivalent. On the one hand, it was stated that the concept is about mitigating "le froid cynisme positiviste".[185] As far as this means to limit or overcome some perceived defects of positive international law, this points to the concept's roots in natural law theories. Historically linked to the inter-war period and scholarly attempts to cope with the atrocities of the time and the crimes of Nazi Germany, much can be said for the interpretation that *jus cogens* was about finding a place in international law for the idea of a 'higher' law beyond state authority. On the other hand, its implementation produced the inherent tension between these conceptual roots and positivist treaty law.[186] Drawing on earlier doctrinal works and controversies, the concept was included in the Vienna Conventions on the Law of Treaties of 1969 and 1986. Here, Art. 53 defines norms of *jus cogens* or a peremptory norm as one "accepted and recognized by the international community of States as a whole as a norm from which no derogation is permitted and which can be modified only by a subsequent norm of general international law having the same character." A central aspect of the effect of a *jus cogens* norm is that obligations conflicting with these norms not only contradict the obligations owed to the international community, but also would be considered null and void.[187] There are some indications for a general understanding that this effect does not only concern treaties, but also, for example, unilateral acts.[188] This effect and its underlying logic, which tries to resolve the conflict between natural law and positivist approaches[189], has been suggested to be an important step towards a certain

---

in *Handbook of climate change and India: Development, politics and governance*, ed. Navroz Dubash (Earthscan, 2012), p. 119 et seq.; for an early example of discussing a potential role for jus cogens in the climate change context, see Jutta Brunnée, "'Common Interest' – Echoes from an Empty Shell? – Some Thoughts on Common Interest and International Enviornmental Law", *Zeitschrift für ausländisches Öffentliches Recht und Völkerrecht* 49 (1989), p. 804 et seq.; See also Malgosia Fitzmaurice, "Responsibility and Climate Change", *German Yearbook of International Law* 53 (2010), p. 89 et seqq.

185 Alain Pellet, "Conclusions", in *The fundamental rules of the international legal order – Jus Cogens and obligations Erga Omnes*, ed. Tomuschat Christian and Thouvenin Jean-Marc (Brill, 2005), p. 419.

186 For a comprehensive overview of the theoretical and historical foundations, see International Law Commission, First report on jus cogens (2016), para. 51–60.

187 H. W. A. Thirlway, *The sources of international law* (Oxford University Press, 2014), p. 144.

188 Simma, "From bilateralism to community interest ", p. 289.

189 Ibid., p. 287.

hierarchy of norms protecting the most fundamental values in an otherwise horizontal legal system.[190] This, however, is not undisputed. In the controversial discussion about the ability of *jus cogens* to adequately protect community values, scholars have pointed to inconsistencies in its legal regime which weaken the protection of community values.[191] These objections mostly concern the invocation of *jus cogens* norms. This is as the invocation of an invalidity of any given norm under the Vienna Convention is reserved to parties of the Convention (Art. 65 (1)). Strictly applying this limitation[192] can mean a limitation to precisely those States that accepted obligations conflicting with *jus cogens* norms and that are likely not to be interested in having their commitments declared void.[193] As this paradox indicates, caution is due when using the concept of *jus cogens* to argue for any substantial move away from consent-based, 'bilateralist' international law towards a more value-based international order.

In recent debates, both in the ILC itself and in the sixth committee, the core characteristics of *jus cogens* norms played a key role. The special rapporteur had submitted that

> *"[n]orms of jus cogens protect the fundamental values of the international community, are hierarchically superior to other norms of international law and are universally applicable."*[194]

Some members insisted that international law did not recognize that *jus cogens* norms "protect the fundamental values of the international community, are hierarchically superior to other norms of international law and are universally applicable". They advocated caution against any significant departure from the VCLT wording on *jus cogens*.[195] The notion of 'fundamental values', in particular, raised criticisms. It was criticized for being too narrow if only referring to norms of humanitarian character. At the same time, the notion was critiqued for blurring the fact that *jus cogens* norms are dependent on the acceptance and recognition by States, and not on any subjective notion of values.[196] In the 6th committee, it was

190 Thirlway, *The sources of international law*, p. 155 and p. 132 et. seqq.
191 Villalpando, "The legal dimension of the international community", p. 411 et seq.
192 For a discussion of the possibility of a less formalistic understanding, see Simma, "From bilateralism to community interest ", p. 289.
193 Villalpando, "The legal dimension of the international community", p. 419 et seq.
194 International Law Commission, First report on jus cogens (2016), Draft conclusion 3, para. 2.
195 For a summary of the debate, see General Assembly, Official Records, Seventy-first session, Supplement No. 10, UN Doc. A/71/10, especially para. 125 et seqq.
196 Ibid., para. 126.

the US delegation who put an emphasis on their critical view towards the notion of *jus cogens* reflecting fundamental values. They stated that this would allow the derivation of such norms from "vague and contestable natural law principles" and to disregarding the actual acceptance and recognition by States.[197] As such objections and reservations show, States are reluctant to accept a more influential role of value considerations through *jus cogens*. They are likewise careful to make this point were discussions like the one in the 6th committee arise with their potential implications for the interpretation of the State's *opinio iuris*.

Obligations *erga omnes* drew considerable attention in scholarship. This attention increased after the *Barcelona Traction* Judgment of the ICJ and has been called a "great leap forward" in the development of community structures.[198] In an *obiter dictum*, the Court emphasized the distinction between bilateral obligations and those obligations "towards the international community as a whole" which "all [S]tates can be held to have a legal interest in their protection".[199] This formulation also points to the interwovenness of *erga omnes* and *jus cogens*.[200] According to the Court, such obligations can derive from basic human rights or the outlawing of major crimes like genocide.[201]

Despite being a major conceptual development towards the idea of a community with values to protect and more than a mere sum of their parts, this notion has been met with criticism. As the ICJ made clear in later decisions, "the erga omnes character of a norm [or its *jus cogens* nature] and the rule of consent to jurisdiction are two different things"[202] and that "the mere fact that rights and obligations *erga omnes* may be at issue in a dispute would not give the Court jurisdiction to entertain that dispute".[203] The Court has dismissed the idea of an international *actio popularis* that was advocated as a tool to effectively protect *erga omnes* norms.[204] The Court's insistence on the principle of consensual

---

197 Statement by the Delegation of the United States of America (Mr. Simonoff), UNGA, Sixth Committee, Summary record of the 26th meeting, 5 Dec 2016, UN Doc. A/C.6/71/SR.26, para. 126.

198 Simma, "From bilateralism to community interest ", p. 293.

199 Barcelona Traction, para. 31.

200 Jochen Frowein, "Obligations Erga Omnes", in *MPEPIL*, ed. Rüdiger Wolfrum (Oxford University Press, 2008), para. 3.

201 Ibid.

202 *Armed Activities on the Territory of the Congo* (Democratic Republic of the Congo v. Uganda), Judgment, Merits, I.C.J. Rep. 2005, p. 168, para. 64.

203 Ibid.

204 Critically discussed by Alfred P Rubin, "Actio popularis, jus cogens and offenses erga omnes", *New Eng. L. Rev.* 35 (2000).

jurisdiction has been criticized as hindering the effective utilization of the potential of *erga omnes* obligations.[205]

Taking a broader perspective on the role both concepts played in the ICJ jurisprudence, much can be said for the argument that the Court is generally reluctant to let community interests prevail over individual interest. A prominent example is the 1996 advisory opinion on the legality of the threat or use of nuclear weapons, which certainly included considerations of community interests, but refrained from using them to limit the States' autonomy by not formulating an absolute prohibition on the use of nuclear weapons.[206] The common denominator of the controversies outlined above is that concepts like *jus cogens* or obligations *erga omnes* are indeed elements of an increased degree of community thinking and the ambition to protect community values in existing positive law and ICJ jurisprudence. At the same time, controversial issues like the invocation of *jus cogens* norms or the procedural enforcement of obligations *erga omnes* show that there are limits to these concepts if they are grounded in the existing rules and mechanism of international law. The most prominent example being the consent dependent jurisdiction of the ICJ. The discussions on *jus cogens* in the ILC and the sixth committee show that in contrast to some early hopes in scholarship for *jus cogens* and *erga omnes* to advance community values in international law, core institutions have either continued or recently chosen to take reluctant approaches to these emphases. This reality in state and institutional practice must be considered when analyzing the prospects of community values in international law. For a value-laden field like climate change, it points to the reluctance of States to allow for one of the key concepts of international law connected to the idea of values to be broadened.

4. The General Principles of International Law

Another conceivable way for community values to achieve practical importance in positive law is by gaining the status of general principles. The General Principles of Law, according to Art. 38 (1) c of the ICJ statute, are among the main sources of international law. The origins of the provision show that it was a response to the need for more completeness of an international legal system that was widely seen as being less clear and coherent than domestic legal systems.[207]

---

205 Villalpando, "The legal dimension of the international community", p. 412.

206 See ibid., p. 413 et seq.

207 Alain Pellet, "Article 38", in *The statute of the International Court of justice: A commentary*, ed. Andreas Zimmermann, et al. (Oxford University Press, 2012), para. 250.

On the one hand, the drafters of the Article wanted to give room for the recurrence on general principles, as they were an important source of inspiration for the founders of international law as a legal system. On the other hand, they were concerned that an inclusion of principles could give undue room to subjectivity in applying the law.[208]

Although there is no clear consensus on the definition of general principles in the sense of the Court Statute, it is sufficiently clear that they are (a) unwritten legal norms of wide-ranging character, (b) recognized in the municipal laws of States and (c) transportable at the international level.[209] Conceptually, the notion of general principles of international law has long been accompanied by scholarly debate as to their nature and functions. Hans Kelsen is a prominent example for the doubt of "whether such principles common to the legal order of the civilized nations exist at all".[210]

There are two main distinctions that mark the demarcation between non-legal notions of principle from the 'general principles' as a source of international law. One is the term 'general' itself, indicating the image of a wide-ranging norm. The other is the conjunction with 'of law' and specifically – in the chapeau of Art. 38 – the association with 'international law'. The two references to (international) law clarify that the principles in questions are and ought to be of a legal nature and that the ICJ would only be entitled to adjudicate based on existing international law.[211] This also holds when the ICJ is applying general principles. The ICJ, in this regard, has differentiated between legal rules and "moral principles" that the Court only can take into account "so far as the[y] are given a sufficient expression in legal form".[212]

Arguably, the practical importance of the general principles provision has remained limited. This is due in part to the controversial formula 'recognized by civilized nations'.[213] The ICJ has rarely used references to Art. 38(1) c in its jurisprudence and has ruled out the application on every occasion to do so.[214]

---

208 Ibid., para. 251 et seq.

209 Ibid., para. 254.

210 Hans Kelsen, *Principles of international law*, ed. Robert W. Tucker, 2nd ed. (Holt, Rinehart and Winston, 1967), p. 539.

211 Giorgio Gaja, "General Principles of Law", in *MPEPIL*, ed. Rüdiger Wolfrum (Oxford University Press, 2013), para. 6; Pellet, "Article 38", para. 256.

212 South West Africa, Ethiopia v. South Africa, Second Phase, [1966] ICJ Rep 6, para. 49.

213 Gaja, "General Principles of Law", para. 2, 16.

214 Pellet, "Article 38", para. 253, citing as the only examples: Right of Passage over Indian Territory, Portugal v India, Merits, Judgment, [1960] ICJ Rep 6, p. 43; South West Africa, Ethiopia v. South Africa, Second Phase, [1966] ICJ Rep 6, para. 91; North Sea

The court differentiates between two sets of principles: (i) those that are recognized in domestic legal system and are derived from those; (ii) those that are inherently principles of international law as they are only relevant on the international level. Both notions of principle share the necessity to be based on the recognition by States. Hence, in the case of the non-municipal principles, States would have to express that the given principle applies to their international relations.[215]

Notwithstanding these specificities surrounding the practices of the ICJ, the general principles of international law and the specific principles of a given field of international law, share the basic considerations that can be made regarding customary international law. That is that the advancement of general principles is largely dependent on a mixture of progressive ideas in general statements of institutions and state practice as well as the consolidation by international courts.

In this vein, the primary difference between the two is the level of generality in their formulation.[216] Hence, similar reservations apply as to the role of general principles in the accommodation of community values. This is amplified by the degree of generality that is necessary for a norm to be accepted as a general principle of international law. While these considerations must be taken into account for any analysis of international law, it is an open *empirical* question whether any norm in climate change law could amount to a general principle of international law.

5. Legal Bindingness and the Contentious Role of Soft Law

Community value considerations become relevant to international law by being formed as norms in a broader, non-legal sense. Analyzing a field of international law focused on community values such as climate change law includes dealing with value-laden norm concepts not always congruent with legal terminology. On the one hand, such developments should be considered in order to develop a holistic picture of the field. Therefore, this section will outline the role of norms below the threshold of legal norms, including insights from political science and legal philosophy. On the other hand, the lines between legal norms and non-legal

---

Continental Shelf, Germany v Denmark, Merits, Judgment, (1969) ICJ Rep 3, para. 17; Avena and Other Mexican Nationals, Mexico v United States, Judgment on Jurisdiction, Admissibility and Merits, [2004] ICJ Rep 12, para. 127.

215 Gaja, "General Principles of Law", para. 19.

216 Dupuy, "Formation of Customary International Law and General Principles", p. 461.

norms must not be blurred. Hence, the tensions between such norms and the sources of international law will be taken into account.

Insightful perspectives on how to deal conceptually with norms below the threshold of legal norms stem from the field of legal philosophy. An influential view suggests a threefold distinction between 'policies', 'legal principles' and 'legal rules'.[217] A policy, in Dworkin's understanding, is "that kind of standard that sets out a goal to be reached, generally an improvement in some economic, political or social feature of the community".[218] He defines a legal principle as a "standard that is to be observed, not because it will advance or secure an economic, political, or social situation deemed desirable, but because it is a requirement of justice or fairness or some other dimension of morality."[219] Legal principles (as distinct from legal rules), he holds, "do not set out legal consequences that follow automatically when the conditions provided are met"[220], but "have a dimension that rules do not – the dimension of weight or importance".[221] A problem with Dworkins distinctions is that he focusses his analysis on the borderline between 'principles' and 'rules'. In international environmental and climate law, however, drawing the line between 'policies' and 'principles' is just as important, as it is here where legal nature and role is most contentious.[222] Scholars have adopted Dworkin's approach to the field of international environmental law. They put forward a distinction between 'principles' as a type of statement of formulation of a norm or 'principles' to describe the legal foundation of a norm, whether in a treaty, in customary law or a general principle of law. In a similar vein, Bodansky suggested that principles "embody legal standards, but the standards they contain are more general than commitments and do not specify particular actions"[223], in contrast to rules. The designation of a norm as a principle itself does not yet offer insights about its legal quality. The legal quality, in turn,

217 Ronald Dworkin, *Taking rights seriously* (Duckworth, 1977), p. 22.
218 Ibid., p. 22.
219 Ibid., p. 22.
220 Ibid., p. 25.
221 Ibid., p. 26.
222 Ulrich Beyerlin, "Different Types of Norms in International Environmental Law Policies, Principles, And Rules", in *The Oxford Handbook of International Environmental Law*, ed. Daniel Bodansky, Jutta Brunnée, and Ellen Hey (OUP, 2008), p. 435 et seq.
223 Daniel Bodansky, "The United Nations Framework Convention on Climate Change: A Commentary", *Yale J. Int'l l.* 18 (1993), p. 501.

can only be analyzed on a case-by case basis.[224] Starting from that such scholars further modified the Dworkin terminology to distinguish 'concepts', 'rules' and 'norms'.[225] As a form of distinction "based on the degree of generality/particularity", they suggest "to consider concepts as guiding norms that are implemented by principles, which, in turn, are realised by rules." The more abstract a norm is, the more potential of controversy there is regarding its application.[226] This potential for controversy is an example of the tension noted above. With a growing proliferation of norms with unclear legal contours being used in legal contexts, conflicts can arise between actors claiming a legal status for (one of) them and others who object. This conflict is conceivable between various actors on different levels, most importantly, between an international court or the International Law Commission (ILC) on the one hand, and a group of States on the other. When, for example, a court or the ILC suggests legal status for a value-laden norm in a manner that is perceived as premature by States[227], the legal role of community value related norms can become connected to the acceptance of international law by the States.

A significant tension between the emergence of community values and the bilateralist structures of international law concerns the question of legal bindingness. Even among those accepting the hypothesis of a general tendency towards the emergence of community value elements in international law, it is disputed what their concrete legal implementation could and should look like. Two aspects of legal bindingness stand out in their significance for such debates. First, the role of norms just below the threshold of formal legal force, which become influential through legal practice like treaty interpretations, court decisions or influential scholarly work (e.g., in UN commissions). Since such norms have a central role in international environmental and climate law, this first aspect is of particular interest for the empirical part of this study. The second aspect relates to the special role ascribed to certain legal norms through dogmatic concepts like *jus cogens* or *erga omnes*.

---

224 Pierre-Marie Dupuy and Jorge E. Viñuales, *International environmental law: A modern introduction* (Cambridge University Press, 2015), p. 52.

225 Ibid., p. 51 et seq.

226 Ibid., p. 52.

227 A salient example is the debate about the status of the 'common concern' concept in the ILC and the 6th Committee of the UN General Assembly, which will be discussed in further detail in Part D.

Public international law is mostly composed of equally co-existing norms, but has nonetheless developed some elements of a hierarchy between norms. This is exemplified by the figure of *jus cogens*.[228] At the bottom of this hierarchy, in the "grey area between international 'hard law' and 'soft law', are an ever-growing number of amorphous 'concepts' and 'principles', whose nature and normative quality are far from clear".[229] The nature, role, influence and effects of such norms have been conceptualized in many ways by different strands of scholarship. Their proliferation in international climate law is a central element of the community value implementation in the field.

The often-contentious role of 'soft law' belongs in this context. The term covers a wide range of instruments differing in nature and function. Their common denominator is the inclusion of non-binding norms in treaties, resolutions, recommendations, codes of conducts, manuals or other texts. Also, norms below the threshold of legal norms can be attributed to this realm. In political science, 'soft law' is defined largely independent from any claim of legal validity, the criterion rather being the mechanisms of binding States to their commitments (e.g., an instrument with reduced 'precision', 'obligation' or 'delegation', like a vaguely formulated international treaty without adjudication would be soft law). Soft law is also used to distinguish between the above realm of norms and both 'hard law' and purely political arrangements.[230] From a legal perspective, the term soft law can be defined as "[s]ocial norms of varying character and relevance influence the behaviour and decisions of actors participating in international relations. As far as their binding quality is concerned, such social norms range from purely moral or political commitments to strictly legal ones."[231]

The meaning, role and importance of soft law is a matter of ongoing dispute among international lawyers. While some have argued that soft law is an important tool of progressive development of international law[232], others insist on its

---

228 See on hierarchy Erika De Wet and Jure Vidmar, eds., *Hierarchy in international law: The place of human rights* (OUP, 2012); See also section III.3. below on *jus cogens* and obligations *erga omnes*.

229 , , p. 426.

230 Kenneth W. Abbott and Duncan Snidal, "Hard and Soft Law in International Governance", *International Organization* 54, no. 03 (2000), p. 422 et seq.

231 Daniel Thürer, "Soft Law", in *MPEPIL*, ed. Rüdiger Wolfrum (Oxford University Press, 2009), para. 1.

232 Mary Ellen O'Connell, "The Role of Soft Law in a Global Order", in *Commitment and compliance: The role of non-binding norms in the International Legal System*, ed. Dinah Shelton (Oxford University Press, 2000), p. 100.

limited relevance and its non-legal character.[233] In the perspective taken here, it is crucial to emphasize the apparent, but often blurred fact that the varying instruments discussed under heading of 'soft law' are not law in the sense of Art. 38 of the ICJ statute.

The point to be made here relates more to the systemic role of soft law in a particular field of international law[234]: In many of the areas where community thinking and value orientation has become influential, so too have soft law provisions. Especially in international environmental law, soft law has played an important and often-ambiguous role.[235] Particularly under multilateral environmental agreements (MEAs) like the UNFCCC, the practice of 'soft' standard setting through plenary bodies with different forms and scopes of application was pivotal in the development of the regime.[236] Even where treaties themselves were adopted as law, soft law-decisions have often been decisive in their implementation and the fostering of their political acceptance.[237] Indeed, the entire development of international environmental law (IEL) has been shaped by soft law documents and agreements.[238]

One of the arguments made in favor of principles – instead of precise and binding rules – is that they are better suited to guide complex regimes like the Climate change regime, notwithstanding the corresponding effect on their legal status.[239] It is argued that one of the most important forms of influence exerted by soft law principles is in expressing emerging norms and catalyzing the making of customary norms.[240] Where principles are put into such prominent positions

---

233 Thirlway, *The sources of international law*, p. 143, see also for the 'absolutist view' Prosper Weil, "Towards Relative Normativity in International Law", *AJIL* 77, no. 3 (1983).

234 The implications for the Climate change regime will be dealt with more extensively in Part D.

235 Jutta Brunnée, "The Sources of International Environmental Law: Interactional Law", in *Oxford handbook on the sources of international law*, ed. Samantha Besson and Jean d'Aspremont (Oxford University Press, 2017), p. 977 et seqq.

236 Ibid., p. 15.

237 Ibid., p.16, naming the Marrakesh accords of 2001 on the implementation of the 1997 Kyoto protocol as an example.

238 Ulrich Beyerlin and Thilo Marauhn, *International environmental law*, 1. print. ed. (Hart u.a., 2011), p. 289 et seqq.; Dupuy and Viñuales, *International environmental law*, p. 34 et. seqq.

239 [redacted]Lluís Paradell-Trius, "Principles of International Environmental Law: An Overview", *Review of European Community & International Environmental Law* 9, no. 2 (2000), p. 93 et seqq.

240 Ibid., p. 96.

(e.g., in the UNFCCC), they are able to develop significant indirect influence on legal practice. Consequentially, where such norms are suggested to gain legal significance, they can also become a hurdle in terms of State acceptance for the instruments and regimes they are in. This is exacerbated by the fact that such norms are often value-laden by nature. This form of tension is also an important link between the move towards community values and the potential decline of international law outlined above.

There is one final dimension in legal bindingness important in the tension produced by the emergence of value-oriented norms. This dimension touches upon a development that has been debated in scholarship as the introduction of 'relative normativity' in international law. Prosper Weil expressed a dogmatic unease with this trend he discerned in the early 1980s.[241] Among the phenomena he summarized under the header of 'relative normativity' were the emergence of soft law, the ILC distinction between international crimes and delicts, as well as underlying concepts like obligations *erga omnes* and *jus cogens* norms. For international lawyers in their capacity as "system builder[s] by vocation"[242], this was a matter of concern. If and where the existence of rights or obligations were to be determined through the importation of material criteria into the formal law, he held, international law would no longer be capable of ordering international relations in a pluralist international society made of equally sovereign States. Such importation would give ambiguous weight to such rights and obligations and would mean abandoning the neutral evaluation offered by the application of formal legal criteria.[243] The arguments he advanced attracted academic praise[244], but also varying degrees of criticism. Even to some authors who shared Weil's positivist theoretical background, his arguments were not entirely convincing. Some held that relative normativity found based on a positivist theory would correlate with that found based on other theoretical approaches.[245] Critiques

241 Weil, "Towards relative normativity in international law", p. 413–442.

242 Ibid., p. 440.

243 Ibid., p. 416 et seqq.

244 For an overview of the discourse, see Dinah Shelton, "International Law and 'Relative Normativity'", in *International law*, ed. Malcolm D. Evans (Oxford University Press, 2010), p. 137 et seqq.

245 Ulrich Fastenrath, "Relative Normativity in International Law", *EJIL* 4 (1993), p. 306, 324 et seqq.

were also advanced on Weil's approach from other theoretical angles.[246] However, the concerns Weil expressed remain important today. For instance, in this study, especially his warning of the potential systemic influence of any normative development beyond the existing and functioning types of legal norms and sources are taken well into account. On the other hand, the existence of what Weil called relative normativity is to a certain extent a matter of fact that international law must and can handle, depending on the ways of implementation and application.

6. Conclusion Community Values, Law-Making and the Sources of International Law

The system of international law-making and its sources have undergone many changes. The debate about community thinking and value orientation has influenced scholarship and policies concerning the sources of international law and their interpretation. This is most tangible in the increasing emphasis on human rights, on protection of common goods like the environment and in the (limited) acceptance of concepts like *jus cogens* or obligations *erga omnes*. Nonetheless, these developments have not led to a fundamental redefinition of the entire system as they concern only certain fields of international law, and 'bilateralism'[247] continues to be the rule.[248] The centrality of state consent has been significantly challenged in very few fields of international law.[249] State sovereignty and individual state interests continue to play a key role and this leads to certain paradoxes and inherent limits of concepts like *jus cogens* or *erga omnes*.[250] Hence, there are existing norms and mechanisms in current positive international law. There are also legal tools that have been used to pursue community values "that were not, at their origins, elaborated for that purpose and are better suited to the protection of individual interests."[251] What existing norms and mechanisms do not do is protect community values by favoring them over individual state interests or values. Instead, what they do, and *can* do, is carefully balance the two.

---

246 For a critique based on natural law reasoning, see John Tasioulas, "In Defence of Relative Normativity: Communitarian Values and the Nicaragua Case", *Oxford Journal of Legal Studies* 16, no. 1 (1996), pp. 85–128.

247 Simma, "From bilateralism to community interest ", p. 230 et seqq.

248 Villalpando, "The legal dimension of the international community", p. 411.

249 Here again, the debate about the 'Responsibility to Protect' is a case in point.

250 Villalpando, "The legal dimension of the international community", p. 408 et seq.

251 Ibid.

As to the different capabilities of the sources of law to accommodate community values, the perspective taken here shares the observation that "international customary law is a natural companion of bilateralism".[252] Consequentially, multilateral treaties are the most promising instruments for the promotion of community values, as similar reservations must apply to the role of general principles of international law being necessarily based in state practice. In both cases, the often-ambiguous nature of customary norms and those potentially seen as general principles further confirms this necessity for caution. That is not to say that customary norms and general principles cannot play a role on some occasions. Where state practice and *opinio iuris* are sufficiently clear or where an international court finds clear indications for the existence of a customary norm or a general principle, this can advance community values in international law. But inversely, caution is necessary in their 'identification' by others, including scholars, to ensure continuing acceptance of the law, both in general and in the field of climate law.

Corresponding to the understanding put forward in this section, any substantial changes to these mechanisms have their limits with regards to the actors involved and the normative grounding of any conceivable instrument. If for instance, the ICJ were to give up the principle of consensual jurisdiction to make some sort of international *actio popularis* possible, this would limit the State's willingness to accept the Courts jurisdiction at all.[253] In the absence of any other normative grounding for an effective international jurisdiction, such a substantial shift away from state consent would not improve the protection of community values. As can be seen regarding the role of soft law, the use of terms like 'international community' or its interests and values, these concepts often serve a political or "ideological"[254] function. This shows that the implications of international law not only concern governments and States, but also concrete human beings and their needs.[255] It is the understanding of the present author that, while these political purposes must not be confused with legally binding norms, this is also an important function of international law. Such provisions can serve as a framework to foster the emergence of political understandings.

252 Simma, "From bilateralism to community interest ", p. 324.
253 As in Villalpando, "The legal dimension of the international community", p. 414, pointing to further examples such as the ILC debate on the immunity of state officials from foreign criminal jurisdiction.
254 Simma, "From bilateralism to community interest", p. 248.
255 Tomuschat, "Obligations arising for states without or against their will", p. 227.

Furthermore, they can advance social norms of commonality and shared responsibility that may in the long run become legal norms.

Thus, to a certain extent, the existing sources and mechanism of international law offer a framework for community values and the norms implementing them to serve a positive function. However, there are inherent limits to this due to the strong bilateralist grounding of sources and law-making mechanisms. If the role of community values is to be made a stronger part of the normative foundation of international law, this would have to include a renegotiation of the mechanisms of international law-making. The same is true for any expansion of the role of non-state actors in law-making. For any such renegotiation, it would need either the will of the States or a true alternative in normative grounding other than state consent. As neither of the two are discernible, the debate surrounding proper balance between individual and community interests must accept the boundaries and limited changeability of the existing law-making structures.

III. Conclusion Part B: Perspective on Community Values and Legality in International Law for the Empirical Analysis

This chapter shows that the relationship between community values and legality in international law is one characterized by conceptual tensions. These tensions decisively inform the further process of this study. Basic objections against the whole concept of an international community based on values or elements of it, the contentious notion of the universalisation of values and the struggle on the role of legal bindingness in their implementation are not mere theoretical exercises. All three aspects, sometimes in overlap with each other, are discernibly shaping both discourse and practice. A focus on these factors allows for a differentiated assessment of implementation practices of community values in international law and identifying tendencies of rise or decline. Before turning to the empirical part of this study, the key insights of the previous sections shall be summarized to clarify the perspective subsequently applied.

As the inquiry above shows, the idea of values being protected and promoted through law is not a unique feature of concepts surrounding the idea of an 'international community'. In fact, to protect and promote *some* set of values is an integral part of every legal system. These values define its purpose and larger objectives. As pointed to especially in the works of Henkin, the classical interstate international law has its own values to protect, primarily the peaceful and largely free interaction of sovereign States, each vested with the right to pursue their own interests. The sheer fact that a regulation or norm is in the interest of a single state, does not rule out the possibility of this interest also being a community interest. There can be goals which are pursued in the interest of both individual States and the international community, such as peace or international security.[256] This is of particular significance here, as it points to the limited usefulness of an artificially constructed dichotomy between community interests (or values) and States.

According to the perspective adopted here, the debate about community values is not about the presence or absence of values *per se*. It is rather a question about the changing prioritization of different sets of values and how far such changes are materialized through legal norms. Correspondingly, the question of *whose values* are in play is important. Put another way, the question of which actors drive such a process and who decides which values should be protected is defining for the discussion at hand.

This observation has a two-fold significance for the matter at hand. First, it points to a flaw in some of the current debates about the relationship between international law and values. The flaw comes from when discussions start from the assumption that the introduction of values into international law was in some way a sudden phenomenon unique to post-1990 international law. The problem with such perspectives is that they are blind to the fact that classical international law is also based on values, and consequentially, these perspectives have difficulties in grasping real challenges concerning community values. Second and following from the first, an analysis of the role community values play in a given field of international law should arguably focus on the concrete ways in which they are introduced and implemented rather than on a meta-debate about the usefulness of values in international law. Concretely, community thinking and value orientation do influence the structures of international law, its self-understood purpose and its ability to function as a system organizing international relations. In doing so, it creates significant tensions with the existing international legal order and its structures.

Regarding the contentious role of universalized values, this study takes into account the possibility of both aspects – definition/subject as well as realization – playing a role in possible objections to community value implementation.

---

256 Alfred Verdross and Bruno Simma, *Universelles Völkerrecht* (Duncker & Humblot, 1984), §§ 451 et seqq., arguing that somewhat in between society and community thinking, Verdross and Simma had argued that a community interest ("Gemeinschaftsinteresse") is present when a certain regulation, at least not directly, serve the interest of a single state.

Where values going beyond the material interest of States are introduced in a way that gives enough room for the differentiation and the assertion of the respective interests, it has the potential to advance international law's normative grounding. Introducing values in that way may then serve as a basis on which further non-legal norms of social cohesion and cooperation may develop and which then might find their way into law. If, on the other hand, values contingent on certain cultural backgrounds and not shared by others are introduced through legal norms without sufficient deliberation, this poses a severe risk for the stability of international law. A combination of the two aspects can indicate the degree to which the respective concepts of *lex feranda* would mean a conceptual threat to existing structures of consent-oriented bilateralist international law or a useful supplementation for it. The hypothesis is that there is a threshold beyond which norms stand little chance to be accepted in state practice.

From the debate of the notion 'international community' itself, the empirical analysis shows that if elements of community value thinking are carefully introduced into international legal norms of treaty or custom, it can help international law overcome its structural weaknesses in a globalized context. Existing scholarship suggests that it can potentially help increase acceptance for multilateral structures. Where, in turn, this scale is 'overstretched', it risks the acceptance by States as the remaining key actors in international relations.

The relationship of community values, as understood here, to law-making and the sources of international law shows the contentious role of legal bindingness in the implementation of community values, calling for careful analysis and differentiation. Especially in a field like climate law, many highly influential norms stem from the non-legal realm. From the perspective of social constructivist perspectives on norm development, it is taken here that there is more to the development and role of community values than what an analysis focused only on formal, positivist international law could reveal. The community values that have become relevant to international law went through a process of being formed as norms. Also, after having been introduced in some form into international law, such processes continue. This is especially true in a legal domain involving so many different actors such as climate change diplomacy. While these processes of framing and re-framing must not be confused with any change in formal law, they do influence the international legal order. Given the social embeddedness of legal norms and the potential impact of norm change on the acceptance for the field or instrument in question, they must also be considered in a legal analysis.

As outlined above, 'concepts' can have different functions, including, by providing a collective identity for a field of international law, by transforming already existing principles, by offering a way to reconcile existing and conflicting concepts, by framing the structure of a regime or by providing a basis for (judicial) decision-making.[257] Taken together, these norms serve as the underpinnings of a more complex regime, framing, informing and shaping the different ways in which policies are implemented in varying legal forms.[258] Such provisions of soft law can thus have an important influence in areas of international law where community thinking and value orientation play an important role. By itself, this is neither a positive nor a negative aspect for the development of international law. The question is rather how precise those applying and interpreting the law are in drawing the respective lines. Principles in MEAs are a good example for that: Understood as guidelines for introducing normative considerations of community values to the interpretation and application of the law, they can play an important and positive role. On the other hand, when understood as a shortcut to norms of customary law, general principles of international law or *jus cogens* norms, they can do serious harm to the acceptance of international law among States. They can also negatively affect State willingness to engage in legal interaction under frameworks like the UNFCCC which are essential to the development of international environmental law and climate law in particular.

Starting from the works of Simma and Paulus, this study shares with them the understanding that community values in international law cannot mean the introduction of abstract pre-ordained convictions of a certain cultural background, if only for the lack of an authority to define them. Any concept that would attempt this comes dangerously close to natural law theories that a pluralist international legal system cannot accommodate. In the absence of this authority, values must be deliberated and accepted by the actors of the international system, especially by States. To reconcile with this difficulty, this study draws on Brunnée and Toope notion of 'shared understandings'. Specifically, I draw on the notion that there needs to be room for such normativity to develop, but that this must also be possible in constellations where there are few shared values to begin with.[259]

Even given these difficulties, I share with Paulus the notion that for these phenomena the term 'values' is best suited. The term 'interests' implies that they are objectively identifiable. It is held here that balancing objective material interests is not the core of what made community thinking so controversial. Rather, I suggest that the controversy stemmed from the difficulty in balancing different

257 Dupuy and Viñuales, *International environmental law*, p. 52 et seq.
258 Ibid., p. 86.
259 Brunnée and Toope, *Legitimacy and legality in international law*, p. 71.

inter-subjective normative conceptions of the protective purpose of international law and the idea that some of them should not be left to the disposition of the States. 'Values' are more culturally informed than 'interests', more open to political deliberation and development and more central to any substantial notion of 'community'. But this, in turn, does not mean that the most relevant group of actors cannot still be the States as they are the closest actors international relations has to stable representation.

From international relations scholarship, the present author's understanding is informed by a combination of realism and social constructivism. Realism adds the recognition of the significance of state power and the need to sufficiently emphasize the role of the state. Likewise, it highlights the importance of state interest in the formation of international law. It needs to be acknowledged that despite the inclusion of other actors and the significance of this development, States remain the main actors as there are no other entities that will be suitable to take their position in the foreseeable future. From legal positivism, the perspective taken accepts positive law's necessary formality and its normative importance. Concurrently, the study shares with social constructivism that this does not capture the role of law exhaustively and that legal norms also have an important role in organizing and sometimes fostering political processes. It is maintained here that the idea of community values is not *a priori* negative or positive for the stability of international law and can be an improvement if wisely implemented.

The hypothesis for the following analysis in Part C and D is that the notion of community values in international law is often considered to be problematic because the concepts connected to these values are necessarily vague and offer room for different kinds of interpretation and implementation. What matters is how this room is being filled. One possibility is that it is filled with a strong community orientation where decisive actors are guided by values of the community even if these conflict with their own short-term interests. This scenario may be perceived by more powerful States as a holding a certain risk; weaker States would possibly benefit (e.g., from concerted action against climate change). The opposite possibility is that the void is filled by value hegemony and 'governing by law'. Hence, both weaker and more powerful States face a certain risk if the implementation of community values would structurally change international law. If, consequently, neither more powerful nor less powerful States would no longer believe in the advantages of international law, a 'decline' of international law would indeed be possible in climate change and beyond. This hypothesis makes it even more important to follow a careful legal implementation of this concept. Community values, therefore, present the risk of destabilizing international law by potentially reducing the acceptance by States while at the same time presenting an opportunity for improving the law's normative foundations.

Part C: Historical Background of Climate Change as a Matter of Community Values and International Law

I. Historical Background of International Climate Change Law

Today's international law concerning climate change did not just start to develop after 1990 but had historical precedents in both substance and form. These shall be elaborated in this section, with special focus on the structural connections of community value-related developments in international law generally.

The evolution of the UN climate regime itself can be divided into four chronological chapters: Firstly, the *agenda-setting phase* (1985–1990) transformed climate change from a scientific to a policy issue, lifting it to the intergovernmental level. Secondly, the *constitutional phase* (1991–1995) included the negotiation and adoption of the FCC itself as well as the way to the first COP in 1995, where the strategic road mapping for further regulatory action took place. Thirdly, the *regulatory phase* (1995–2005), from the Berlin mandate (1995) to the Kyoto Protocol's entry into force (2004), was characterized by the negotiation and implementation of the Kyoto Protocol. Finally, the *second constitutional phase* (2005–2016), was concerned with developing a post-2012 and later a post-2020 regime to succeed the Kyoto Protocol. This phase came to an end with the 2015 Paris Agreement and the beginning of its implementation.[260] While drawing on this historical periodization, the present study – in this part as well as in the subsequent analytical Part D – focusses on the conceptual evolution, pointing to those strands of development that came to be relevant for the community value orientation in the field and the norm concepts implementing it.

---

260 Daniel Bodansky, Jutta Brunnée, and Lavanya Rajamani, *International climate change law* (Oxford University Press, 2017), p. 96 and 97 et seqq.; see as well Daniel Bodansky and Lavanya Rajamani, "The Evolution and Governance Architecture of the United Nations Climate Change Regime", in *Global climate policy: Actors, concepts, and enduring challenges*, ed. Detlef F. Sprinz and Urs Luterbacher (MIT Press, 2018), p. 13 et seq.

1. Early Forms of International Law on Environmental Protection (1941–1985)

Before the evolution of the climate regime in the narrower sense, it took some time for climate change to enter the legal arena. Two moments can be distinguished as decisive for the inception of international climate change law, i.e., the early arbitral decisions bringing environmental issues and international law together (a) and on a multilateral level, the 1972 Stockholm Conference (b).

Initially, the phenomenon now referred to as 'climate change' was primarily an issue in the scientific sector. As early as 1896, the 'greenhouse warming theory' was put forward by Swedish chemist Svante Arrheniuse. He was the first scientist to quantify the influence of changes in the concentration of carbon dioxide (CO_2) in the atmosphere on the temperature of the earth's surface.[261] After World War II, the discussions about climate change also originated in the scientific arena. In the early 1960s, researchers established that atmospheric concentrations of CO_2 were increasing. The 'Keeling Curve' illustrating this came to be one of the few undisputed facts in the early debates on global warming and climate change.[262] Later still in the 1960s, environmental movements politically promoted issues like wildlife conservation and human health related environmental measures, thus putting them on the national political agenda. On the international level, these efforts resonated most prominently in the 1972 Stockholm Declaration produced by the UN Conference on the Human Environment. This internationalization of environmental concerns can be seen as one of the earliest examples of emphasizing a shared responsibility of the entire international community for a given problem. Although up until then, in a purely political sense. As elaborated earlier, three years after the VCLT acknowledging the existence of *jus cogens* norms and two years after the *Barcelona Traction* decision mentioning *erga omnes* obligations, this turn towards an emphasis on a shared responsibility for the environment in the early 1970s blends in well with the phase of increasing engagement with community aspects of the international order at this time.

Principle 21 of the Stockholm Declaration elaborated a connection of national sovereignty over resources to the obligation not to cause transboundary harm.

---

261 Henning Rodhe, Robert Charlson, and Elisabeth Crawford, "Svante Arrhenius and the Greenhouse Effect", *Ambio* 26, no. 1 (1997), p. 2; see also James Rodger Fleming, *Historical Perspectives on Climate Change* (Oxford University Press, 2005), p. 65 et seqq.

262 Bodansky, Brunnée, and Rajamani, *International climate change law*, p. 97.

This dated back to the *Trail Smelter* arbitral decision of 1938 and 1941[263], often quoted as the outset and beginning of modern international environmental law.

(a) Establishment of the No-Harm Rule: The Trail Smelter Arbitration

In the *Trail Smelter* case, the arbitral tribunal submitted to by the parties, had to decide whether Canada was responsible for damage caused to the crops and lands of the State of Washington. This damage was caused by the sulphur dioxide emissions stemming from a Canadian smelter of zinc and lead ores, based in British Columbia. In its decision of March 11, 1941, the tribunal held that:

> *[U]nder the principles of international law, as well as the law of the United States, no State has the right to use or permit the use of its territory in such a manner as to cause injury by fumes in or to the territory of another or the properties or persons therein, when the case is of serious consequence and the injury is established by clear and convincing evidence."*[264]

On this basis, the tribunal held Canada responsible for the damage caused by the Canadian smelter and granted compensation to the United States. Despite the significance of this case, it's importance has perhaps at times been overstated. Already in 1971 – some thirty years after *Trail Smelter* – it was remarked that the "heavy reliance on a single precedent breeds overstatement" and that "the time has come to re-examine the precedential value of the Trail Smelter Arbitration, to restore it to its rightful place as a landmark case in a continuum of developing law and remove from its shoulders the burdens heaped upon it by two generations of publicists".[265] Certainly there is some truth to the assessment of the case being overstated at times. Nonetheless, the case is of landmark significance for giving a first legal expression to environment-related concerns and for defining their relationship to international law: The States remain sovereign in their decision on how to use the resources linked to their territory, but the freedom of this use is linked to the obligation not to cause harm to other States, signifying a limitation to the idea of absolute sovereignty.

In 1963, another arbitral tribunal deciding a transboundary dispute between France and Spain relating to the use of the waters of Lake Lanoux, endorsed

---

263 Trail Smelter Arbitration (United States v. Canada) [1938] and [1941], 3 R.I.A.A., p. 1905.

264 Trail Smelter Arbitration (United States v. Canada) [1941], *3 R.I.A.A., p. 1963.*

265 Alfred P. Rubin, "Pollution by Analogy: The Trail Smelter Arbitration", *Oregon Law Review* 50, no. 3 (1971), p. 259.

again the rather narrow conception of environmental protection laid out by the Trail-Smelter-Arbitration:

> *"The Spanish government has also sought to establish the contents of contemporary positive international law [...]. Certain principles that it seeks to demonstrate are, assuming it succeeds, without relevance for the issue under review. Thus, assuming there is a principle prohibiting the upstream State from altering the waters of a river in such a way as to seriously harm the downstream State, in any event such principle would not apply in the present case, to the extent that it has been admitted by the Tribunal [...] that the French project does not alter the waters of the river Carol. In fact, States are nowadays perfectly aware of the importance of the contradictory interests involved in the industrial use of international watercourses, and of the need to reconcile them through mutual concessions. The only way to achieve such interest compromises is the conclusion of agreements, on an increasingly comprehensive basis."*[266]

This section of the *Lake Lanoux* decision illustrates one of the central ambiguities of these early forms of international environmental law: It was unclear whether environmental protection was required as such, meaning for the sake of the environment itself (or as a common resource), or whether the environment was to be protected only where damages to another state could result from a given conduct.[267] In these early examples of case law, it is difficult to find evidence for the first alternative. This ambiguity would later find its perpetuation in the ambiguity between norms based on environmental or climate protection for its own sake and those based on the idea of environmental goods being protected in the interest of human beings, thus rooted in (individual) human rights norms.[268]

---

266 Affaire du Lac Lanoux (Spain v. France), 12 R.I.A.A. 285 (1963), para. 308. In the original French, it reads: "[L]e Gouvernement espagnol s'est efforce d'établir également le contenu du droit international positif actuel [...]. Certains principes dont il fait la démonstration sont, à supposer celle-ci acquise, sans intérêt pour le problème actuellement examiné. Ainsi, en admettant qu'il existe un principe interdisant à l'Etat d'amont d'altérer les eaux d'un fleuve dans des conditions de nature à nuire gravement à l'Etat d'aval, un tel principe ne trouve pas son application à la présente espèce, puisqu'il a été admis par le Tribunal [...] que le projet français n'altière pas les eaux du Carol. En réalité, les Etats ont aujourd'hui parfaitement conscience de l'importance des intérêts contradictoires, que met en cause l'utilisation industrielle des fleuves internationaux, et de la nécessité de les concilier les uns avec les autres par des concessions mutuelles. La seule voie pour aboutir à ces compromis d'intérêt est la conclusion d'accords, sur une base de plus en plus compréhensive."

267 Jorge E. Vinuales, "The Contribution of the International Court of Justice to the Development of International Environmental Law: A Contemporary Assessment", *Fordham Int'l LJ* 32 (2008), p. 238.

268 See chapter III below.

This early heritage of arbitral decisions, which would form into the 'no-harm rule', was firmly based in classical bilateral international law.

(b) *Stockholm 1972 – the Birth of Modern International Environmental Law*

The Conference on the Human Environment, held at Stockholm in June 1972, was hailed at the time as "in many respects the most successful international conference held in recent years".[269] In retrospect, it is generally seen as the foundational moment of modern international environmental law.[270] The conference certainly was productive: The final document contained a set of 'common principles to inspire and guide the peoples of the world in the preservation and enhancement of the human environment' ('The Stockholm Declaration'). It proposed to the UNGA the establishment of an international Governing Council for Environmental Programmes, an Environment Secretariat, an Environment Fund and an interagency Environmental Co-ordinating Board for ensuring cooperation and coordination among all bodies concerned.[271] The institutional outcome of these suggestions was the establishment of the UN Environment Programme (UNEP), which despite lacking legal personality on its own (in contrast to UN specialized agencies) has come to exercise considerable influence on the law-making processes in the field.[272] The Stockholm Conference also set in motion a period of increased engagement with environmental policies on the national and regional level, such as the adoption of the EU (then European Communities) environmental protection rules or the creation of an Environment Committee at the OECD.[273]

Although the Stockholm Conference and its outcomes were not yet directly linked to climate change, it brought about structural developments that became influential on the emerging climate regime. Arguably the most important one

---

269 Louis B. Sohn, "The Stockholm Declaration on the Human Environment", *Harv. Int'l. LJ* 14, no. 3 (1973), p. 423.

270 Dupuy and Viñuales, *International environmental law*, p. 8.

271 Sohn, "The Stockholm Declaration on the Human Environment", 423 et seq.

272 'Institutional and Financial Arrangements for International Environmental Cooperation', 15 Dec 1972, UN Doc. A/Res/2997/XXVII. See also, Dupuy and Viñuales, *International environmental law*, p. 9; Beyerlin and Marauhn, *International environmental law*, p. 8.

273 Philippe Sands, *Principles of international environmental law*, 3rd ed. (Cambridge University Press, 2012), p. 34, with further references.

was the Stockholm Conference's contribution to the relationship between human rights and environmental protection.[274] Building on the ambiguity of the reason to protect the environment outlined above, Stockholm emphasized the synergies between the two areas of international law: It insisted that a healthy environment was necessary for the realization of human rights (Principle 1). This nexus informed the legal and political processes in both areas. The impact on the human rights discourse is well summarized in the 2011 analytical study of the Office of the High Commissioner for Human Rights (OHCHR), according to which, three main approaches have characterized the relationship between human rights and the environment: The first approach sees the environment as a pre-condition to the enjoyment of human rights. The second submits that human rights are tools to address environmental issues, both procedurally and substantively. The third approach aims to integrate both human rights and the environment under the concept of sustainable development.[275] The three approaches are expressions of different ways to resolve the aforementioned ambiguity and its respective consequences: The first approach implies that environmental protection has merely an instrumental value to the efforts in protecting human rights. The second, rather inversely, sees human rights as a legal tool in the effort to ensure environmental protection. Only the third has the explicit ambition to resolve the existing contradictions. However, the translation of this approach into the language of legal obligations is one of its biggest challenges and disadvantages in comparison to the other two.[276] As will be seen in Part D, where 'sustainable development' is analyzed in more detail as a legal concept, an inherent problem is its lack of clarity – making it difficult to formulate it as a legal norm that could be applied in a concrete manner. While some aspects of the 'sustainable use' of resources can be formulated sufficiently clear to form the basis of legal rules, this is much more difficult for the imperative to balance different concerns (primarily environmental against economic and developmental ones) in a given case or policy decision.

One aspect of the political and legal development surrounding the Stockholm Conference is particularly noteworthy with regard to the connection between environmental issues and community thinking in international politics and law at the time. That is, how closely the introduction of environmental protection

274 Dupuy and Viñuales, *International environmental law*, p. 298.

275 Office of the High Commissioner for Human Rights (OHCHR), Analytical Study on the Relationship between Human Rights and the Environment, (2011) para. 7 et seqq.

276 See especially part D, section II.4., discussion the concept of 'Sustainable Development'.

into the international arena has been linked to a normative agenda of some actors, who aimed to broaden the range of the relevant constituents of IEL and the rights conferred to them.

For instance, before the conference, a group of economic experts from developing countries called for an inclusion of development aspects into the Agenda.[277] At the conference, developing States sought to further connect environment- and development-related human rights in the deliberations.[278] The negotiation and adoption of the Stockholm declaration gave rise to an intensive discussion in legal scholarship about how far the declaration could be cited as an enforcement of an 'international principle of solidarity'. Through this, individuals would be entitled, based on a human right to a healthy environment, to acts of environmental protection by the whole international community.[279] The connection of a human rights-based entitlement with a 'principle' conceptually directed at States and international institutions, to create some form of community-bound (sense of) obligation, preludes themes that became central in the post-Cold War changes.

As alluded to, parts of the ICJ jurisprudence from the 1970s contributed to the foundations of a debate about community related legal developments. Two cases did this in particular: The *Nuclear Tests* case of 1974[280], confirming previous case law on transboundary damages[281], as well as the obiter dictum made in the *Barcelona Traction case*[282] on obligations *erga omnes*. Both were soon perceived as potentially applicable to environmental norms. Thus, although not directly linked to environment, let alone climate law questions, the apparent trends in jurisprudence fostered community related legal development.[283]

---

277 Steven Bernstein, *The compromise of liberal environmentalism* (Columbia University Press, 2001), p. 42.

278 UN Doc. A/CONF.48/14/Rev.1, para. 44 on the proceedings in the General Debate; see also para. 310 (Statement by the Philippines).

279 Brunnée, "'Common Interest' – Echoes from an Empty Shell?", p. 798 et seq. with further reference.

280 *Nuclear Tests* (Australia v. France), Judgment, IC.J. Rep. 1974, p. 253; *Nuclear Tests* (New Zealand v. France), Judgment, I.C.J. Rep. 1974, p. 457.

281 In its Corfu channel case, the ICJ had already invoked "every State's obligation not to allow knowingly its territory to be used for acts contrary to the rights of other States", see Corfu Channel (United Kingdom v. Albania), Judgment, I.C.J. Rep. 1949, p. 4 [hereinafter Corfu Channel], para. 22.

282 *Barcelona Traction*; See already in Part A, III. 3. above.

283 Vinuales, "The Contribution of the International Court of Justice to the Development of International Environmental Law: A Contemporary Assessment", p. 237.

2. The 'Agenda-Setting Phase' and 'Pre-Negotiation-Phase' (1985–1991): Growing Awareness and the Struggle for Appropriate Legal Concepts

The increasing awareness in the 1980s of global climate change and its anthropogenic causes could build on the scientific, political and to a certain extent legal-institutional frameworks outlined above. Political initiatives developed to meet the challenges with new instruments on the national, regional and international level. These initiatives coincided with three significant trends alluded to in Part A: First, a growing focus on the 'common' elements in international politics, finding expression in early concepts like the 'common heritage of mankind' (a). Second, an ongoing tendency towards a multilateral approach to environmental and climate governance (b), combined with an increasing emphasis on legal bindingness and the structural role the law should play in this field of international relations (c). Quantitatively, this can be seen exemplified in the growing density of the MEAs being concluded during that period.[284] Qualitatively, regarding the legal density of the codification projects at the time, what happened with the Brundtland commission's report is a case in point. With remarkable speed – compared for example to the genesis of the ITLOS – the developing efforts led to the inclusion of climate change in the agenda of the UN and eventually to the adoption of the UNFCCC, the multilateral framework governing the area ever since.

(a) The Common Heritage Principle Informing the Process: ITLOS

The concept of common heritage of mankind was developed primarily[285] in context with the management of the seabed and its resources.[286] After being

---

284 Beyerlin and Marauhn, *International environmental law*, p. 10 et seq. For an overview of the MEAs deposited with the UN, see UN Treaty Collection, Multilateral Treaties Deposited with the Secretary General, Chapter XVII: Environment, available at https://treaties.un.org/pages/Treaties.aspx?id=27&subid=A&clang=_en . See Pauwelyn, Wessel, and Wouters, "When structures become shackles", p. 734, for an overview of the number of new multilateral treaties concluded during the 1950s, 1960s, 1970s, 1980s and 1990s.

285 The concept was also used in the Agreement Governing the Activities of States on the Moon and Other Celestial Bodies, 18 December 1979, U.N.T.S., vol. 1363, p. 3 (Moon treaty). Due to its very limited number of ratifications, especially among the States actively pursuing space programs, the influence of the treaty remained limited. See Dupuy and Viñuales, *International environmental law*, p. 84 et seq. with further reference to the few other references to the principle.

286 See ibid., p. 84 with further references.

mentioned first in the UNGA resolution of 1970[287], it was reiterated by inclusion into Part XI of UNCLOS. The basic idea behind it was to exclude the appropriation of the resource in question by a single state, while putting exploitation under common management. Apart from the negative aspect of precluding appropriation, it introduced a new element into the law of the sea by indicating that the control and management of the deep seabed is vested in mankind as a whole. Hence, it was assigned to an international body (the ISA).[288]

Although the program conveyed by the common heritage concept is distinct from the 'common concern' concept that would come to be at the center of the climate regime, the former has in some ways preluded the latter: The conceptual approach of the common heritage principle is to put an emphasis on co-operation when it comes to the utilization of the administered common resource. The common concern concept, on the other hand, is different in putting its main emphasis on a resource that is accessible to all, but where collective action is needed to protect it.[289]

Moreover, the common heritage concept is one of the early and very few examples of a tangible allusion to community-based concepts in positive international law, despite its vagueness concerning the concrete obligations following it.

(b) Multilateralising Climate Law: The Vienna Convention 1985 as a Blueprint for the UNFCCC

Among the environmental instruments concluded before the UNFCCC, arguably none was more influential than the Vienna Convention for the Protection of the Ozone Layer of 1985.[290] During the preparatory work for the UNFCCC, two models were seriously considered. First was the UNCLOS model envisaging a general agreement on a 'law of the atmosphere'. The second was a framework convention specifically on climate change, with the possibility of further developing the convention through protocols and subsequent agreements under it. The latter prevailed not least because of the comparatively successful step-by-step approach of the Ozone regime. This is especially evident when compared to

---

287 'Declaration of Principles Governing the Seabed and the Ocean Floor, and Subsoil Thereof, beyond the limits of national jurisdiction', UN Doc. A/RES/25/2749.

288 Rüdiger Wolfrum, "Common Heritage of Mankind", in *MPEPIL*, ed. Rüdiger Wolfrum (Oxford University Press, 2009), para. 14.

289 A more detailed account of the 'common concern' concept is given in Part D, II.

290 Vienna Convention for the Protection of the Ozone Layer, U.N.T.S., vol. 1513, p. 293 [hereinafter 1985 Vienna Convention].

the complicated and lengthy negotiations for the UNCLOS regime.[291]During a meeting of the INC Working Group III in October 1989, there was "[full] support for a framework convention" on climate change "based on [the] format of [the] Vienna Convention for the Protection of the Ozone Layer".[292] The Vienna system consisted of both a framework convention setting forth general principles and a series of specific protocols, including the 1987 Montreal Protocol.[293] The Working Group correspondingly also acknowledged its "support" to establish, within a framework convention, "general principles and obligations with respect to climate change" and an "institutional framework and mechanisms to monitor and assess climate change, and manage the responses" as well as to "take into account the needs, technological and financial, of developing countries".[294] The Vienna Convention was largely procedural, establishing very general obligations such as co-operation (Art. 2(2), Art. 4) and exchange (Art. 3,4). It, however, mainly established an institutional framework under which States were invited to participate and elaborate more substantive regulations in subsequent protocols.[295]

The *Montreal Protocol* is the most significant protocol adopted under the 1985 Vienna Convention. It created incentives to both reduce the consumption and the production of Chlorofluorocarbon (CFC).[296] Scholars have argued that it was more successful than any of the climate agreements for reducing greenhouse gas emissions.[297] The Montreal protocol's success has been argued to be due to its

---

291 Daniel Bodansky, "The History of the Global Climate Change Regime", in *International relations and global climate change*, ed. Urs Luterbacher and Detlef F. Sprinz (MIT Press, 2001), p. 31 with further reference; Durwood Zaelke and James Cameron, "Global Warming and Climate Change – An Overview of the International Legal Process", *American University International Law Review* 5, no. 2 (1990), p. 272 et seq.

292 See WMO/UNEP/IPCC Working Group III, Second Session, Geneva, 2 – 6 Oct 1989, Legal Measures and Processes: Synopsis of Contributions (submitted by Chairman Working Group III) [hereinafter Legal Measures Synopsis], para. 2–5.

293 Montreal Protocol on Substances that Deplete the Ozone Layer, U.N.T.S., vol. 1522, p. 3 [hereinafter Montreal Protocol].

294 Legal Measures Synopsis, para. A(2).

295 Bodansky, "The history of the global climate change regime", p. 33.

296 Scott Barrett, "The Paris Agreement: We Can Do (and Have Done) Better", in *Paris agreement and beyond: International climate change policy post-2020*, ed. Robert N. Stavins and Robert C. Stowe (Cambridge, Mass.: Harvard Project on Climate Agreements, 2016), p. 76.

297 Guus J. M. Velders et al., "The Importance of the Montreal Protocol in Protecting Climate", *Proceedings of the National Academy of Sciences* 104, no. 12 (2007) p. 4814.

approach of combining asking countries to coordinate their behavior with changing incentives in trade policies and ensuring broad participation.[298]

(c) An Increasing Emphasis on Legal Bindingness – the 'Brundtland' Commission

During the 1980s, the momentum to develop an international environmental law initiated by the Stockholm Conference brought about a growing number of legally relevant MEAs, with the treaty practice covering a much broader spectrum than before.[299] Still, the approach taken by most agreements of that time – the Vienna Convention being the notable exception – was still predominantly utilitarian rather than ecological, directed more at transboundary harm than at global environmental problems. Moreover, the legal substance of many agreements, especially regarding the operative norms, remained relatively poor.[300]

At the same time and to a certain extent in contrast to this trend of rather 'thin' agreements, "a rush of international initiatives for the trans-sectoral codification of environmental law 'principles'", as it has been called, unfolded.[301] After the 'World Charter for Nature', adopted by the UNGA[302] and underscoring the growing relevance of environmental issues on the international level[303], instruments such as the 'Montreal Rules of International Law Applicable to Transfrontier Pollution', adopted by the non-governmental 'International Law Association' (ILA)[304], were further examples of this trend.[305]

---

298 Barrett, "The Paris Agreement: We Can Do (and Have Done) Better",

299 Beyerlin and Marauhn, *International environmental law*, p. 10 et seq.; Dupuy and Viñuales, *International environmental law*, p. 11; For a broader overview, see Andronico O. Adede, "The Treaty System from Stockholm (1972) to Rio de Janeiro (1992)", *Pace Environmental Law Review* 13, no. 1 (1995), pp. 33–48.

300 Beyerlin and Marauhn, *International environmental law*, p. 11.

301 Peter H. Sand, "The Evolution of International Environmental Law", in *The Oxford handbook of international environmental law*, ed. Daniel Bodansky, Jutta Brunnée, and Ellen Hey (OUP, 2008), p. 38.

302 UN Doc. A/Res/37/7.

303 Dupuy and Viñuales, *International environmental law*, p. 11.

304 International Law Association, "Draft Rules of International Law Applicable to Transfrontier Pollution", *Umwelt- und Planungsrecht* 3, no. 1 (1983), p. 21 et seqq.

305 Further examples are the ILC working on 'responsibility and liability for environmental harm' and some years later, the Institut de Droit International (IDI) beginning to work on its own set of rules applicable to the environment and to environmental damage in 1991 (finished in 1997), cf. Sand, "The Evolution of International Environmental Law", p. 38 with further reference.

A major contribution in this regard was the Brundtland Commission's work: Its strong emphasis on legal implementation is tangible in the 22 'Proposed Legal Principles for Environmental Protection and Sustainable Development' it contains. Twenty-one of these include the obligatory formulation "[S] tates shall", except for principle 1, which reiterates the "fundamental right to an environment adequate for their health and well-being".[306] Where the 1985 Vienna Convention was coined by a framework approach with little substantively obligatory rules and the mentioning of principles took place only in its preamble, the Brundtland Commission emphasized the obligatory role principles could play in environmental contexts. This emphasis is arguably not a coincidence of a single internationally minded group of experts, but to a certain extent an expression of one of the predominant perspectives at the time. This perspective gained even further traction after 1990: For the emerging international climate regime, as in many fields of international relations at the time, it was not yet clear what role legal norms and legal form would play. This included the question about the relationship between rules and principles in multilateral instruments. It was yet clarified how far community related rhetoric would produce tangible legal quality in the field. For instance, the introduction of *jus cogens* or obligations *erga omnes* would need to gain acceptance and translation into the various fields of international law to result in legal relevance. Reminiscent of the early 1970s and the debates surrounding the Stockholm declaration, opinions differed between wide-ranging normative aspirations and minimalistic, technical and procedural approaches.

Regarding the value-orientation of the legal development in this period, in the discussion whether there are norms in international environmental law which can be identified as 'shared values' – on which, according to rather cautious assessments of *jus cogens* such norms would have to be based – it was suggested that this was (already) possible. Pollution reaching a degree at which it would represent a threat to the entire international community, it was suggested (climate change being cited as an example), "would be in conflict with a peremptory rule of international law", albeit without specifying which jus cogens norm is referred to.[307] The connection of values and principles in the field of international

306 World Commission on Environment and Development, *Our common future* (Oxford University Press, 1987), Annex 1: Summary of Proposed Legal Principles for Environmental Protection and Sustainable Development Adopted by the WCED Experts Group on Environmental Law.

307 Brunnée, "'Common Interest' – Echoes from an Empty Shell?", p. 804. The argument is based on a comparison to the dangers of atomic weapons, regarding what others had

environmental law with legal structures as strong and rich in prerequisites as *jus cogens* speaks for the strong connection between the regulatory ambitions and an emphasis on legal instruments to implement them. The same author observed "that international law is at a turning point from a system balancing conflicting sovereign interests to one of constructive interaction for the common good".[308] With this alleged shift in scholarship and legal development, the historical turning point to the 1990s approached.

II. Climate Change as a Community Issue

At the outset of the idea of co-operation in international relations is the notion that certain problems, challenges, aspirations and goals are too large for single nation-States to handle alone and independent from one another. Later, ideas surrounding the conception of an 'international community' and the protection and promotion of values through international law built on that notion. Taking this notion seriously, few phenomena require such a high level of international cooperation as climate change. From a value perspective, few other problems make it necessary to take so many interwoven political and ethical challenges into account in political and legal considerations. Reflecting these two perspectives, the protection of the environment and combating climate change had a pivotal role in the historical emergence of community thinking and value orientation in international law. This is particularly salient during the period chosen as a frame of reference for the present thesis. In this section, the ethical implications of climate change will be outlined, and a summary of global public opinion surveys will be given. The latter will show how climate change has become a value-related matter in public perception. A brief conclusion on the historical background of climate change as a matter of community values will lead over to the empirical analysis.

1. Community Value Orientation Regarding Climate Change (After 1990)

Environmental protection and especially efforts to deal with climate change have been a prominent example for the development of community-oriented thinking

---

argued before that their use and other means of mass destruction were prohibited as they threatened the existence of the entire international community, see Mosler, "The international society as a legal community", p. 18.

308 Brunnée, "'Common Interest' – Echoes from an Empty Shell?", p. 792.

in international law and a focal point of the debate on community values. While early developments like the *Trail Smelter* case[309] had been strictly bilateral, the focus shifted slightly after World War II and the decolonization period. In the Stockholm Declaration of 1972, which established environmental protection as a matter of international politics, 'common convictions' are stated, and principle 18 speaks of the 'common good of mankind'. Nevertheless, the declaration echoes traditional bilateralist international law[310]: Principle 21, generally seen as the Declaration's core, elaborates the 'no-harm'-rule and links national sovereignty over resources to an obligation not to cause harm beyond one's own territory. The 'no-harm'- rule today is widely regarded as a norm of customary international law.[311] During the 1980s, many UN-level efforts were made to strengthen international cooperation regarding the environment, most notably the 'Brundtland Commission'[312] with its report 'Our common future'.[313] In 1988, the UN General Assembly recognized climate change as a 'common concern of mankind'[314] and thus contributed to establishing terminology for the underlying phenomenon and the multilateral cooperation concerning it.

During the 1990s and early 2000s, the international trend of advocacy for international action on climate change gained momentum. The number of internationally operating NGOs in the field increased significantly, as did the media coverage on climate change related issues.[315] Numerous policy efforts were made to formulate and promote values related to climate change and sustainable development on the political agenda. The 2000 Millennium Declaration[316] by the UNGA, the 'Earth Charter' or the Global Scenario Group[317] are some

309 Trail Smelter Arbitration (United States v. Canada) [1938] and [1941], 3 R.I.A.A., p. 1905.

310 Simma, "From bilateralism to community interest ", p. 238 et seq.

311 On 'no-harm', see Section II.6.

312 World Commission on Environment and Development (WCED), commonly referred to as 'Brundtland Commission' for its chair, former Norwegian Prime Minister Gro Harlem Brundtland.

313 World Commission on Environment and Development, *Our common future*.

314 UN Doc. A/Res/43/53.

315 Andreas Schmidt, Ana Ivanova, and Mike S. Schäfer, "Media Attention for Climate Change around the World: A Comparative Analysis of Newspaper Coverage in 27 Countries", *Global Environmental Change* 23, no. 5 (2013), p. 1240 et seq.

316 UN Doc. A/RES/55/2.

317 The Global Scenario Group was founded in 1995 as an independent, international and interdisciplinary body to examine world prospects and ways of fostering a more sustainable and equitable future. This was established by the Tellus Institute and

examples of these policy efforts. The Millennium Declaration points out "certain fundamental values to be essential to international relations in the twenty-first century"[318] and at least three of them (solidarity, respect for nature and shared responsibility) are directly linked to climate change. The Earth Charter Initiative – a civil society effort – originated in the Brundtland commission's call for a "universal declaration" to "consolidate and extend relevant legal principles" and to create new norms "needed to maintain livelihoods and life on our shared planet" as well as to "guide state behavio[u]r in the transition to sustainable development".[319] The initiative was launched in 1994 as an open and participatory consultation process including NGOs and individuals from around the world. The Charter produced four general values, namely 'community of life', 'ecological integrity', 'social and economic justice' and 'democracy', then elaborated 16 intermediate-level principles and 61 specific values.[320]

A possible reservation against counting these developments as indicators for an increasing community value orientation could be to understand them as mere political rhetoric. Indeed, the use of highly ambitious terms in speeches or resolutions is a quite common phenomenon in international diplomacy. However, two factors distinguish the discussed instruments and the period they exemplify from the 'usual' invocation of ambitious rhetoric. One is the sheer breadth of allusions to community values not only in international politics, but also in scholarly debates during this period. The other is the increasing engagement of actors on the UN level promoting community value related issues. It is one thing for advocacy NGOs to invoke community value references in their work, but it is quite another for UN level commissions or the UNGA to do so. With the inclusion in UN documents, agendas, and discussions, the arguments make an institutionally decisive step towards the state-consent-based channels of law making on the international level.

Stockholm Environment Institute to engage a distinguished and diverse international group in an examination of the prospects for world development in the 21st century. For their first report, see Paul Raskin et al., Great Transition: The promise and lure of the times ahead. A report of the Global Scenario Group (2002) https://greattransition.org/documents/Great_Transition.pdf.

318 UN Doc. A/Res/55/2.

319 World Commission on Environment and Development, *Our common future*, para. 85.

320 Earth Charter International (ECI), "The Earth Charter" (2000), available at http://earthcharter.org/invent/images/uploads/echarter_english.pdf.

(a) Climate Change as an Ethical Problem

Values, as understood in this study and outlined above[321], are informed by and thereby connected to moral and ethical considerations. In this vein, the ethical implications of climate change need to be considered in explaining the interconnection between the development of community values and that of the climate change regime. They exemplify the historical and theoretical considerations outlined earlier in this study, and thereby depict how climate change is not only a complex problem regarding natural science or the organisation of policies. From a general *ethical* perspective, climate change amplifies many of the challenges humanity is facing, such as poverty, famines or loss of land. In view of this, climate change has been called the "perfect moral storm".[322] From an ethical perspective focusing on *human security*, climate change has been argued to be a 'threat multiplier'[323], influencing and exacerbating conflicts over resources and borders.

Following from the above, for those arguing for justice as the normative core of international law, it is imperative to argue that international law should consider itself with this impediment to justice. Approaching these questions from a *utilitarian* and pragmatic perspective, it is argued that the protection of the global climate is something that cannot be accomplished by bilateral efforts alone.[324] Even States that abide by the no-harm rule would lack any effective influence on others.

Corresponding to the ethical implications of climate change, religious communities also increasingly engage in the public discourse on the issue: The US Conference of Catholic Bishops called upon the US government to live up to their "special responsibility in its stewardship of God's creation to shape responses that serve the entire human family". The 2001 statement called for the global action on climate change to be based on social and economic justice and to avoid unfair burdens for poor and developing countries.[325]

---

321 See Part B., I.

322 Stephen Mark Gardiner, *A perfect moral storm: The ethical tragedy of climate change* (Oxford University Press, 2011).

323 Gordan R. Sullivan and et al., National Security and the threat of climate change, (2007).

324 Simma, "From bilateralism to community interest ", p. 239.

325 United States Conference of Catholic Bishops, Global Climate Change: A Plea for Dialogue Prudence and the Common Good (Statement), (2001) http://www.usccb.org/issues-and-action/human-life-and-dignity/e...ate-change-a-plea-for-dialogue-prudence-and-the-common-good.cfm.

A key figure in the contemporary debate on the ethics of climate change is Pope Francis. Already by choosing his papal name upon his election in 2013, he linked his work to that of Saint Francis of Assisi, an important figure in catholic teaching for the relationship between humankind and the environment. In his widely discussed 2015 encyclical 'Laudato Si', he focused on environmental concerns and emphasized climate change.[326] Explicitly aiming to influence the process leading up to the Paris Summit later that year[327], he called for an "ecological conversion"[328] of all Catholics and linked action against climate change to his stance on social justice. The letter found wide resonance, even among policymakers from various governments and organizations[329] as well as pertinent NGOs.[330] Comparable efforts emphasizing the combat against climate change as a value issue have been made by other religious communities: The Organisation of Islamic Cooperation (OIC) included climate change as a priority area in their recent ten-year program of action.[331] The Coalition on the Environment and Jewish Life (COEJ), an initiative founded in 1993 by numerous Jewish communities, has continuously contributed to the debate about climate change, energy policies and GHG reduction.[332]

(b) Integrated Approach to Climate Change and Development Policies

The ethical ramifications of climate change are also closely linked to a third dimension, which entails the economic aspects of climate change. On the one hand, an economic perspective on climate change is concerned with the efficient organisation of the fight against climate change – producing the highest

326 Francis I., Laudato Si: On Care for Our Common Home, (2015) .

327 Philip Pullella, "Pope Demands 'action now' to Save Planet from Environmental Ruin", *Reuters online* (2015).

328 Francis I., Laudato Si: On Care for Our Common Home (2015), para. 16–221.

329 UNFCCC Secretariat, "Pope Francis Releases Encyclical on Climate and Environment – UN Leaders React," *News release*, http://newsroom.unfccc.int/unfccc-newsroom/pope-francis-releases-encyclical-on-climate-and-environment/.

330 See e.g. Giuseppe Onufrio, "The Encyclical: Spirituality and Ethics Join the Climate Debate," *Greenpeace International news blog*, https://www.greenpeace.org/archive-international/en/news/Blogs/makingwaves/the-encyclical-blog/blog/53267/.18 June 2015.

331 Organisation of Islamic Cooperation, Programme of Action 'OIC-2025' (2016), available at https://www.oic-oci.org/docdown/?docID=16&refID=5.

332 Coalition on the environment and Jewish life, Jewish Energy Guide, ed. David Krantz, (2014) http://aytzim.org/JewishEnergyGuide-web.pdf.

net benefit for all actors involved.[333] On the other hand and more pertinent for the matter at hand, these links account for the entanglement of climate change and development in the political as well as the legal development of the field. The above-mentioned 'Brundtland commission' and the later 'Earth charter'-initiative exemplify a trend which, as will be elaborated below, has its roots in the late 1960s and early 1970s, and especially in the 1972 Stockholm declaration. The international engagement against environmental problems and climate change was discursively and politically linked to human rights-based approaches to development. This had significant effect on the development of the climate regime as conflicts about the purposes, i.e., which policies and norms were to be pursued, lingered on. One example of this conflict is the protection of the environment in the interest of human beings versus an approach which sees the environment as an end in itself. A further illustration of this conflict is the conflicting priorities of environmental protection and human economic development. The norm concept of 'sustainable development' is the best illustration of this linkage and will be hence be scrutinized in this regard.[334] This chapter depicts in how far the field of climate change law has come to be interwoven with issues of (community) values, their prioritization and the relationship of these processes with legal structures.

(c) *Perception of Climate Change as a Community Value: Global Public Opinion*

"Values", political analyst Robert Worcester suggested, are "the deep tides of public mood, slow to change, but powerful."[335] This definition rightfully points to a further dimension of values as understood and defined in this study. Their origin is not primarily in positive law, but rather situated in the political realm influenced by moral and ethical considerations. Because of the increasing role of community values in international relations and law, a certain importance is accorded to public opinion regarding community value related issues. Showing how the broader field of international engagement with climate change is an issue of community value orientation, is further confirmed by an, albeit cursory,

---

333 Bodansky, Brunnée, and Rajamani, *International climate change law*, p. 6 et seq., pointing to economic insights such as that adaptation to CC is cheaper than mitigating the effects of CC as a possible basis for political decisions from such perspectives.

334 See part D, section II.4.

335 W. Phillips Davison, "Public Opinion", in *Encyclopædia Britannica online*, ed. Dale H. Hoiberg (Encyclopædia Britannica, inc., 2017).

look at international public opinion surveys. These show strong indications that among societies, climate change is increasingly perceived as a serious global threat that requires coordinated international action and is significant for the entire international community.

In 1995, a year at the peak of the reference period for community values outlined earlier, a clear majority (62 %) worldwide said they "would agree to an increase in taxes if the extra money were used to prevent environmental damage," whereas only 33 % said they would oppose such policies.[336]

A survey of 11 developed and 23 developing countries in 2000 found that 83 % of respondents expressed fair to high levels of concern about the environment. Large majorities selected the strongest response possible (very serious) for seven of eight environmental problems assessed. Climate change was graded at an average 56 % into this category.[337] The 2000 World Values Survey also asked about which political level certain policy decisions should be made. Overall, a majority preferred UN-coordinated national policy for areas like human rights or international peace-keeping. But remarkably, this was not the case for environmental protection: Here, an overall majority of 46 % preferred those decisions to be made on the national level alone, with much higher numbers in developing countries. Interpretations of this outcome suspected the desire to maintain sovereignty over resources to be a key motivating factor.

Looking at more recent inquiries, it seems that the view of climate change as a common challenge has largely continued or even proliferated. That is, such opinions are shared across the divide between the Global North and the Global South, which is a pivotal factor in identifying community values as understood here. A 2017 survey on climate change throughout EU countries showed that a steadily increasing number of people support the view that national governments, but increasingly also other actors such as businesses, are responsible for acting on climate change.[338] A survey conducted by the Yale University on the perception of climate change among the US population shows that here as well,

336 Ibid., p. 421.

337 Anthony Leiserowitz, Robert Kates, and Thomas Parris, "Sustainability Values, Attitudes and Behaviors: A Review of Multi-national and Global Trends.", *Annual Review of Environment and Resources* 31 (2006), p. 421 et seq. with further references.

338 European Commission, Special Eurobarometer 459 'Climate Change' – Report, ISBN 978-92-79-70220-4 (2017) https://ec.europa.eu/clima/sites/clima/files/support/docs/report_2017_en.pdf, p. 23.

a growing number of people perceive climate change as a threat.[339] Of respondents, 71 % said that climate change is threatening future generations. Similarly, 24 % of respondents stated that their most important motivator for climate action was a desire to provide a better life for their children and grandchildren. Hence, the intergenerational aspect of climate change is predominant. Likewise, the impact climate change will have on the world's poor and on people in developing countries is a salient feature of the American perception: 62 % think that these groups will be harmed by global warming and 4 % name saving people from poverty and starvation as a reason for fighting climate change.[340]

Looking at large societies in the Global South, similar trends have been described. In India, awareness of climate change and its adverse effects have risen. India is a highly relevant player both in terms of the feelings the impacts of climate change and contributing to the problem: It is one of the world's countries most vulnerable to climate change with roughly half of its population dependent on climate change-sensitive sectors like agriculture. However, India also became the third largest emitter of GHG, e.g., by tripling its CO_2 emissions from fuel combustion alone between 1990 and 2011.[341] However, in a 2012 survey, 41 % of respondents said that the government of India should be doing much more (24 %) or more (17 %) to address global warming. A large majority said that India should be making substantial efforts to reduce global warming, even if this comes at an economic cost. A majority (53 %) of respondents even stated that in case of conflict between the two, protecting the environment is more important than promoting economic growth.[342] Of the respondents, 38 % stated that India should reduce its own emissions of the gases that cause global warming immediately, without waiting for other countries.[343] These opinions coincide with an overall emphasis on egalitarian values. A large majority agreed that "in an ideal society, all basic needs (food, housing, health care, education) would be guaranteed by the government for everyone" (76 %). Statements like "the world

---

339 Anthony Leiserowitz et al., Climate change in the American mind, (2017) http://climatecommunication.yale.edu/wp-content/uploads/2017/07/Climate-Change-American-Mind-May-2017.pdf.

340 Ibid., p. 3, 24.

341 Jagadish Thaker and Anthony Leiserowitz, "Shifting Discourses of Climate Change in India", *Climate Change* 123, no. 2 (2014), p. 107.

342 Anthony Leiserowitz and Jagadish Thaker, Climate change in the Indian mind, (2012) http://climatecommunication.yale.edu/wp-content/uploads/2016/02/2012_08_Climate-Change-in-the-Indian-Mind.pdf, p. 31 et seq.

343 Ibid., p. 2.

would be a more peaceful place if its wealth were divided more equally among nations" also found support.[344] Comparably, according to a local 2017 survey, China shows growing support for policies on climate change, both nationally and internationally. Regarding the national level, respondents generally thought that the government should do more to address climate change.[345] Concerning China's international engagement, a staggering majority of 96.8 % supported international cooperation in the fight against climate change, including support for less developed countries.[346] Of respondents, 96.3 % either "somewhat support" or "strongly support" (59.3 %) China's participation in the Paris Agreement. The decision of the government to stay committed to the Agreement even after the US's 2016 withdrawal announcement was supported by 94 % of respondents.[347]

As the present thesis is not focusing on public perceptions of climate change (policies), these exemplary results shall suffice. What they – and the broader empirical patterns they stand for – indicate, is how broad the support for action on climate change has become internationally and that this support is connected to the phenomenon of internationalized concerns for political challenges. This forms a key feature of the discourse in international politics and law of the 1990s.

2. Interim Conclusion: Climate Change Established as a Value-Laden Community Issue

Being a "*collective action*"[348] or "*wicked*"[349] problem, climate change dealings include self-interested States incapable or unwilling to act for the global good along with incentives for free-riding by certain actors.[350] Already in the late 1980s and

344 Ibid., p. 43.

345 BB. Wang et al., Climate change in the Chinese mind, (2017) http://www.efchina.org/Attachments/Report/report-comms-20171108/Climate_Change_in_the_Chinese_Mind_2017.pdf, p. 22.

346 Ibid., p. 27.

347 Ibid., p. 25 et seq.

348 Stephen M Gardiner, "A Perfect Moral Storm: Climate Change, Intergenerational Ethics and the Problem of Moral Corruption", *Environmental values* 15 (2006) p. 400 et seqq.

349 Kelly Levin et al., "Overcoming the Tragedy of Super Wicked Problems: Constraining Our Future Selves to Ameliorate Global Climate Change", *Policy sciences* 45, no. 2 (2012), p. 126 et seqq.

350 On free-riding, see Daniel Bodansky, "What's in a Concept? Global Public Goods, International Law, and Legitimacy", *European Journal of International Law* 23, no. 3 (2012) p. 658 et seq.; Paulus, "Reciprocity revisited", p. 124 et seqq.

early 1990s, scholars alluded to international climate change law as being an example for a challenge to the classical state-centerd notion of international law and international relations.[351] Parts of the international legal scholarship saw common interests as "motivating and consolidating agents" in the development of rules and concepts and pointed to "the catalytic function of common or coinciding interests" as well as to the restricted prospects and the limited usefulness of cooperative practice without such underlying interests.[352] The 1990s depicted a time of struggle for appropriate answers. A great variety of suggestions were made, from rather classical regulatory approaches to ideas like that of guardianships for nature.[353] Meanwhile, climate change has been increasingly perceived as a *global* challenge calling for concerted action by the international community.

351 Zaelke and Cameron, "Global Warming and Climate Change – An Overview of the International Legal Process", p. 250 et seq.

352 Brunnée, "'Common Interest' – Echoes from an Empty Shell?", p. 795.

353 Christopher D. Stone, "Defending the Global Commons", in *Greening international law*, ed. Philippe Sands (Earthscan, 1993), p. 39 et seqq.

Part D: Structural and Conceptual Analysis of the International Climate Regime Since 1992

"Galileo discovered the fact that the sun is not circulating around the earth, but that the earth travels around the sun. [...] Climate risk teaches us that the nation is not the centre of the world."[354]

Ulrich Beck

"Foreign leaders in Europe, Asia, and across the world should not have more to say with respect to the [US] economy than our own citizens and their elected representatives. Thus, our withdrawal from the [Paris] agreement represents a reassertion of America's sovereignty."[355]

US President Donald J. Trump

The previous part (C.) has shown that the historical background of international climate change law is deeply interwoven with the broader themes of community thinking and value orientation elaborated in Part B. The present part of this thesis scrutinizes climate change as a prototype for the community value-orientation after 1990 and the way international law has addressed the issue.

The analysis consists of three sections. The first analyzes the overall structure of modern international climate change law (I.). During the quarter century that passed since the adoption of the UNFCCC, different regulatory approaches have tried to accommodate climate change in international law. The section elaborates the central conflict of approaches specific to the field of climate law between a

354 Beck, *Metamorphosis*, p. 7.

355 The White House, Statement by President Trump on the Paris Climate Accord, 1 Jun 2017, available at https://www.whitehouse.gov/briefings-statements/statement-president-trump-paris-climate-accord/.

top-down and a *bottom-up* approach. The first approach, culminating in the 1997 Kyoto Protocol, wants to use classical instruments of international law making and implementation to centrally affix obligations in GHG emission reduction, financial contributions or adaptation efforts. The latter, being exemplified by the 2015 Paris Agreement, gives greater leeway and (legal) flexibility to States, aiming for them to act faithfully to less concrete commitments, and claims to foster acceptance among States by reducing legal pressure.[356] The section develops the argument that especially after the Kyoto Protocol, climate law has experienced an overall shift indicating a 'decline' of international law through a trend of informalisation. This shift is noticeable in comparison to the 1990s' strong and combined emphasis on multilateralism, legal bindingness and value-underpinning.

Against the backdrop of the findings of this section, Kyoto will be considered as a watershed moment in the subsequent section (II.). This section will zoom in to analyze the community value-related norm concepts of the climate regime. This context poses questions as to the relationship between community values and legal norms, and the influence of the former on the latter. The fact that climate change is to such a large extent an ethical problem has not only been influential in bringing it as an issue into the international realm but has also shaped many of the norm concepts comprising community value considerations. To accommodate such – in the classical sense extra-legal – considerations in norms that are supposed to be legally relevant is a challenge both in a technical sense of application and in a political sense, as it tests the States' willingness to accept it. It entails the inherent risk of blurring the lines between applicable law, political ambitions and rhetorical embellishment. As this section will show, their legal status and role in the political and legal process remains contentious.

Finally, section III. complements the structural (I.) and conceptual (II.) perspectives by looking at the prospects of adjudication fostering the implementation of community values by legal means. This includes both recent trends in climate litigation on the national and regional level as well as the estimated chances of international courts, especially the ICJ, engaging in the field.

Together, these sections aim at answering the key question underlying this study, i.e., whether elements of 'rise or decline' can be identified in the development of the climate regime since the 1990s. The analytical lenses for this have been outlined in Part A and B: The elements of legal bindingness, the emphasis on multilateralism and the underpinning of the two with notions community

356 Steve Rayner, "How to Eat an Elephant: A Bottom-Up Approach to Climate Policy", *Climate Policy* 10, no. 6 (2010), p. 615 et seqq.

values have been identified as key factors for rise and decline. As central tensions, the notion of community itself, the idea of universalized values and the role of legal bindingness were pointed to. As this part will show, these elements matter differently and to varying degrees in the overall structure. In particular, the relevance of said elements differs between the analysis of the norm concepts themselves on the one hand and the analysis of the legal implementation of the climate change regime on the other. For instance, where in the overall structure the emphasis on legal bindingness is important in the design of the treaties and agreements, the underlying community values are more highly visible in the analysis of the concrete concepts.

I. The Changing Structure of Modern International Climate Law: Community Values at the Heart of a Dynamic Field of Law

The phase of international climate change law's transition into a comprehensive intergovernmental and multilateral framework coincided with the final years of the Cold War and the first years of the new, yet to be defined historical period. Between 1988 and 1990 – a period often called "transitional"[357] – governments began to assume a greater role in the process of that transition, where non-governmental actors had been preeminent thus far. The foundation of the Intergovernmental Panel on Climate Change (IPCC), established by the World Meteorological Organization (WMO) and the UN Environmental Programme (UNEP) in 1988 testifies to this. Also in 1988, the UNGA acknowledged climate change to be a 'common concern' for the first time.[358] This was a pivotal moment in the evolution of the climate regime. With the UNGA mandating the INC in December 1990[359] and the five negotiation sessions for the UNFCCC taking place between February 1991 and its adoption in May 1992, this transition covers nearly the same period as the developments leading to the end of the Cold War, from the beginning transition in Poland, via the fall of the Berlin wall to the end of the Soviet Union in 1991. Apart from the practical significance of changing parameters for the negotiations, this further exemplifies how deeply interlinked

357 Bodansky and Rajamani, "The Evolution and Governance Architecture of the United Nations Climate Change Regime", p. 18.

358 UN Doc. A/Res/43/53.

359 UN Doc. A/Res/45/212, 'Protection of global climate for present and future generations of mankind'.

the evolution of the climate regime is with the historical period under consideration in this study. The UNFCCC's adoption took place during the UN Conference on Environment and Development (UNCED) in Rio de Janeiro. One of the explicit ambitions of the conference was to "promot[e] the further development of international environmental law", and, more specifically, to "examin[el the feasibility of elaborating general rights and obligations of States in the field of the environment".[360]

The modern international climate change regime's main subject matter became; the mitigation of climate change, adaptation to climate change, financing mechanisms as well as the oversight of the respective implementations.[361] This section explores the core elements of the regime's structure, with a special look at the role of principles and the overall objective incorporating community values (1.). Subsequently, the changing approach of the regime from a centralized, 'top down'-approach (2.) to a decentralized 'bottom-up' approach (3.) will be discussed. Finally and in conjunction, this section conducts a review of the Paris Agreement as the latest and most far-reaching example of climate governance (4.).

1. The Central Role of Principles and the Normative Force of the Overall Objective of Climate Protection

The establishment of the international climate regime as a set of legal norms started at the beginning of the 1990s. Implementing the UNGA mandate, the intergovernmental negotiating committee for a framework convention on climate change began to work in March 1991. During the negotiations, the issue whether the convention should include a list of principles in its operative part – as opposed to an inclusion in a preamble only – became controversial. Many developing countries supported the idea, with China being the first delegation to make the proposition.[362] Many developed countries, particularly the US delegation, opposed the idea. Some countries argued that the principles would only serve as an expression of the parties' intentions and providing context for the

360 UN Doc. A/Res/44/228, para. 15(d). With this resolution, the UNGA decided to convene the UNCED and formulated its agenda and ambitions.

361 Bodansky, Brunnée, and Rajamani, *International climate change law*, pp. 11–17.

362 Ibid., p. 126; see as well: Intergovernmental Negotiating Committee, Set of informal papers provided delegations related to the preparation of a Framework Convention on Climate Change (23 Jul 1991), UN Doc. A/AC.237/Misc.1/Add.4/Rev.1, p. 3 (4 et seq.).

operative part, and therefore, should only be part of the preamble. Others argued that the principles should be included as commitments, but then be indicated as such.[363]

The text of the UNFCCC as adopted the following year is a compromise between the two approaches: The developing countries were successful in championing the inclusion of principles in Art. 3, hence including them into the operative part. Likewise, the US position was considered by including several changes aiming at reducing the legal implications of the provision: Art. 3 came to include a chapeau expressly specifying its guiding function. Moreover, the term 'States' was replaced by 'Parties' – a move aiming at disabling arguments that the principles of Art. 3 would constitute general customary international law.[364] The effect of the provision was to be confined to the FCCC regime. There was a footnote added to the header of Art. 1 stating that the headers of the articles were only to assist the reader.[365] This footnote aimed especially at Art. 3 to make clear that they were not to be understood as strictly legal principles.[366] In addition, the term *"inter alia"* was added to make clear that parties would be free to consider other principles and guidelines during the implementation of the Convention.[367] One of the main concerns of the US and other 'common law' delegations was that the provisions of Art. 3 could be subject to dispute settlement or create specific commitments outside of Art. 4.[368]

Compromises were also made regarding the substance of Art. 3: Some principles were moved to the preamble instead of including them in Art. 3.[369] Some

363 Bodansky, "UNFCCC commentary", p. 501; Bodansky, Brunnée, and Rajamani, *International climate change law*, p. 126 et seq.

364 Bodansky, "UNFCCC commentary", p. 502.

365 It reads "Titles of articles are included solely to assist the reader".

366 Philippe Sands, "Climate Change and the Rule of Law: Adjudicating the Future in International Law", *Journal of Environmental Law* 28, no. 1 (2016), p. 28.

367 Bodansky, Brunnée, and Rajamani, *International climate change law*, p. 127.

368 Sands, *Principles of international environmental law*, p. 233 et seq. Here, Sands also points to the fact that a parallel debate developed during the negotiations for the 1992 Biodiversity convention, where the United Kingdom eventually made a declaration upon signature implying that the Principles in Art. 3 of that convention would have no legal consequence outside the convention. The declaration reads *"The Government of the United Kingdom of Great Britain and Northern Ireland declare their understanding that article 3 of the Convention sets out a guiding principle to be taken into account in the implementation of the Convention"*, see https://treaties.un.org/pages/ViewDetails.aspx?src=IND&mtdsg_no=XXVII-8&chapter=27&clang=_en .

369 The principle of sovereignty is mentioned in the para. 9 of the Preamble, but not in Art. 3. An early proposal in the responsible working group of the INC had suggested

others, which had been discussed before as potential principles, were discarded from the Convention altogether.[370] In comparison to the Rio Declaration negotiated parallel to the UNFCCC, the initiatives by developed and common law countries in particular had the effect of narrowing the UNFCCC principles. Arguably, this was influential during the negotiations making those of the latter less politicized than those of the former.[371]

In the Convention, the principles in Art. 3 are preceded by an explicit formulation of its overall objective. Art. 2 accordingly reads:

> *"**The ultimate objective of this Convention** and any related legal instruments that the Conference of the Parties may adopt **is to achieve**, in accordance with the relevant provisions of the Convention, **stabilization of greenhouse gas concentrations in the atmosphere at a level that would prevent dangerous anthropogenic interference with the climate system**. Such a level should be achieved within a time-frame sufficient **to allow ecosystems to adapt naturally to climate change, to ensure that food production is not threatened and to enable economic development to proceed in a sustainable manner**."*[372]

Albeit formulated separately from the principle on which the focus lies here, the overall objective to jointly protect the global climate from climate change is an important normative element of the UNFCCC regime. The objective can be understood as translating the central governance problem and legal challenge of the field into a treaty provision: Climate change, the collective action problem to which the above-mentioned 'tragedy of the commons' is inherent, is turned into a joint problem of all parties to the UNFCCC. All subsequent actions under the Convention would have to achieve this provision and all subsequent regulations would have to be in line with it. However, the legal weight of this is not entirely clear as the legal status of Art. 2 is uncertain. This concerns primarily the question whether Art. 2 is a specification of the treaty's 'object and purpose' in the sense of Art. 18 and 19 of the VCLT.[373] In the 26 years since the adoption of the

---

its inclusion, see Bodansky, "UNFCCC commentary", pp. 499 and 502, both with further reference.

370 Proposed, but ultimately not included principles were on the right to development, an equal right to ocean sinks, the principle that the GHG emissions of developing countries *must* grow, the principle that no environmental conditions should be imposed on aid, and the 'main responsibility' principle as well as related principles on liability and compensation, see Ibid., p. 502 with further reference.

371 Compare UNFCCC, Art. 3 with Rio Declaration, Articles 3, 7 and 13; Ibid., p. 502.

372 UNFCCC, Art. 2, emphasis added.

373 Bodansky, Brunnée, and Rajamani, *International climate change law*, p. 126, who hint at the possibility that the formulation of Art. 2 including the wording "*ultimate*

Convention, parties have not yet specified the concentration of GHG that the regime should achieve, but have instead resorted to objectives defined in terms of temperature rise and long-term-emissions.[374] Nevertheless, the overall objective has been rightly called – alongside the concept of 'common but differentiated responsibilities' (CBDR) – one of the "lynchpins" of the regime's development.[375]

2. Strong on Legalization and Top-Down Organisation – from Rio to Kyoto

The early years of the FCCC regime leading up to the 1995 Berlin mandate and the resulting 1997 Kyoto Protocol were characterized by the effort to adopt "a protocol or another legal instrument"[376] aiming to "set quantified limitation and reduction objectives within specified time-frames, such as 2005, 2010 and 2020, for their [the States'] anthropogenic emissions [...] of Greenhouse Gases".[377] The design of the Convention featured a sharp differentiation between developed and developing countries: The definition of the commitments of state parties (Art. 4) designated general commitments to all parties, which were rather qualitative than quantitative. They included GHG inventories, national or regional strategies, reporting and scientific exchange. For Annex I countries (OECD members and the former eastern bloc) and to Annex II countries (OECD countries), additionally specific commitments were formulated concerning sources and sinks as well as financial resources and technology transfer respectively.[378]

The main features of the Kyoto Protocol were a top-down regulatory approach including internationally negotiated emission targets and accounting rules, the continuously sharp division between developed and developing States, the legally binding nature of the agreement as well as market mechanisms for effective implementation.[379] The protocol also established a concrete obligation (for developed countries) to provide financial and technical assistance.[380]

---

objective" could have been a measure by States to exclude the effect of Art. 2 expressing the 'object and purpose'.

374 Ibid., p. 126, with further reference; on the temperature objective, see also section I.4. on the Paris Agreement.

375 Brunnée and Toope, *Legitimacy and legality in international law*, p. 130.

376 UN Doc. FCCC/CP/1995/7/Add.1 [hereinafter 'Berlin mandate'], preamble, para. 3.

377 Berlin mandate, para. II, 2. (a).

378 Bodansky, "UNFCCC commentary", p. 505.

379 Bodansky, Brunnée, and Rajamani, *International climate change law*, p. 105.

380 Kyoto protocol, Art. 11 (2).

For the matter at hand, the first three of these features are relevant: The top-down approach of the Kyoto Protocol had been negotiated in the Berlin mandate during COP 1 in Berlin in 1995. It was a consequence of the assumption that the nationally determined climate policies that the UNFCCC had prescribed in its Art. 4 would not be sufficient to reach its goals in emission reduction. The legally binding nature of key provisions to the protocol was strongly connected to the top-down approach. The Berlin mandate was not entirely clear on the legal nature of the future agreement, as the emission targets had been called 'objectives' rather than 'commitments'. At the second COP in Geneva in 1996, a ministerial declaration settled this matter by making the targets legally binding.[381] In terms of hard obligations, Kyoto confirmed and further specified only the hard obligation established by the UNFCCC: The obligation to exchange information and to co-operate in scientific research.[382]

The protocol was largely appreciated for its legally binding character and the stringency of the emission targets – a feature that the EU countries especially had put a large emphasis on and could consider themselves successful in that regard. But many observers annotated that the agreements character – combining legal bindingness and strong emission targets – came at a certain price, being also a trade-off between the EU and two other different interest groups, namely the US and the group of developing countries: The US could regard the important role of market mechanisms and hence the increased flexibility as their achievement, although they had to accept much stronger emissions targets[383] than initially planned in order to get it. First and foremost, this flexibility through market mechanisms included the development of an international trading system for emissions. Moreover, the CDM was created, a financial mechanism enabling industrialized countries to receive credits for emission reduction projects in developing countries. Finally, flexibility was fostered by providing for certain sink activities to be credited under the financial mechanism.[384] The sharp differentiation between developed and developing countries that originated in the framework convention was continued and in some way deepened by calling for (Berlin

381 Report of the Conference of the Parties on its second session, held at Geneva from 8 to 19 July 1996, FCCC/CP/1996/15/Add.1, Annex: The Geneva Ministerial Declaration; cf. Bodansky, Brunnée, and Rajamani, *International climate change law*, p. 106.

382 Kyoto Protocol, Art. 1(b),3,4,7,8,10(d).

383 Minus 7 % in comparison to the 1990 levels.

384 Bodansky and Rajamani, "The Evolution and Governance Architecture of the United Nations Climate Change Regime", p. 33 et seqq.

mandate), negotiating and adopting (Kyoto Protocol) the quantified emission limitation and reduction objectives (QELROs) for developed States only.[385] This was a notable success of the developing countries as the third interest group in play.[386]

The result of the Kyoto Protocol regime cannot be regarded as satisfying in terms of climate change mitigation ambitions: As of 2015, the commitments under the Kyoto Protocol covered a mere 14 % of global annual emissions. The main emitters, specifically China and the United States, which account together for almost half of global annual emissions, were not bound by any clear commitments.[387] Reasons for this limited success are manifold. Some limitations can be regarded as singular political decisions, but in sum, parts of the structure of the protocol itself proved not to be viable and revealed deeper underlying problems of the UNFCCC architecture.

A major blow to the development of the Kyoto Protocol was dealt by the withdrawal of the USA. The government of President Bill Clinton of the Democratic Party had signed the Protocol in November 1998, but the US Congress refused to ratify it, with the predominant argument being possible damages to the US economy.[388] After George W. Bush of the Republican Party succeeded Clinton in office, the government called the Kyoto Protocol "fatally flawed" and announced withdrawal in March 2001.[389] This meant that the largest emitter of GHG among the developed countries would no longer be bound to the protocol. However, the instant demise of the instrument – as predicted by many –, did not materialize. The EU took the role of the negotiation pacemaker and in November 2001, the Marrakesh Accords were adopted, a set of draft decisions designated to be adopted after the entry into force of the protocol. They concretised its provisions

385 Bodansky, Brunnée, and Rajamani, *International climate change law*, p. 105.

386 Ibid., p. 106.

387 Jorge E. Viñuales, "The Paris climate agreement: An initial examination" (C-EENRG Working Papers: Cambridge Center for Environment, Energy and Natural Resource Governance, University of Cambrige, 2015)), p. 8.

388 Helen Dewar and Kevin Sullivan, "Senate Republicans Call Kyoto Pact Dead", *The Washington Post*, 11 Dec 1997; For a broader analysis on the US relationship with the Kyoto Protocol, see Jon Hovi, Detlef F. Sprinz, and Guri Bang, "Why the United States Did Not Become a Party to the Kyoto Protocol: German, Norwegian, and US Perspectives", *European Journal of International Relations* 18, no. 1 (2012).

389 International Institute for Sustainable Development, "Summary of the resumed sixth session of the Conference of the Parties to the UN Framework Convention on Climate Change: 16-27 July 2001", *Earth Negotiations Bulletin* 12, no. 176 (2001), p. 2.

and set them on a path towards broader acceptance.[390] In 2004, upon the ratification by Russia and Canada, the Protocol entered into force.[391]

Another structural factor was that the differentiation between developed and developing countries became increasingly uneven and harder to reconcile with ecological and economic realities: Emissions from most developing countries remained comparatively low in per capita terms, but their growth became rapid in absolute terms and was projected to be responsible for roughly 75 % of the emission-increase over the next 25 years. With China surpassing the USA in 2006[392], a developing country in Kyoto nomenclature became the world's largest CO_2 emitter.[393]

For the second commitment period of the protocol, instituted by the Doha Amendment and originally envisaged to cover the period from 2013 to 2020, there was from the outset limited participation by the developed countries responsible for large parts of global GHG emissions[394]: At the Durban COP 2011, States such as Canada, Russia and Japan refused to accept a new commitment period.[395] Canada withdrew from the Kyoto Protocol effectively by December 2012[396], again diminishing the level of support for the protocol from developed countries.

The Kyoto Protocol, in hindsight, stands for a set of regulatory ambitions and legal strategies that are closely intertwined with the overall ambition to progressively develop international law in the 1990s. Starting from the UNFCCC – strongly characterized by the community value-related normative ambitions in commitment and principles – it combined this heavy normative

390 Beyerlin and Marauhn, *International environmental law*, p. 165.

391 See, U.N. treaty collection, CHAPTER XXVII, 7. a, available at https://treaties.un.org/Pages/ViewDetails.aspx?src=IND&mtdsg_no=XXVII-7-a&chapter=27&clang=_en.

392 PBL Netherlands Environmental Assessment Agency, "China Now No. 1 in CO2 Emissions; USA in Second Position," *News release*, 19 Jun 2007, http://www.pbl.nl/en/dossiers/Climatechange/Chinanowno1inCO2emissionsUSAinsecondposition.

393 i.e. in GHG emissions per year, not cumulatively.

394 By 2013, the USA contributed more than one-fifth of global CO2 emissions and all OECD countries roughly half, see Bodansky and Rajamani, "The Evolution and Governance Architecture of the United Nations Climate Change Regime", p. 14 with further reference.

395 Dupuy and Viñuales, *International environmental law*, p. 149 with further reference.

396 In accordance with article 27 (2) of the Kyoto Protocol […], the Government of Canada notified the Secretary-General that it had decided to withdraw from the Kyoto Protocol as from 15 Dec 2012, see UN treaty collection as referenced above.

superstructure with a comparatively strong legal form. Spoken in the 'legalization'-terminology[397] of the late 1990s, this approach was strong on 'obligation' and 'precision', although 'delegation' of enforcement to international bodies continuously played a minor role. The decline in acceptance from States had diverse reasons – the most frequently invoked in scholarly explanations range from industrialized countries' decreasing willingness to carry a burden perceived to be increasingly asymmetric vis-a-vis emerging economies to widespread discontent with players such as the United States not adhering to their part of the burden-sharing. A common denominator arguably is what the present author calls the overstretching of the States' willingness to accept limitations on their sovereignty in the context of a community value-oriented legal regime: The regulatory effort represented by the Kyoto Protocol relied on the formulation of substantial, legally binding obligations on the international level. Starting from the normative frame laid out by the Convention and its community-oriented emphasis on legal principles and the objective of the overall regime, it sought to translate this frame into effective action by means of international law. This combination arguably demanded from States a twofold acceptance – of the normative frame as well as the regulatory translation. The latter meant to accept compromises such as the strong differentiation between groups of actors – a feature specific to the approach of bringing actors with immensely different interests together to act in broad common interest.

The implementation of the Kyoto Protocol showed the limits of this effort. The tensions sketched out in Part A of this study produced a tangible result: With many decisive actors deciding to prioritize other interests before the obligations of the climate regime, the emphasis on sovereignty seemed to outweigh the trend towards community orientation. The underpinning of the Protocol with (allegedly) universalized values failed to bind actors with diverging interests together and the legal bindingness of community oriented obligations proved to be sufficiently controversial to provoke decisive reluctance among States.

This apparent failure of the Kyoto approach led to an important change in international climate policies, i.e., the differentiation between the normative superstructure on one hand and the legal implementation of the regime increasingly occupying a rather procedural role, on the other.[398] This changed strategy

---

397 Abbott et al., "The Concept of Legalization", p. 401 et seqq.; see already: Part A and Part B., Section I and II.

398 cf. Duncan French and Lavanya Rajamani, "Climate Change and International Environmental Law: Musings on a Journey to Somewhere", *Journal of Environmental Law* 25, no. 3 (2013), p. 445 et seq.

would come to put an increased emphasis on differentiation, i.e., giving room for the accommodation of specific national circumstances.[399]

3. The Road to the Paris Agreement: Bottom-Up Approach and a New Dawn for Climate Change Policies with Legal Bindingness in Decline

As soon as the Kyoto Protocol, despite the obstacles outlined above, entered into force in 2005, negotiations began on how climate policy should proceed after the end of the Protocal's commitment period in 2012. As the first major document of this new period of climate negotiations, the 2007 Bali Action Plan[400] launched a process[401] – envisaged to end at the Copenhagen COP in 2009 – to produce an 'agreed outcome' on how to proceed in designing the future climate regime.[402] Already the ambiguity of the term 'agreed outcome' mirrored the lack of agreement on both legal form and level of ambition of the envisaged outcome.[403] The Copenhagen summit of 2009 was hence widely perceived as a failure against the background of the expectations raised by the Bali Action Plan with the summit falling short of delivering a binding agreement for the post-2012 era. Observers were divided on who and what to blame for this failing. Depending

399 On differentiation, see Susan Biniaz, "I Beg to Differ: Taking Account of National Circumstances under the Paris Agreement, the ICAO Market-Based Measure, and the Montreal Protocol's HFC Amendment," *Sabin Center for Climate Change Law, Columbia Law School* (2017), http://columbiaclimatelaw.com/files/2017/01/Biniaz-2017-01-Taking-Account-of-National-Circumstances.pdf.

400 Decision 1/CP.13, Bali Action Plan, in Report of the Conference of the Parties on its Thirteenth Session, held in Bali from 3–15 December 2007, Addendum, Part Two: Action taken by the Conference of the Parties at its Thirteenth Session, FCCC/CP/2007/6/Add.1 (14 March 2008) (hereinafter Bali Action Plan).

401 Most prominently, the 'Ad Hoc Working Group on Long-Term Cooperative Action' (AWG-LCA) was initiated, following up on the dialogue on long-term cooperative action under the FCCC after 2012, established in 2005 at the first COP after the entry into force of the Kyoto protocol. This dialogue was concerned with actions by all parties in demarcation to the parallel structure that engaged in negotiations about possible further obligations for industrialized States after 2012.

402 Bali Action Plan, para. 1.

403 Lavanya Rajamani, "Addressing the 'post-Kyoto' Stress Disorder: Reflections on the Emerging Legal Architecture of the Climate Regime", *International & Comparative Law Quarterly* 58, no. 4 (2009), p. 806 et seq.

on the perspective, the reluctance of the US[404] to take part in the Protocol was blamed, but China was also understood by some to be the 'villain' hindering an effective outcome.[405] When neither the Cancun (COP 16/CMP 6, 2010)[406] nor the Durban (COP 17/CMP 7, 2011) conference produced such an agreement, increasing concern developed whether the multilateral framework under the UNFCCC was still capable of responding to the challenge.[407] The issue of legal form was important during all steps of the negotiations. Disagreements over the legal form made the adoption of a treaty impossible at Copenhagen, with the US being ready to accept a legal instrument only if applied equally to all parties. Conversely, China and India were only willing to sign the agreement if binding emission reduction obligations would exclusively apply to developed States.[408]

The three COPs also played a pivotal role in re-framing the approach the negotiation process would take. This eventually lead to the Paris Agreement four years later.[409] Many parties did not regard the Copenhagen Accord or the Cancun Agreements as bringing the Bali Action Plan Process to an end. Hence, negotiations continued with many States continuously pressing for a new legal agreement.[410] Moreover, the Copenhagen Accord also brought about a positive development often overlooked in the overall negative assessment of the conference. For the first time, the 'BASIC' countries (Brazil, South Africa, India and China), being the major emerging economies, subscribed to at least some general commitment on climate policy and GHG reduction efforts, albeit without any bindingness. Given the background of the UNFCCC- and Kyoto-version of

---

404 E.g. Friends of the Earth, "Copenhagen: A Disaster for the World's Poorest," *News release*, 17 Dec 2009, https://www.foei.org/no-category/copenhagen-a-disaster-for-the-worlds-poorest., lamenting the "failure of rich country governments to secure a strong and fair UN agreement to tackle climate change".

405 Mark Lynas, "How Do I Know China Wrecked the Copenhagen Deal? I Was in the Room", *The Guardian*, 22 Dec 2009; for a more nuanced account, see Andrew Hurrell and Sandeep Sengupta, "Emerging Powers, North–South Relations and Global Climate Politics", *International Affairs* 88, no. 3 (2012), p. 464 et seq.

406 Report of the Conference of the Parties on its sixteenth session, held in Cancun from 29 November to 10 December 2010, UN Doc. FCCC/CP/2010/7 [hereinafter 'Cancun outcome'].

407 Robyn Eckersley, "Moving Forward in the Climate Negotiations: Multilateralism or Minilateralism?", *Global environmental politics* 12, no. 2 (2012), p. 24.

408 Daniel Bodansky, "The Paris Climate Change Agreement: A New Hope?", *American Journal of International Law* 110, no. 2 (2016), p. 295.

409 Viñuales, "The Paris climate agreement: an initial examination", p. 8 et seq.

410 Bodansky, "A New Hope?", p. 295.

differentiation leaving 'non-Annex I' countries (including all four BASIC countries) out of defining substantive obligations, this was an important step forward in fixing one of Kyoto's major deficiencies, for the four COP decisions combined show a distinct shift in the notion of differentiation under the UNFCCC regime. Where the regime had previously been defined by differential treatment in favor of developing countries, there was now a trend towards symmetry in the legal requirements for both developed and developing countries.[411] Furthermore, many of the structural characteristics of the regime that gained attention after the Paris Agreement, have their roots in this phase of the negotiations between Copenhagen and Durban. Those are, in particular, the development towards greater deference to national circumstances, more discretion for individual States, a more circumscribed role for the legal instruments on the international level and a corresponding expansion of sovereign power.[412] The structural reasons for the changing notion of differentiation, however, exceeds the frequently quoted geopolitical shift caused by some developing countries entering the sphere of middle-income economies with simultaneously growing interests.[413] Another side of it was likely the growing discontent of some developed countries with the system of differentiation, especially given attempts by developing countries to convey, for instance, the principle of 'common but differentiated responsibilities' to other areas of international law. Thereby, there was an attempt made to extend the existing notion that developed countries would have to carry the primary burdens of policy making.[414] The gradual abandonment of the distinction between Annex I (or II) and non-Annex I countries was arguably the most

---

411 French and Rajamani, "Climate Change and International Environmental Law", p. 440. For an extensive textual analysis see Lavanya Rajamani, "From Berlin to Bali and Beyond: Killing Kyoto Softly?", *International & Comparative Law Quarterly* 57, no. 4 (2008); "Addressing the 'post-Kyoto'stress disorder: Reflections on the emerging legal architecture of the climate regime"; "The Cancun Climate Agreements: Reading the Text, Subtext and Tea leaves", *International & Comparative Law Quarterly* 60, no. 2 (2011).

412 French and Rajamani, "Climate Change and International Environmental Law", p. 440.

413 Daniel W. Drezner, "The New New World Order", *Foreign Affairs* 86, no. 2 (2007), p. 34 et seq. with further reference.

414 French and Rajamani, "Climate Change and International Environmental Law", with further references quoting examples from fields like the regulation of aviation or maritime emissions, where notably China has been advocating the application of the CBDR principle in these areas. For a more detailed account of the debates surrounding 'CBDR', see Section II.2. of this part.

demanding among the structural changes. The Kyoto Protocol, in particular, had hardened this division of the UNFCCC to an extent where some called it a 'Chinese Wall'. Hence, it was clear that one of the foremost challenges of a reformed climate regime would be to include major developing countries (including large emitters such as the BASIC countries, Mexico and others) under the new form of emission reduction commitments.[415]

In an effort to set the climate regime on track for the time after 2012, there was again an increased resort to political rhetoric conjuring a spirit of community and shared responsibility. The Bali Action Plan had already been setting the tone for the following negotiations by, despite the unclarified issues, setting the goal to develop a "shared vision for long-term cooperative action".[416] The Durban platform for enhanced action (the new negotiation format that would lead to the Paris Agreement), initiated at the 2011 COP, clarified what the Bali Action Plan had left open. It did so by defining the aim to develop "a protocol, another legal instrument or an agreed outcome with legal force" for the post-2020 period.[417] Moreover, the Durban Platform made clear that the envisaged instrument would continue to be rooted in the principles of the UNFCCC.[418] Over the course of the COPs in Doha (2012), Warsaw (2013) and Lima (2014), the groundwork was laid for making a next attempt to adopt a comprehensive instrument. The Paris Agreement, then, was adopted on the last day of COP 21 in Paris on 12 December 2015. It's acceptance by States and the rapidity of its entry into force exceeded even optimistic expectations: Opened for signature by parties to the UNFCCC from 22 April 2016 to 21 April 2017 at the UN headquarters in New York, the Paris Agreement was signed by 174 States and the EU on the first day alone. That the same day, celebrated as 'Earth Day' since 1970, more than 20 countries issued statements of intent to join as soon as possible. When the EU ratified the agreement on 4 November 2016, the Agreement reached the

415 Viñuales, "The Paris climate agreement: an initial examination", p. 8.

416 Bali Action Plan, para. 1 (a).

417 Establishment of an Ad Hoc Working Group on the Durban Platform for Enhanced Action, UNFCCC Decision 1/CP.17, UN Doc. FCCC/CP/2011/9/Add.1(15 Mar 2012) [hereinafter Durban Platform]. For a legal analysis of the Durban Platform decision, see Lavanya Rajamani, "The Durban platform for enhanced action and the future of the climate regime", *International & Comparative Law Quarterly* 61, no. 2 (2012).

418 References to 'under the Convention' and the 'principles of the Convention' in Durban Platform, para. 2; Decision 2/CP.18, 'Advancing the Durban Platform', in FCCC/CP/2012/8/Add.1 (28 Feb 2013), preamble, para. 4; and Decision -/CP.19, 'Further advancing the Durban Platform', preamble, para. 4.

necessary threshold of 55 countries producing at least 55 % of the world's GHG emissions as of 2015, to enter into force. The Agreement was widely acclaimed by the public, media and leading politicians[419] as a success after years of failure in producing a legally binding treaty for the post-Kyoto era. The Agreement seems to have a pragmatic way of managing climate change. Some have argued that it did so at the expense of legal quality, weakening international law's role in the field.[420] The Paris Agreement, in this sense, stands for the detrimental shift from traditional intergovernmental structures to other fora and more decentralized structures including business communities, NGOs and sub-national actors like cities. But among those seeing the Agreement as an example for a reduced role of international law were also voices that nonetheless came to a positive overall assessment, claiming that it would exemplify a new and promising approach in global governance.[421]

(a) Architecture

The Agreement sets three main action areas: *Mitigation* (Articles 3–6), *adaptation* (Article 7) and *loss and damage* (Article 8). The former two are arguably given more weight than the more conflictual and, consequentially, largely circumscribed latter article.[422] A clear focus of the Paris Agreement is on climate change mitigation, with the goal of "[h]olding the increase in the global average temperature to well below 2 °C above pre-industrial levels and to pursue efforts to limit the temperature increase to 1.5 °C above pre-industrial levels" (Art. 2 (1) (a)).

In the section dedicated to mitigation, the flexibility of the newly established 'nationally determined contributions' (NDCs) is the key element.[423] The

---

419 See e.g. Slaughter, "The Paris Approach to Global Governance".

420 Peter Lawrence and Daryl Wong, "Soft law in the Paris Climate Agreement: Strength or Weakness?", *Review of European, Comparative & International Environmental Law* 26, no. 3 (2017), pp. 277, 285 et seq.; others have been more cautious in their assessment: For instance, Krieger and Nolte, "The International Rule of Law – Rise or Decline? Points of Departure ", p. 21 et seqq. put forward the question whether this shift will ultimately lead to a decline of traditional international law or if it would simply indicate a change of the ways in which international law operates.

421 Slaughter, "The Paris Approach to Global Governance".

422 Viñuales, "The Paris climate agreement: an initial examination".

423 David G. Victor, "Making the Promise of Paris a Reality", in *Paris agreement and beyond: International climate change policy post-2020*, ed. Robert N. Stavins and Robert C. Stowe (Cambridge, MA: Harvard Project on Climate Agreements, 2016).

mechanism of the NDCs (Art. 3 and 4) is both a major factor in explaining the success of the Paris Agreement in terms of acceptance by States during the negotiations and the adoption process as well as it is the central element of its operating mode. The state parties get to choose their level of ambition in emission reduction and de-carbonization of their economies. This great level of discretion is accompanied by the duty to regularly (at least every five years, Art. 4 (9)) update the contribution plans and a duty of non-regression. The non-regression obligation ("Each Party's successive nationally determined contribution **will** represent a progression [...]" [Art. 4 (3), emphasis added]) is one of the innovative aspects of the Agreement.[424] Its political as well as legal implications will foreseeably have a pivotal role in the debates surrounding the Agreement's implementation.[425]

The Paris Agreement significantly increases the role non-state actors like businesses, cities and others hold in climate governance. This development as such is not entirely new: The growth of transnational governance initiatives dates back to the late 1990s. Further, that climate change is no longer governed through a single multilateral, interstate institution, has already been theorized by scholars discussing the 'regime complex'[426] of climate change or a 'global climate-governance landscape'.[427] One recent change to this is that actors within the UNFCCC started trying to connect with many of the existing initiatives in a coordinated way. The decisions taken in Paris amplify this.

In decision 1/CP. 21 for instance, the commitments from all actors are recognized, including those launched through the Lima–Paris Action Agenda. The decision emphasizes the urgent need to scale up the global response to climate change by mobilizing non-party stakeholders and to support greater ambition

424 Zou Ji, "Enhancing Climate Mitigation Ambition Successively: The Drivers", in *Paris agreement and beyond: International climate change policy post-2020*, ed. Robert N. Stavins and Robert C. Stowe (Cambridge, MA: Harvard Project on Climate Agreements, 2016), p. 29 et seq.

425 Viñuales, "The Paris climate agreement: an initial examination", p. 12, who even argues that the non-regression duty could "signal what perhaps will become a major new principle of international environmental law in the years to come".

426 Robert O. Keohane and David G. Victor, "The Regime Complex for Climate Change", *Perspectives on politics* 9, no. 1 (2011), p. 7 et seqq.

427 Michele Betsill et al., "Building Productive Links between the UNFCCC and the Broader Global Climate Governance Landscape", *Global Environmental Politics* 15, no. 2 (2015).

from governments. The 'Non-State Actor Zone for Climate Action activities'[428] has become the platform to collect information on the actors involved and to connect their action to the UNFCCC process. A 'High-Level Event on Accelerating Climate Action' was held to highlight outcomes from the Action Events throughout the COP 22 and the 'Marrakech Partnership for Global Climate Action', a new framework to catalyze and support climate action, was launched.

The Paris Agreement draws a strong link between the efforts to combat climate change and human rights issues. In paragraph 12 of the preamble, it emphasizes that parties are

> *"[a]cknowledging that climate change is a common concern of humankind[.] Parties should, when taking action to address climate change, respect, promote and consider their respective obligations on human rights, the right to health, the rights of indigenous peoples, local communities, migrants, children, persons with disabilities and people in vulnerable situations and the right to development, as well as gender equality, empowerment of women and intergenerational equity, [...]".*

The Paris Agreement, "in enhancing the implementation of the [UNFCCC], including its objective, aims to strengthen the global response to the threat of climate change" (Art. 2(1)). In doing so, it adheres to the principles and objectives set out by the UNFCCC, in part explicitly by re-emphasizing and singling out parts of them. Art. 2 singles out CBDR and equity (Art. 2(2)) as well as sustainable development and "eradicating poverty" (Art. 2 (1)). The Paris Agreement thus follows up on the Convention in being anchored in the principle of common but differentiated responsibilities and respective capabilities, in light of different national circumstances. That is the case despite that the way it operationalizes this principle is distinctly different from that in the FCCC and its Kyoto Protocol.[429] The NDCs allow for much more detailed differentiation in accordance with CBDR than any other instrument under the modern climate regime. Politically, that was part of the price of getting the large emitters among the developing countries to join the system.[430]

---

428 See UNFCCC secretariat, Non-State Actor Zone for Climate Action, http://climate-action.unfccc.int.

429 Lavanya Rajamani, "Differentiation and Equity in the Post-Paris Negotiations", in *Paris agreement and beyond: International climate change policy post-2020*, ed. Robert N. Stavins and Robert C. Stowe (Cambridge, MA: Harvard Project on Climate Agreements, 2016), who argues that the equity principle is the second anchor of the Paris Agreement.

430 Viñuales, "The Paris climate agreement: an initial examination", p. 12.

(b) Open Questions and Potential Pitfalls

The complex structural changes brought about by the Paris Agreement have various pitfalls. Their impact can only be fully assessed several years into the implementation process. Although a compromise has been reached on differentiation in Paris, many questions remain open, and "the devil of differentiation will be in the detail of its operationalization in the post-Paris negotiations". How the terms "developed" and "developing" countries are to be applied, is as unclear as how conditional NDCs from developing countries are to be understood and treated or how equity is to be operationalized in the global stocktake.[431]

The success of the broadly discussed 'bottom-up' approach of the Agreement will depend on how well the information exchange regarding country preferences will work, as many of the actor networks will form outside the formal convention process. A similar caveat is to be made concerning the implementation of the regular stocktaking.[432] It also remains to be seen how the Paris Agreement process will relate to the dynamic of global trends, international interactions, multilateral and bilateral agendas, and the parties' expectations regarding their own development level and the dynamic of their interests in the future.[433] Another critical issue in this regard will be whether the Agreement's assessment and review framework will be able to create sufficiently strong incentives for countries to reduce their emissions.[434] The interaction between the inter-state level and the non-state actors involved requires a special non-hierarchical coordination effort. It is not necessarily self-evident that initiatives like the 'C 40' Cities, or the institutional investors involved in the CDP, will see themselves as accountable to the UNFCCC.[435]

---

431 Rajamani, "Differentiation and Equity in the Post-Paris Negotiations",

432 Victor, "Making the Promise of Paris a Reality".

433 Ji, "Enhancing Climate Mitigation Ambition Successively: The Drivers".

434 Barrett, "The Paris Agreement: We Can Do (and Have Done) Better", who argues that the Paris Agreement is in fact unlikely to create strong incentives for countries to reduce their emissions relative to the levels that would have resulted anyway or without the Agreement.

435 Matthew Paterson, "Networks and Coordination in Global Climate Governance", in *Paris agreement and beyond: International climate change policy post-2020*, ed. Robert N. Stavins and Robert C. Stowe (Cambridge, MA: Harvard Project on Climate Agreements, 2016), p. 83.

(c) The Issue of Legal Bindingness

That international agreements are shaped by the wording negotiators use and by on which nuances of formulation they agree upon is evident. But in climate diplomacy, the significance of the last punctuation mark, is perhaps even higher than in many other areas of international relations.[436] The debates on the legal bindingness of the Paris Agreement in general and on some of its key provisions are a good example for this only seemingly mundane insight. At the last minute of the negotiations, the Agreement almost collapsed because of the very issue of the legal bindingness of Art. 4(4), which defines the respective obligations for developed and developing countries. In its adopted version, the provision reads:

> *"Developed country Parties **should** continue taking the lead by undertaking economy-wide absolute emission reduction targets. Developing country Parties **should** continue enhancing their mitigation efforts, and are encouraged to move over time towards economy-wide emission reduction or limitation targets in the light of different national circumstances."*[437]

In the final version discussed in the plenary, the orthographically minor but immensely meaningful difference was that it included the word "shall" instead of "should", concerning developed countries taking the lead in emission reduction. This would have turned a re-iteration of the respective formulation of the UNFCCC (Art. 3 (1)) into a legal valorisation of the developed countries' obligations.[438] Dramatic last-minute negotiations included the US delegation insisting on having erroneously accepted the provision and some developing countries' delegations protesting a change (back) to the weaker 'should'. In the end, a re-opening of the plenary debate with an unpredictable outcome was avoided when the French conference presidency introduced a changed text. The text was presented as the correction of typing mistake made in the process of transferring formulations from one draft to the other.[439] This instance of facilitating

---

436 On the use of language in the climate regime, see generally Susan Biniaz, "Comma but Differentiated Responsibilities: Punctuation and 30 Other Ways Negotiators Have Resolved Issues in the International Climate Change Regime", *Mich. J. Envtl. & Admin. L.* 6 (2016).

437 Emphasis added.

438 See also section II.2. on this 'taking the lead' provision.

439 David A. Wirth, "Cracking the American Climate Negotiators' Hidden Code: United States Law and the Paris Agreement", *Climate Law* 6, no. 1 (2016), p. 153 et seq.; John Vidal, "How a 'typo' Nearly Derailed the Paris Climate Deal", *The Guardian*, 16 Dec 2015.

the diplomatic success of the Paris Agreement by diminishing the legal bindingness of a substantial provision, is characteristic for the role of the law in the Agreement.

Unlike the 1995 Berlin mandate[440] and the clarifying Geneva COP outcome, the Bali Action Plan did not specify the specific legal form of the envisaged agreement. Although the Durban Platform was clearer in that regard, the adoption of the Paris Agreement reinvigorated the debate about the legal bindingness of the international instruments on climate change, which accompanied the international climate regime throughout its development. Some authors have argued, surrounding the Paris summit, that large parts of the debate on legal bindingness are futile at best, or even a 'red herring'. That is, for realist scholars, the 'obsession' about legal bindingness is puzzling – only for international lawyers would it seem to be "important to confirm [their] self-standing".[441] The debate, according to this argument, would divert attention from the questions that "really matter" about substance, ambition, follow-up procedures and buy-ins on the domestic level. Others have argued that quite to the contrary, the Durban 2011 and Paris 2015 negotiations are examples of how important the 'legal obligation factor' still is for States – in both negotiations, the legal form itself was an integral part of the debate about the respective instruments.[442]

A valuable contribution to the debate was the suggestion to differentiate between different aspects of legality: The legal character of the agreement itself (such as the broad question whether it is a treaty under international law) is to be distinguished from the question whether individual norms create legal obligations. The question whether certain provisions are sufficiently precise is connected to, but distinct from, if and how courts can apply the Paris Agreement. The enforceability of the agreement as a whole, or of parts of it, differs from the Agreement's accountability mechanism. The legal status of the Agreement finally, is also connected to the various domestic implementation procedures.[443]

---

440 Here, the aim was explicitly to adopt a 'Protocol or another legal instrument', see Berlin Mandate, para. 3, Preamble, Decision 1/CP.1.

441 Pauwelyn and Andonova, "A 'Legally Binding Treaty' or Not?, EJIL talk 04/12//2015"; as for the matter itself, the authors conclude that the Paris Agreement is a treaty in the broader sense as most international agreements, but that it is not a treaty seen from a US constitutional law perspective.

442 Daniel Bodansky, "The Legal Character of the Paris Agreement", *Review of European, Comparative & International Environmental Law* 25, no. 2 (2016), p. 143.

443 See for a detailed account of the set of questions, ibid., p. 142 et seqq.

A decisive part of the Agreement's legal bindingness concerns the NDCs and their negotiation enroute to Paris via the COPs in Warsaw and Lima, and especially their legal nature.[444] NDCs are already and will often be codified through targets set in domestic law or European law for the States concerned, thus having a higher impact on private individuals or companies. Some have argued that under international law, NDCs may qualify as both a binding unilateral act and as a 'subsequent agreement' (Art. 31 (3)(a) VCLT) interpreting the provisions of the UNFCCC and the Paris Agreement.[445] On a few issues, such as accounting of the NDCs and their implementation, the CMA may adopt decisions governing the conduct of the parties, but these will not be legally binding, unless the implementation of the Paris Agreement would make them so.[446] On the other hand, much speaks against a potential legal bindingness of NDCs, even in combination with 'non-regression'. Examples are both the fact that an obligation of result was explicitly not agreed upon in the Paris Agreement and the overall systematic architecture of the agreement.[447]

4. After the Paris Agreement

The Paris Agreement calls for further elaboration of many subjects through the decisions of the upcoming COPs and CMAs. Although an important contrast to the Kyoto Protocol implementation process is that the elaboration of additional procedures and rules is not necessarily essential to the domestic implementation, still, guidance by the CMAs will be necessary to operationalize the institutional re-arrangements made by the Agreement. Most prominently, this will concern the mitigation and sustainable development mechanism, the transparency framework and the compliance mechanism.[448] Coordination across the many different non-state actor initiatives accompanying the UNFCCC has the potential to increase ambition and catalyze action to meet the Paris Agreement

---

444 Ibid., p. 146.

445 Viñuales, "The Paris climate agreement: an initial examination", p. 13.

446 Daniel Bodansky, "Elaborating the Paris Agreement's Rules", in *Paris agreement and beyond: International climate change policy post-2020*, ed. Robert N. Stavins and Robert C. Stowe (Cambridge, MA: Harvard Project on Climate Agreements, 2016), p. 26 et seq.

447 As in, Harald Winkler, "Mitigation (Art. 4)", in *The Paris agreement on climate change: Analysis and commentary*, ed. Daniel Klein, et al. (Oxford University Press, 2017), p. 148 and 155 with further reference.

448 Bodansky, "Elaborating the Paris Agreement's Rules", p. 27 et seq.

goals. The social networks evolving from these frameworks can contribute to building trust and spreading ideas across various initiatives.[449] Understanding the functioning of those networks of actors in climate governance could help identify ways of improving coordination and thus raise ambition.[450] Improving the level of ambition embodied by the NDCs will be an important priority in the years to come. The development of the NDCs and the way States will be handling the non-regression provision will reveal what countries are willing and capable to do.[451] That, in turn, is connected to the elaboration of the oversight and reporting mechanism.

The assessment of the Paris Agreement and its key provisions yields mixed results. On one hand, the Paris Agreement and the political and societal debates surrounding it indicate that there is a growing momentum that further action could build upon.[452] After the 2016 withdrawal of the US, other actors on the sub-national level showed their willingness to fill the gaps in financial contributions and emission reductions on the state level or through business activities. Other States like China showed their readiness to introduce rather large-scale climate policies. Especially after the US re-joined the Agreement under President Biden in 2021, politically, there is reason for optimism on climate change policies after Paris. As seen throughout the development of the climate regime thus far, the momentum and political force of the regime has been significantly built on the normative developments connected to the progressive international law and relations of the 1990s and its historical precedents.

Considering the role of law in the field, the balance is different and rather negative. The analysis of the Paris Agreement shows to what extent there has been a trade-off between far-reaching policies and the weakening of legal structure. As will be further elaborated vis-à-vis individual norm concepts and principles, the Paris Agreement also stands for growing discrepancy between the normative pervasiveness of community value orientation on the one hand and the ambition of strong legal structures implementing them on the other.

---

449 Paterson, "Networks and Coordination in Global Climate Governance", p. 83 et seq.

450 Ibid.

451 Victor, "Making the Promise of Paris a Reality", p. 14 et seq.

452 Peter Christoff, "The Promissory Note: COP 21 and the Paris Climate Agreement", *Environmental Politics* 25, no. 5 (2016), p. 780 et seq.; On civil society and the Paris Agreement, see Michael Jacobs, "High Pressure for Low Emissions: How Civil Society Created the Paris Climate Agreement", *Juncture* 22, no. 4 (2016), p. 322 et seq.

5. Interim Conclusion: A 'Decline' of Legal Form in the International Climate Change Regime

The analysis of the international climate change regime's historical evolution has shown an overall shift indicating a 'decline' of international law as understood in the framework of this thesis. In the 1990s, a strong and combined emphasis on multilateralism, legal bindingness and value-underpinning shaped the field. Up to the Paris Agreement, a steady trend towards a more informalized regime re-emphasizing national circumstances and flexibility is discernible.

In the period between the conclusion of the UNFCCC and the Kyoto Protocol, the climate regime overlapped to a great extent the progressive development trends in international law of the 1990s. The Kyoto Protocol, in particular, translated the efforts in multilateralism and value-underpinning into far-reaching legal obligations. This regulatory approach seems to have overstretched state's willingness to accept legal bindingness in the field. Facing the looming failure of the Kyoto Protocol, a shift in emphasis is recognizable nearly from the start of the negotiations for the post-Kyoto-period. After the Copenhagen conference failed to produce a legally binding instrument capable of replacing the Kyoto Protocol, this shift gained critical traction for bringing about the much-discussed change from a 'top-down' to a 'bottom-up' approach in the climate regime. From a purely practical perspective on the regime, the Paris Agreement has been rightly acclaimed for embodying positive aspects of this shift: After years of frustration among climate policymakers and speculations that climate diplomacy would be incapable of producing a lasting agreement, the Agreement has built on a critical and positive momentum and brought about the unlikely result of an instrument that gained almost universal acceptance among States. It did so by combining multilateralism with underpinnings of many references to the value and principle orientation that gained traction in the 1990s. Despite the US' 2016 withdrawal impeding the Agreement's implementation, positive trends are recognizable. Some example include, other US actors trying to make up for the US contributions during the Trump presidency, China's apparent willingness to deliver on its commitments notwithstanding the US position and an unprecedented level of climate advocacy that seems to have favorably shifted public opinion internationally. In sum, prospects for a value-oriented climate change policy are considerably higher today than they were in any other previous occasion.

As alluded to in the introduction to this study, one of the pertinent questions in the field is whether the Paris Agreement and the approach it stands for is an example for forward-looking developments or, conversely, a figurative 'declaration of bankruptcy' for the 'progressive' international law of the 1990s? Moreover, if the latter is true, does this show that the law is incapable of exceeding certain limits? For the view represented here, the above statements all have some truth components. The issues discussed in this study are all structural examples for the hypothesis that the existing international law, which is based on a "bilateralist framework" as its fundamental source of legitimacy and effect, has certain inherent limits it cannot exceed however normatively aspirational the drivers of change may be. The design and implementation of an international agreement on mitigating climate change must be consistent with countries' strategic interests to find acceptance.[453] The design of the Paris Agreement pays tribute to this. Its reduced legal force was in many regards the price to pay for a comprehensive agreement on climate change to be internationally adopted. The drivers of enhanced mitigation ambition (as the context of the Paris Agreement) provide cause for cautious optimism that the Agreement may be successful. The example of introducing community values into international law was successful from a value perspective. The actors driving the process managed to establish a relatively broad consensus regarding central norm concepts introducing community values into the field. An important factor in this success, in terms of community value orientation, was to refrain from overstretching States' acceptance. It allowed for differentiation and made it possible for States to accept the shifting of priorities towards a more community-oriented legal regime.

Still, it must be noted that if one considers legal form and legal bindingness as important factors, a distinctly different perspective emerges. While – shaped by the debates in many democratic cultures – the notion of a 'bottom-up' approach is positively connoted, standing for enhanced participation and legitimacy, in international law this move away from a 'top-down' approach signifies a lower level of legal bindingness and an overall reduced role of the law in exercising its classical functions. This decline in legal bindingness seems to have been the price for the Paris Agreement's existence.

This assessment of a historical development confirms the assumption that the role of international law shifted compared to the 1990s for the specific field subject of this study. This assessment will now serve as the backdrop for the further analysis, focusing on specific norm concepts embodying community values in the climate regime and their role in the above analyzed shift.

453 Ji, "Enhancing Climate Mitigation Ambition Successively: The Drivers", p. 31.

II. Community Value Based Concepts and Legality in Contemporary Climate Change Law and Policy Since 1992

Climate law, or for this matter environmental law in general, consists of a variety of different types of norms that differ in their degree of generality/particularity, their bindingness and normative force.[454] This section analyzes the different norm concepts identified as embodying community values, i.e. the core principles enshrined in Art. 3 of the UNFCCC ('common but differentiated responsibilities', inter- and intragenerational 'equity', 'sustainable development', 'precaution' and 'prevention'), as well as the 'common concern' concept which is at the outset of any notion of community orientation in modern climate law. Finally, the no-harm rule is included in the analysis, presenting the oldest and most basic notion of obligations to other States in IEL and is the cornerstone of bilateralist legal thinking in connection to the environment. According to the perspective taken in this study, special focus lies on a comparison between scholarly and political expectations connected to such norm concepts in the 1990s and the degree of acceptance by States in legal practice since then.

The analysis proceeds by delineating the debates surrounding the inception of the above-mentioned norm concepts and retraces their development throughout the regime development from the UNFCCC to the time after the Paris Agreement. Each section will be split into the conception and development of the respective concept and the expectations connected to it in the 1990s on the one hand, and the further development in the 'post-Kyoto'- period on the other. As indicated, this period can be situated in the time following 2005.[455] The analysis will show in how far different actors (States, courts, but also non-state-actors) have influenced and shaped the concepts and their interpretations. Tensions between the normative ambitions of certain norms and their community value-related underpinnings and conversely, the legally relevant state practice of States, will be pointed out. Lastly, conclusions will be drawn from the

454 For an overview, see Beyerlin, "Different Types Of Norms in IEL", p. 425 et seqq.; Dupuy and Viñuales, *International environmental law*, p. 51 et seqq.; See already Part B, section II.2. and 3.

455 Note: The historical segmentation is not applied categorically. For reasons of better legibility, sometimes developments between the adoption of the Kyoto Protocol (1997) and 2005 are included in the 'post-Kyoto' sub-sections where they are informative for the section's perspective.

concept-based analysis regarding the systemically relevant state of community value-implementation through law in the field and what this indicates for the overall relationship of community values and international law.

1. The Notion of 'Common Concern': Outset and Frame of the Debate

The notion of climate change being a 'common concern of (hu)mankind' is widely regarded as being among the most accepted concepts[456] in modern climate law. Emerging in the late 1980s and early 1990s, the concept has been re-emphasized in almost all important documents shaping the field. Nonetheless, the program conveyed by the concept as well as the substantial consequences following from it still contain ambiguities and uncertainties, which keep affecting and significantly limiting its legal influence. The concept recently was the subject of an intensive debate on the UN level, yielding important insights as to the States' (un)willingness to allow for community value provisions to gain more substantive legal weight.

(a) Conception, Development and Expectations in the 1990s

Recognizing the global nature of the greenhouse effect and that anthropogenic climate change is a challenge shared by all humankind dates to the late 1980s. The formulation of it being a 'common concern' was first used by the UNGA in 1988.[457] Historical precedents can be found as early as 1949 when tuna and other fish were of "common concern" to the parties of the relevant treaties.[458]

The basic conceptual approach of common concern is tangible especially in differentiation to the 'common heritage of mankind': The latter is concerned with the joint management of access to and exploitation of a resource that is common to mankind. The common concern, in turn, is concerned with a resource (here, a functioning atmosphere of the planet) that is accessible to all, but where collective action is needed in order to protect it. Consequentially, common concern is about subjecting States to certain requirements regarding the exploitation of a shared resource.[459] Positively, the core of the concept is that

456 Classifying 'common concern' as a concept, see e.g. Dupuy and Viñuales, *International environmental law*, p. 85 et seq.

457 See already Part C, Section I.2.

458 Sands, *Principles of international environmental law*, p. 286, with further reference.

459 Dupuy and Viñuales, *International environmental law*, p. 85.

addressing common concerns together also provides benefits to all States.[460] Unlike the 'common heritage' or, for that matter, the concept of 'common areas', the 'common concern' is more open ended, as it does not share the inherent limitation of the other concepts to certain geographic areas and their resources.[461] A notable example from international practice which indicates the differences between the concepts were the negotiations for the Convention on Biodiversity (CBD). Here, it was primarily the reluctance of developing States that prevented the application of the 'common heritage' concept. As the holders of most of the Earth's biological resources, those countries felt that their sovereign rights to the use of their resources would have been limited by declaring these resources a common heritage.[462]

Also regarding the climate change regime, there was an early proposal by Malta in the UNGA to declare the climate a 'part of the common heritage of mankind', which was rejected during the negotiations for the respective resolutions.[463] In Resolution 43/53, the initiative was still referenced, but in the operational part, the UNGA then "[r]recognize[d] that climate change is a **common concern of mankind**, since climate is an essential condition which sustains life on earth".[464] In the subsequent annual session, that recognition was explicitly recalled and connected to the initiatives for developing an international framework convention on climate change.[465] One year later, the resolution establishing the INC which then prepared the UNFCCC, recalled the two previous resolutions and linked the start of the negotiation process with the 'common concern' concept.[466]

The concept's implications regarding global environmental issues have also been examined at a meeting of the UNEP Group of Legal Experts in 1990.

---

460 Jutta Brunnée, "Common Areas, Common Heritage, and Common Concern", in *The Oxford handbook of international environmental law*, ed. Daniel Bodansky, Jutta Brunnée, and Ellen Hey (OUP, 2008), p. 553.

461 Ibid., p. 564.

462 Dupuy and Viñuales, *International environmental law*, p. 85; see as well Marie-Angèle Hermitte, "La convention sur la diversité biologique", *Annuaire français de droit international* 38 (1992), p. 844 et seqq.

463 For the report on the negotiations of the UNGA, see UN Doc. A/43/905; For the original draft resolution proposed by Malta, see UN Doc. A/C.2/43/L.17.

464 UN Doc. A/Res/43/53, para. 1, emphasis added.

465 UN Doc. A/Res/44/207, preambular para. 1, paras. 2, 10–13.

466 UN Doc. A/Res/45/212, preambular para. 1, paras. 1–5.

Here, it was noted that the 'common concern' concept has at least two important facets: spatial and temporal. The spatial aspect means that common concern implies cooperation of all States on matters being similarly important to all nations, to the whole international community. The temporal aspect arises from the long-term implications of major environmental challenges which affect the rights and obligations not only of present but also of future generations.[467] That analysis – albeit still wide-ranging in the possible implications it ascribes to the concept – already pre-empts some of the developments the concept would experience with ambitious propositions of its usage in connection with the realities of the international practices containing them. For instance, the World Conservation Union in their 'Draft International Covenant on Environment and Development', suggested that the "global environment" be a common concern of humanity.[468]

That a given phenomenon is defined as a 'common concern' shows the willingness of the international community to act collectively in order to ensure the action necessary in the interest of the objective.[469] It is because of this connection, that the Special Rapporteur of the ILC held "that common concern forms the soundest basis for international cooperation to protect the atmosphere".[470] Indeed, the way in which common concern is used in the UNFCCC text is closely linked to the duty of cooperation to address the "adverse effects of climate change".[471] Such adverse effects, in this case, are designated as a common concern of

467 UNEP, "The Implications of the Common Concern of Mankind Concept on Global Environmental Issues – Note from the UNEP Secretariat to the Meeting of the Group of Legal Experts to Examine the Concept of the Common Concern of Mankind in relation to Global Environmental Issues, 13–15Dec 1990", *Revista Instituto Interamericano de Derechos Humanos* 13 (1991), p. 239 (para. 5).

468 Commission on Environmental Law of IUCN – The World Conservation Union in Cooperation with the International Council of Environmental Law, *Draft International Covenant on Environment and Development*, 3rd ed., vol. 31, Rev. 2 Environmental Policy and Law Paper (IUCN, 2004), Art. 3.

469 Brunnée, "Common Areas, Common Heritage, and Common Concern", p. 566; The implications concerning international co-operation are discussed more in detail in section II.,2. in context with the 'principle of co-operation'.

470 International Law Commission, Second report on Protection of the atmosphere by Shinya Murase, UN Doc. A/CN.4/681 (2015), para. 36; see also III., 2. below.

471 UNFCCC, Preamble, para. 1.

humankind."[472]

Remarkably, it is thus not the atmosphere as a resource or even 'the climate' in general that is the common *concern* in the understanding of the Convention, but the process of climate change and its direct and indirect results and effects.[473] Still, the resource with which the common concern as applied in the UNFCCC regime is connected is still indirectly defined in Art. 2 of the Convention. That is, a stable climatic system, which must be preserved through the control of anthropogenic interference with the atmospheric composition. Although this resource is global, as it transcends the territory of all States respectively, its preservation nevertheless requires the adoption of appropriate measures by each state on the national level and/or in cooperation with other States on the international level.[474]

The inception and development of the concept thus shows a combination of – at least politically – using it as the broadest possible framing for the emerging climate change regime and early initiatives to use it legally. Early discussions about the legal use show a certain variety between a usage that was in demarcation from concepts that were ascribed with more legal ramifications (like 'common heritage') and approaches that wanted to attribute the 'common concern' concept itself with legal effects, especially regarding international co-operation. From its inception, 'common concern of mankind' ignited lively debates about whether it had any legal meaning and if this meaning could be conceptually conceivable. An early scholarly assessment of IEL discussing 'common concern' concluded that the concept was not concise enough to be more than a potential frame of reference.[475] Others had more confidence in the concept, seeing it as one important facet of the "comprehensive and all-pervading character of the concept of 'common interest'" and comparing it metaphorically to a "shell" producing "echoes including some so powerful that they spell out legal obligations".[476]

---

472 The commonly used formula changed from *man*kind to the more gender-neutral *human*kind during the 1992 negotiations, see Edith Brown Weiss, "The Coming Water Crisis: A Common Concern of Humankind", *Transnational Environmental Law* 1, no. 1 (2012) p. 163 with further reference.

473 Brunnée, "Common Areas, Common Heritage, and Common Concern", p. 565.

474 Dupuy and Viñuales, *International environmental law*, p. 86.

475 Meinhard Schröder, "Instrumente des internationalen Umweltrechts unter Berücksichtigung der Noumea-Konvention vom 24./25.11. 1986", *Jahrbuch des Umwelt- und Technikrechts* (1987), p. 280.

476 Brunnée, "'Common Interest' – Echoes from an Empty Shell?", p. 792.

As for the climate change regime, the notion was used in continuation of the UNGA parlance. The Convention itself acknowledged "that change in the Earth's climate and its adverse effects are a common concern of humankind".[477] In the Kyoto Protocol, reference to the common concern was only indirectly made, when Parties were "[r]ecalling the provisions of the Convention".[478]

(b) Further Development: Post-Kyoto Until Today

From today's perspective and hence roughly 30 years into the concept's development, the question of whether the concept has gained any status under international law as recognized in Art. 38 of the ICJ statute is still pertinent. However, now with more treaty and state practice to base an assessment on. The concept of common concern has found application in two major treaty regimes in international environmental law – the CBD and the UNFCCC – and various positions exist on the customary nature of the concept as a whole and certain elements of it. The Bali Action Plan, other than referring to the Convention and its objectives in general, made no explicit reference to the 'common concern', neither did the Copenhagen Accord. In the Preamble of the Paris Agreement, the concept was again referenced.[479] The legal ramifications of the concept are disputed and depend on the varying interpretations. However, one common denominator is that even a thorough literature review barely uncovered clearly sceptical views about the concept's implications. Some interpretations want the concept to be the basis for the creation of rights for individuals and future generations.[480] Other broad interpretations hold that the concept could give all States a legal interest and standing in the enforcement of rules regarding the common concern – here the

---

477 UNFCCC, preamble, para. 1.

478 Kyoto Protocol, preamble, para. 3.

479 Preamble, para 11, reads "Acknowledging that climate change is a common concern of humankind, Parties should, when taking action to address climate change, respect, promote and consider their respective obligations on human rights, the right to health, the rights of indigenous peoples, local communities, migrants, children, persons with disabilities and people in vulnerable situations and the right to development, as well as gender equality, empowerment of women and intergenerational equity".

480 Laura Horn, "Climate Change and the Future Role of the Concept of the Common Concern of Humankind", *Australian Journal of Environmental Law,* (2015, vol. II), p. 30 et seqq.

climate or the atmosphere.[481] Others hold that the concept could lead to the creation of more concrete substantive obligations for States.[482]

The ILC Project on the Protection of the Atmosphere

In line with this tendency in literature, it has been argued that recent state practice supports the emergence of the concept of 'common concern' as reflected in the 1992 UNFCCC.[483] Given the scarcity in treaty practice on 'common concern' beyond the mentioning in preambular sections, the question is primarily whether the concept has gained a significant status under customary international law or as a general principle of law. A case in point to test what positions States have recently been taking on the concept is the project of the ILC on 'protection of the atmosphere' and the debates surrounding it. They offer a broad and important example for the ramifications of the concept of common concern on the international level. In 2013 (65th session), the ILC decided to include the topic "Protection of the atmosphere" in its program of work and appointed Mr. Shinya Murase of Japan as the Special Rapporteur responsible for the topic. In his first report, the Special Rapporteur alluded to the possible role the concept could play in the project:

> *"The legal content of the concept of common concern is that States can no longer claim that atmospheric problems are within the reserved domain of domestic jurisdiction because the issues now legitimately fall under "matters of international concern". It will certainly lead to the creation of substantive legal obligations on the part of all States to protect the global atmosphere as enforceable erga omnes. It may be too early at present to interpret the concept of common concern as giving "all States a legal interest, or standing, in the enforcement of rules concerning protection of the global atmosphere", in view of the absence of appropriate procedural law to implement such an interpretation. It may also be premature to consider the concept of common concern as creating rights for individuals and future generations."*[484]

---

481 Alan E. Boyle, "International Law and the Protection of the Global Atmosphere: Concepts, Categories and Principles", in *International law and global climate change*, ed. Robin Churchill and David Freestone (Graham and Trotman, 1991), p. 11 et seq., connecting the question to international crimes concerning the environment and deducing that all States have an interest in suppressing such violations of international law. According to Boyle, the same conclusion would follow from the logic of *erga omnes*.

482 Ibid., p. 13.

483 Sands, *Principles of international environmental law*, p. 287.

484 International Law Commission, First report on Protection of the atmosphere by Shinya Murase, UN Doc. A/CN.4/667 (2014), para. 89.

The Special Rapporteur went on to state that it "may be concluded that the atmosphere has the legal status of an international resource, whether shared or common, indispensable for sustaining life on earth, human health and welfare, crops and the integrity of ecosystems; and that consequently its protection is a common concern of humankind." He added as a caveat that the draft guidelines included in the report were not intended to prejudice in any way the status of airspace already established in international law.[485] In the subsequent report, the common concern concept was elaborated and incorporated into draft guideline 3, which read

> "*The atmosphere is a natural resource essential for sustaining life on Earth, human health and welfare, and aquatic and terrestrial ecosystems, and hence the degradation of atmospheric conditions* ***is a common concern of humankind.***
>
> *As outlined above, application of the concept of the common concern of humankind has two important corollaries as regards the protection of the atmosphere (which are considered below):* ***the general obligation of States to protect the atmosphere and international cooperation for the protection of the atmosphere.***"[486]

At the 67th session one year later, its Chairman presented the first report of the Drafting Committee.[487] In doing so, he highlighted the controversial role that the 'common concern' concept had played during the negotiations of the Commission: Regarding the preambular paragraphs of the special rapporteur's draft guidelines, he quoted "some members" being "concerned that the use of the 'common concern' concept could trigger legal consequences for States".[488] While other members considered the proposed use of the term a merely factual statement not carrying any legal consequences, still others were comfortable with the prospect of the phrase possibly carrying legal implications into the draft guidelines.[489] As a consequence, the Commission agreed that draft guideline 3 would be moved to the preambular section of the draft guidelines. Furthermore, the Drafting Committee recommended that instead of 'common concern

485 Ibid., para. 90.

486 Second report on Protection of the atmosphere (2015), para. 34–40, draft guideline at para. 39 et seq., emphasis added.

487 UN Doc. A/CN.4/L.851.

488 International Law Commission, Sixty-seventh session, *Protection of the Atmosphere*, Statement of the Chairman of the Drafting Committee, Mr. Mathias Forteau, 2 Jun 2015, p. 9 et seq., available at http://legal.un.org/docs/?path=../ilc/documentation/english/statements/2015_dc_chairman_statement_atmosphere.pdf&lang=EF.

489 Ibid., p. 10.

of humankind', the expression 'pressing concern of the international community as a whole' should be used.[490] The newly adopted preambular section now held:

> *"Recognizing therefore that the protection of the atmosphere from atmospheric pollution and atmospheric degradation is a pressing concern of the international community as a whole"*[491]

Later that year, the sixth committee of the UNGA discussed the matter, with States giving their explicit opinion on the use of 'common concern'.[492] A minority wanted to keep the original formulation including the reference to the 'common concern': The German representative held that the "[p]rotection of the atmosphere was indeed a pressing concern for all States", and that "it might therefore be justifiable to follow the Special Rapporteur's initial recommendation and classify it as a common concern of humankind."[493] The Portuguese delegation held that the 'common concern' concept "would provide an adequate framework for addressing the legal questions relating to the atmosphere", as it would be established in state practice and the UNFCCC regime.[494] The clearest and legally most explicit expression of discontent with the commission's decision was expressed by the representative of Micronesia. His delegation criticized the conversion of guideline 3 into a preambular paragraph as stripping the text of its operative essence. The changing of expressions, in his opinion, "implied that the Commission had shied away from explicitly acknowledging that the degradation of atmospheric conditions was a common concern that all States were legally obligated to address cooperatively, comprehensively and urgently". He argued that the concept had been sufficiently established in numerous treaties and the conclusions of the Commission to the contrary were not in accordance with the current state and development of international law.[495]

A clear majority of State delegations, however, agreed with the changing of expressions and thus to the weakening of the role that the 'common concern'

---

490 International Law Commission, Third report on Protection of the atmosphere by Shinya Murase, UN Doc. A/CN.4/692 (2016), para. 3.

491 Fourth report on Protection of the atmosphere by Shinya Murase, UN Doc. A/CN.4/705 (2017), Annex I, preambular para. 4.

492 UNGA, Sixth Committee, Summary record of the 17th meeting, UN Doc. A/C.6/70/SR.17 (13 Nov 2015); Summary record of the 18th meeting, A/C.6/70/SR.18 (18 Nov 2015) and Summary record of the 19th meeting, A/C.6/70/SR.19 (20 Nov 2015).

493 A/C.6/70/SR.19, para. 12.

494 A/C.6/70/SR.19, para. 24.

495 A/C.6/70/SR.18, para. 13.

concept could play in the development of the ILC project[496], although to varying degrees: The delegation from Sri Lanka, for instance, "approved of the newly adopted third paragraph of the preamble" as "the atmosphere was vital to the existence of life on Earth. Member States could not turn a blind eye to the fact that it was being degraded" without further relating this statement to the 'common concern' and its deletion.[497] Similarly, China expressed their approval with the replacement of formulations and placement in the preamble, however, did so without going into more detail regarding their legal motivation.[498]

Other delegations discussed more explicitly the legal implications: The Nordic countries, spoken for by Finland, "agreed with the Commission's decision" both regarding the expression of the international community's concern "as a factual statement in the preamble to the draft guidelines rather than as a normative statement" as well as with the changed formulation.[499] The delegation from Singapore based their agreement on the position that "the legal consequences of the concept of 'the common concern of mankind' remained unclear".[500] In the same vein, Israel called it "too vague".[501] Poland positively "welcomed the revised phrase", stating that "concern of the international community as a whole", was "clearly better established in international law than the previous formulation".[502]

The Japanese delegation offered a middle ground position, considering that "it would be appropriate to include the concept 'common concern of humankind' in the preamble, as several related legal documents, such as the [UNFCCC], referred to the concept." The delegation's reason for not deeming the usage problematic was seemingly the assumption that "the concept would not necessarily

---

496 International Law Commission, Third report on Protection of the atmosphere (2016), para. 5.

497 A/C.6/70/SR.18, para. 41; Similarly, the Delegation from the Republic of Korea only welcomed "the overarching and comprehensive acknowledgement of the importance of the atmosphere and the fact that its protection was described as a "pressing concern of the international community as a whole" without further differentiating it from the 'common concern' concept, A/C.6/70/SR.18, para. 81.

498 A/C.6/70/SR.18, para. 18; The French delegation also only expressed that "the new formulation "pressing concern of the international community" seemed preferable to 'common concern of humankind'", A/C.6/70/SR.20, para. 15.

499 A/C.6/70/SR.17, para. 37.

500 A/C.6/70/SR.17, para. 46.

501 A/C.6/70/SR.18, para. 4.

502 A/C.6/70/SR.18, para. 63.

entail substantive legal relationships among States; rather, it attributed a certain legal value, broadly speaking, to the project's objectives".[503]

Finally, the discussion also gave rise to more fundamental concerns regarding the entire ILC project which, despite their generality, also apply to the debate on 'common concern'. The US delegation reiterated their original opposition to the inclusion of the topic in the Commission's program of work, as existing instruments would already provide sufficient guidance to States on the development and implementation of treaty regimes. Any exercise aimed at extracting broad legal rules from specific environmental agreements would not be feasible and potentially undermine carefully negotiated differences among regimes.[504]

As a consequence, from the third report onwards, the 'common concern' concept practically ceased to play a role in the further development of the ILC project. One of the few examples is a statement by Poland, quoted in the fourth report of the Special Rapporteur[505]: In a sixth committee debate – now after the adoption of the Paris Agreement – the delegation suggested to include a sentence in the commentary to draft guideline 3 referring to the Agreement's acknowledgment of climate change as a common concern of humankind.[506] Whether this minor inclusion of the concept will prevail remains to be seen.

As a result of the previously depicted process however, the draft guideline 3 ("Obligation to protect the atmosphere") in its latest available version reads

> *"States have the obligation to protect the atmosphere by exercising due diligence in taking appropriate measures, in accordance with applicable rules of international law, to prevent, reduce or control atmospheric pollution and atmospheric degradation."*[507]

Any reference to the 'common concern' concept has thus been erased from the draft. With the sixth committee debates informing this change being the latest and most tangible example of States engaging in the legal ramifications of the concept, it seems reasonable to assume that this answers the question about any further customary law status for the concept, at least for the foreseeable future.

503 A/C.6/70/SR.18, para. 25.

504 A/C.6/70/SR.19, para. 18.

505 International Law Commission, Fourth report on Protection of the atmosphere (2017), para. 4.

506 UNGA, Sixth Committee, Summary record of the 26th meeting, A/C.6/71/SR.26 (5 Dec 2016), para. 55.

507 International Law Commission, Seventieth Session, A/CN.4/L.909 (6 Jun 2018), p. 2.

(c) Conclusion

The 'common concern' is a concise example for both the potential and the limitations of norm concepts incorporating community values into international law. Originating in a period of transition for international relations and formed at a time when internationalist optimism was at a still increasing high, the concept grew in the context of multilateral treaty regimes. 'Common concern' captures the ambition to dissolve the collective action problem of climate change by initiating new forms of cooperation and by transcending the classical interaction of sovereign States along with the strict limitations for international law connected thereto. But the ILC project and the intensive debates surrounding the inclusion of the concept are also salient examples for the different ways of and motivations for resistance to such an inclusion and its legal consequences for States. The debate broadly reflects two motivations: The first seems to be based on the concern that tangible legal consequences *could* follow from an inclusion into international instruments. The other seems to rest on the assumption that concepts like 'common concern' cannot carry legal weight and should, if at all, only play the role of political statements.

Drawing the developments together, the legal ramifications the concept has come to have, remain limited. In treaty law, the UNFCCC regime used the notion, but infrequently. The fact that the Paris Agreement included the concept, might be an indicator that the concept will continue to have a role. But the concept did not undergo sufficient clarification in treaty law to support a clear legal status. Looking at customary international law, the perspective is not much different. An insightful perspective on state practice is offered by a comparison of the first UNGA resolutions with the debates on the ILC project on the protection of the atmosphere. Certainly, their comparability is limited. The former was a predominantly political context, in the latter, it was clear that the subjects were possible legal ramifications. Correspondingly, it is much easier to agree on a given formulation in a political resolution. But nonetheless, different attitudes of States towards the issue are reflected in the two debates. Although being a compromise to begin with, the 'common concern' formula was readily used by States at the end of the 1980s. In the 2010s, the situation looks both more differentiated and bleaker. Whether it be for concerns of legal uncertainty or principled opposition, a clear majority of States are against the derivation of legal obligations from the concept. Arguments about the concept building a basis for concrete rights for individuals, let alone future generations, therefore have no discernible basis in international law as it is currently standing. The concept of common concern has not developed to an extent where it would imply specific rules for the conduct of States.[508] The ILC project can also be assumed to be telling regarding the prospects for a treaty (provision) that could foster the legal status.

Given the limited usage of the concept in national jurisdictions or systems of regional cooperation, it is also not sustainable to assume the establishment of the 'common concern' concept as a general principle of international law. It does not automatically follow that the concept cannot have an influence on the future development of obligations. Ever since the UNGA resolutions discussed above, the 'common concern' has been an argumentative frame of reference in the development of the climate change regime. The concept certainly has established as a norm (in the non-legal sense) that there are limits to actions with detrimental effect on the climate even outside of the context of another State being directly affected in classical terms of transboundary harm. The controversy surrounding the ILC project on the protection of the atmosphere shows that at least some States feel the necessity to exclude certain conclusions as to the legal consequences that, in their opinion, *could* be drawn from the concept. But given that the concept *as such* and as referenced to existing instruments, it cannot in and of itself lead to concrete obligations.[509] In comparison to the actual legal status during the 1990s, this development of 'common concern' is one of stagnation. In comparison to the significant number of expectations attributed to the concept in the scholarly debates of the 1990s, there is a 'decline' of what seems to have been an overestimation of the concept's legal potential.

2. Common but Differentiated Responsibilities: Lynchpin of the Climate Regime

The principle of CBDR is arguably *the* central concept of modern climate change law, certainly in the sense of being the one most frequently used and argued over regarding its content. During the conception of the modern climate regime around the 1992 convention, it was mostly used in framing the argument for regulations placing the primary burden of emission reduction and financial contributions towards climate change mitigation on developed countries. CBDR's structure and approach of striving for a somewhat fair differentiation along the lines of varying capabilities among States in contributing makes it a key example for a community value provision, especially given that this is an effort necessarily

508 As in, Brunnée, "Common Areas, Common Heritage, and Common Concern", p. 566.
509 As in, International Law Commission, Second report on Protection of the atmosphere (2015), para. 37; Alexandre Kiss, "The Common Concern of Mankind ", *Envtl. Pol'y & L.* 27, no. 4 (1997), p. 246.

to be made by the international community as a whole. During the development of the regime, including the recent process of adopting and implementing the Paris Agreement, CBDR has undergone a constant process of re-framing, re-emphasis and partial re-definition. Many of the debates surrounding it are indeed mirroring those regarding the regime as a whole. As during the negotiations leading to up to the Paris Agreement the focus shifted away from the clear-cut differentiation between developed and developing countries that the UNFCCC had introduced, doubts have been raised whether CBDR remains intact as a normative concept.[510]

(a) Conception, Development and Expectations in the 1990s

The principle of CBDR originates from two earlier concepts, highlighting that the principle consists of two complementary dimensions: One was the idea of a 'community of interest' regarding certain specific areas like the Antarctica, the other was the idea of 'differential treatment' used by international trade law or the law of the sea.[511] Analytically, it can also be differentiated between the 'common' – dimension and the 'differentiation' – dimension: The words 'common responsibilities' dictate that all States have the general – and common – obligation to protect the environment, here the climate system, at the national, regional or global level, while the degree of 'responsibilities' should be 'differentiated' according to differing circumstances relating to each state's contribution and their 'respective capabilities'.[512] Both dimensions have links to previously existing concepts, but CBDR should nevertheless be considered as a new principle.[513]

CBDR, as indicated earlier and still influential today, could be seen as reflecting different ways of thinking about the relationship between industrialized and developing countries, between the Global North and the Global South. Either CBDR could simply be a reflection of a rather pragmatic way of accepting

510 In a recent publication, former Indian Foreign Secretary Saran criticised that the CBDR's original meaning, putting the main burden in combatting climate change on developed countries, has been "hollowed out in favour of a 'pledge and review' mechanism applicable to all countries", referring to process leading up to the Paris Agreement, see Shyam Saran, *How India sees the world: Kautilya to the 21st century* (Juggernaut Books, 2017), p. 180.

511 Dupuy and Viñuales, *International environmental law*, p. 73 et seq.

512 International Law Commission, Second report on Protection of the atmosphere (2015), para. 51; Sands, *Principles of international environmental law*, p. 286.

513 Dupuy and Viñuales, *International environmental law*, p. 74.

different levels of development and resourcefulness between countries. Or it could be viewed as embodying an acknowledgment of wide-ranging historic, moral and legal responsibilities.[514] The gradual differences between the views on CBDR can be exemplified by a comparison of the UNFCCC formulation to two other instruments:

CBDR also finds articulation in Art. 7 of the Rio Declaration, which reads:

> *"States shall cooperate in a* ***spirit of global partnership*** *to conserve, protect and restore the health and integrity of the Earth's ecosystem.* ***In view of the different contributions to global environmental degradation, States have common but differentiated responsibilities.*** *The developed countries acknowledge the responsibility that they bear in the international pursuit to sustainable development in view of the pressures their societies place on the global environment and of the technologies and financial resources they command."*[515]

During the negotiations for the Rio Declaration, the G77 had presented a proposal putting even more emphasis on the developed countries' contributions:

> *"All States share a common but differentiated responsibility for containing, reducing and eliminating global environmental damage and for restoring the ecological balance of the Earth, in accordance with their respective responsibilities and capabilities.* ***The major cause of the continuing deterioration of the global environment is the unsustainable pattern of production and consumption, particularly in the developed countries.*** *All countries, particularly developed ones, shall make commitments to address their unsustainable patterns of production and consumption.* ***In view of their main historical and current responsibility for global environmental degradation and their capability to address this common concern, developed countries shall provide*** *adequate, new and additional financial resources and environmentally sound technologies […]."*[516]

In comparison to the G77-formula, the Rio-wording is more cautious and excludes direct references to historic contributions to environmental damage.[517] Yet, the UNFCCC is even more cautious in its version of using the CBDR, with the relevant Art. 3(1) reading:

> *"The Parties should protect the climate system for the benefit of present and future generations of humankind, on the basis of equity* ***and in accordance with their common but differentiated responsibilities and respective capabilities.*** *Accordingly, the developed*

---

514 Karin Mickelson, "South, North, International Environmental Law, and International Environmental Lawyers", *YB Int'l Env L.* 11 (2000), p. 70.

515 Emphasis added.

516 UN. Doc. A/CONF.151/PC/ WG.III/L.20/Rev.1 (1992), emphasis added.

517 Mickelson, "South, North, International Environmental Law, and International Environmental Lawyers", p. 71.

country Parties should take the lead in combating climate change and the adverse effects thereof."[518]

Here, in contrast, no reference is made to the States' different historic contributions to global environmental degradation as an element linked to CBDR. As the basis for differentiation, the UNFCCC formula only recognizes "respective capabilities"[519], i.e., factual differences that lie in the present, as opposed to the historic contingencies in the other formulations. The variety between the proposals point to the differences in tone and approach between the instruments and the reach of the norms included.

CBDR's relationship with the sovereign equality of States requires clarification: The differentiation dimension, explicitly aiming at unequally distributing the burdens of environmental efforts or in this case, climate protection, is arguably a departure from or a violation of sovereign equality.[520] On the other hand, it can be argued that sovereign equality of States alone is incapable of ensuring just interstate relations, and that therefore differential treatment may be essential in order to achieve "real equality".[521] In this latter sense, exercising equal sovereignties in a world shaped by material and other *de facto* inequalities between States would result in unequal rights and duties.[522] Moreover, CBDR needs to be differentiated from the 'polluter pays' – principle, which diametrically differs from CBDR, i.e., in its field of application: The 'polluter pays' – principle is primarily about the internal relation between State authorities and the actual causes of pollution, originating in most cases from civil society, especially economic actors. CBDR, in contrast, comes into play at the interstate level only, regulating the relationships between different groups of States.[523]

518 Emphasis added.

519 The addition "respective capabilities" is also the reason why in some parts of literature on the climate regime, CBDR is instead abbreviated with CBDRRC.

520 International Law Association, Washington Conference (2014): Legal Principles Relating to Climate Change – Report of the International Law Association's Committee on Legal Principles Relating to Climate Change (2014) p. 13.

521 Oscar Schachter, *Sharing the world's resources* (Columbia University Press, 1977), p. 7; Beyerlin and Marauhn, *International environmental law*, p. 63.

522 Lavanya Rajamani, *Differential treatment in international environmental law* (Oxford University Press Oxford, 2006), p. 2 et seqq.

523 Beyerlin and Marauhn, *International environmental law*, p. 64. The primarily internal direction of the polluter-pays- principle is also the reason why the concept is not discussed in this study in a more detailed manner, despite being often discussed as an important 'principle' or 'concept' rooted in values in the field of international environmental law, see e.g. Dupuy and Viñuales, *International environmental law*, p.

(aa) 'Taking the Lead' by Developed Countries

One aspect of CBDR's differentiation deserves further scrutiny, namely the formula that developed countries "should take the lead" in combating climate change and its adverse effects. Being the flipside of exempting developing countries from obligations in the original approach in the UNFCCC and Kyoto, it is an expression of the idea of a group of States being given special responsibilities in the interest of realizing the community values of the climate change regime. The wording of Art. 3 (1) UNFCCC ("accordingly") suggests that the application of the concepts of equity and CBDR require developed States to take the lead in combatting climate change and its effects.[524] As explicated above, this special role of developed countries could, despite attempts by developing countries, not be established based on historical responsibilities for contributions to climate change. Rather, their taking the lead in combatting climate change should be based on their advanced material capacities and technical resources. This provision is an important community value aspect of CBDR and the climate regime in general. Whereas, the climate regime is based on the insight that no state can solve the problem of climate change alone and CBRD was based on the notion that there is a shared responsibility in need of differentiation, the aspect of 'taking the lead' added some version of fairness to the equation: Simply given their economic advantages, developed States would be called upon to bring more to the efforts of protecting the global climate, than those with less advantages. This logic made 'taking the lead' a key feature in the aspirations for CBDR to be the application of distributive justice in the climate regime.[525]

(bb) A Principle of 'Co-Operation'?

International 'co-operation' – although never defined by treaty or UN resolution – can be described as the voluntary, coordinated action of two or more States under a legal regime serving a specific objective or the effort of States to accomplish an objective by joint action where the activity of a single State cannot

---

71 et seqq., who nevertheless come to a similar conclusion on the internal / external application, see p. 72.

524 International Law Association, Legal Principles Relating to Climate Change (2014), p. 9.

525 Jutta Brunnée, "Climate Change, Global Environmental Justice and International Environmental Law", in *Environmental law and justice in context*, ed. Jonas Ebbesson and Phoebe Okowa (Cambridge University Press, 2009), p. 325 with further reference.

achieve the same result.[526] The CBDR concept has been accurately called the "flipside of the concept of common concern".[527] That is because of its encapsulation of the 'common concern' approach of putting the main emphasis on the equitable sharing of the burdens of co-operation and problem solving. CBDR, in turn, is deeply interwoven with 'co-operation' by the same token, as the 'common dimension' of CBDR essentially contains what is being discussed as 'the principle of co-operation'.[528] Indeed, the Rio Convention and especially the UNFCCC did not call 'the climate' (or biological diversity respectively) in general a 'common concern'. Instead, a major emphasis was put on the necessity for international co-operation regarding these issues. Some authors have concluded that the dimension of collective responsibility to act is in fact the *raison d'être* of the 'common concern' concept.[529] Given this connection, 'co-operation' is being discussed by many as a principle on its own.[530] Other scholars have submitted that "[n]otwithstanding its highly abstract wording, the character of the principle of co-operation is that of a rule, rather than a principle, because it attempts to direct conduct towards a particular goal" which, by making reference to the 'spirit of global partnership', "gives some substantive, although rather abstract, guidance for assessing the performance of inter-state cooperation."[531] Given these interconnections and the 'co-operation concept's' meaning for the community value orientation in climate law, it deserves inclusion in the discussion of the matter at hand. That States have a general duty to co-operate has been acknowledged in instruments such as the 'Friendly Relations- Declaration'[532] and can be regarded as well established in international law, while in IEL, it has taken many different forms.[533] In the scholarly debates of the 1990s, a differentiation was often made

526 Rüdiger Wolfrum, "International Law of Cooperation", in *MPEPIL*, ed. Rüdiger Wolfrum (Oxford University Press, 2010), para. 2, recurring to the 'Friendly Relations Declaration' (UN Doc. A/RES/2625) as an important basis for this definition.

527 Brunnée, "Common Areas, Common Heritage, and Common Concern", p. 566.

528 Beyerlin, "Different Types Of Norms in IEL", p. 442.

529 Duncan French, "Common Concern, Common Heritage and Other Global(-ising) Concepts: Rhetorical Devices, Legal Principles or a Fundamental Challenge?", in *Research Handbook on Biodiversity and Law*, ed. Michael Bowman, Peter Davies, and Edward Goodwin (Edward Elgar, 2016), p. 347.

530 Sands, *Principles of international environmental law*, p. 249 et seqq.

531 Beyerlin, "Different Types Of Norms in IEL", p. 442.

532 UN Doc. A/Res/25/2625.

533 Dupuy and Viñuales, *International environmental law*, p. 64 et seq.

between a reading of 'co-operation' that aims at a 'spirit of global partnership'[534] and another that entails a general duty to co-operate in transboundary contexts.[535] For the above-mentioned interconnection of CBDR, common concern and co-operation, the first interpretation is the crucial intersection.

In the most common understanding, it is co-operation that would have crystallized into the other concepts/principles, which therefore follow from 'co-operation'.[536] The most salient example of this version being alluded to in the climate regime is the Bali Action Plan with its ambition to develop a "shared vision" for long-term cooperative action under the Convention.[537] This emphasis is a further example for the community value-orientation in the climate regime. Earlier 'co-operation' threads in the climate regime found reception in scholarly debates about a possible transformation of sovereignty in the early 2000s.[538] The second view – co-operation in transboundary contexts – is responsible for most of the basic procedural aspects and varieties of 'co-operation', i.e. notification and consultation, prior informed consent or the performance of 'environmental impact assessments' (EIA).[539] Connected to the community-orientation, elements of co-operation have also been suggested for establishment with a broader range of actors: While the principle traditionally applies between States, co-operation between States and other actors is also required – UN, inter-governmental organisations (IGOs) and relevant NGOs[540], but also, and especially in the climate context, entities such as cities or international corporations.

---

534 Principle 27 of the Rio Declaration states: "States and people shall cooperate in good faith and in a spirit of partnership in the fulfilment of the principles embodied in this Declaration and in the further development of international law in the field of sustainable development".

535 United Nations Commission on Sustainable Development, Report of the Expert Group Meeting on Identification of Principles of International Law for Sustainable Development, (1995) uses this differentiation between the 'spirit of global partnership' dimension (para. 75–102) and the 'transboundary Context' (para. 105–122).

536 Dupuy and Viñuales, *International environmental law*, p. 65; Perrez, *Cooperative sovereignty*, p. 330, who went further stating that a version of 'co-operation' would become a general principle of international law that he viewed as being confirmed by principles of IEL such as sustainability, precaution, common concern and CBDR.

537 Bali Action Plan (2007), para. 1(a).

538 Perrez, *Cooperative sovereignty*, p. 318 et seq.

539 Dupuy and Viñuales, *International environmental law*, p. 65 with further references. On EIAs, see also the section II.,5. on 'Prevention and Precaution'.

540 An example for this variety is Art. 7 of the ILC Draft articles on the protection of persons in the event of a disaster iterates that "*States shall, as appropriate, cooperate among*

As for the legal status of 'co-operation', differentiation is necessary between (the principle of) 'co-operation' in general as well as its substantial and procedural varieties in IEL and climate law. Concerning the first, despite some non-binding instruments alluding to co-operation[541], there is no evidence for a general customary international law-based obligation for States to co-operate unreservedly. Rather, there are treaty-based obligations to co-operate made by sovereign consent by the States.[542] Given the proliferation of such treaty-based duties for co-operation, some have concluded that there is a general principle of international law on co-operation which, although admittedly its scope is controversial, could give normative direction to the actions of States.[543] As for the more concrete aspects of co-operation, several concrete obligations can be linked to both the principle and the community value-development of the climate regime and IEL more general. For instance, numerous MEAs explicitly oblige parties to co-operate, such as the 1985 Vienna Convention[544] or the 1989 Basel Convention.[545] The ILC draft articles on transboundary harm consider co-operation as a foundational concept for the obligation to prevent transboundary harm.[546] In the UNFCCC, one concrete exemplification of this is that all States

---

themselves, with the United Nations, with the components of the Red Cross and Red Crescent Movement, and with other assisting actors.", see International Law Commission, Report of the Commission to the General Assembly on the work of its sixty-eighth session, Draft articles on the protection of persons in the event of disasters, UN Doc. A/71/10 (2016), para. 48.

541 UN Doc. A/Res/1802 ('International Co-operation in the peaceful uses of outer space', 14 Dec 1962), Section I, para. 2; UN Doc A/Res/2749 ('Declaration of Principles Governing the Sea- Bed and the Ocean Floor, and the Subsoil Thereof, beyond the Limits of National Jurisdiction' 17 Dec 1970), para. 11.

542 Jost Delbrück, "The International Obligation to Cooperate–an Empty Shell or a Hard Law Principle of International Law?–a Critical Look at a Much Debated Paradigm of Modern International Law", in *Coexistence, cooperation and solidarity - Liber Amicorum Rüdiger Wolfrum* ed. Holger P. Hestermeyer, et al. (Martinus Nijhoff Publishers, 2012), p. 13, 15 et seq., with further reference.

543 International Law Association, Legal Principles Relating to Climate Change (2014), p. 27.

544 Vienna Convention for the Protection of the Ozone Layer, 22 Mar 1985, United Nations Treaty Series, vol. 1513, p. 293 (323).

545 Basel Convention on the Control of Transboundary Movements of Hazardous Wastes and their disposal, United Nations Treaty Series, vol. 1673, p. 57 (126).

546 International Law Commission, "Report of the Commission to the General Assembly on the Work of Its Fifty-third Session, Draft Articles on the Prevention of

have to develop, periodically update, publish and make available national inventories of anthropogenic emissions by sources and removals of sinks.[547] States shall promote and co-operate in the exchange of relevant scientific, technological, technical, socio-economic and legal information.[548] They must inform the Conference of the Parties on the implementation of measures adopted to fight climate change[549] and should provide any other information considered relevant to the mitigation of climate change.[550] Moreover, they shall promote and co-operate in the research and the development of data archives related to the climate system.[551] It is further applied in Annex I to the UNFCCC, which States commit to continuous review and law-making "until the objective of the Convention is met".[552] The 'loss and damage' mechanism, which has been formally established[553] can also be cited as an example for co-operation, but its exact contours remain to be developed.

(b) Further Development: Post-Kyoto Until Today

The CBDR principle has undergone a process of significant re-framing and partial re-definition during the evolution of the climate regime, especially regarding differentiation. This shift has been primarily one away from the original understanding.[554]

As noted earlier, the differentiation between industrialized and developing countries was among the primary structural features of the UNFCCC. For instance, regarding information and co-operation obligations in the research and development of data archives related to the climate system, developed countries are subject to a more stringent reporting system.[555] The Kyoto Protocol was

---

Transboundary Harm from Hazardous Activities, with commentaries", *Yearbook of the International Law Commission* 2, no. 2 (2001), p. 155 et seq.

547 Art. 4.1 (a) and 12.1(a).

548 Art. 4.1 (h).

549 Art. 4.1 (j) and 12.1 (b).

550 Art. 12.1(c).

551 Art. 4.1(g) and 5.

552 Art. 4.2(d).

553 Decision 3/CP.18, 'Advancing the Durban Platform', FCCC/CP/2012/8/Add.1 and Decision 2/CP.19, 'Warsaw international mechanism for loss and damage associated with climate change impacts', FCCC/CP/2013/10/Add.1.

554 For an overall assessment, see Lavanya Rajamani, "Ambition and Differentiation in the 2015 Paris Agreement: Interpretative Possibilities and Underlying Politics", *International & Comparative Law Quarterly* 65, no. 02 (2016), p. 493 et seqq.

555 Bodansky, "UNFCCC commentary", p. 511.

prototypical for this diversity of CBDR in its clear-cut differentiation. Combining highly asymmetrically distributed substantial obligations with mechanisms of compliance assistance between the different groups of States, it implemented this approach in practice.[556]

The Durban negotiations of 2011 showed how divided the opinions on CBDR's application in the climate regime had become: Developed countries were almost unanimous in their insistence that any reference to CBDR would have to be qualified with a statement that this principle must be interpreted in the light of 'contemporary economic realities'. Developing countries meanwhile had an interest in keeping the role of CBDR's original meaning as influential as possible, as its political and legal implications had thus far benefitted them.[557] In the end, the Durban outcome documents did remarkably not (!) refer to CBDR. In the Durban parlance, it was rather noted that a new instrument should be "applicable to all"[558], which did, although, signal universality rather than uniformity of application. Yet still, developed countries were successful in including it, while some developing countries argued that this would be in some way a *de facto* amendment to the UNFCCC. While not doing away with differentiation, this suggested that a future climate agreement may be based on a more nuanced form of differentiation than before.[559]

Reversing the decision of excluding CBDR in Durban, the Paris Agreement, in Art. 2(2), again uses CBDR, stating that the Agreement is to be implemented to reflect the principle of CBDR (and equity).[560] The Paris Agreement also marks the temporary peak of the evolution of the CBDR principle. The arguably most important turn is indeed older than the negotiations directly preceding the Paris Agreement: One of the central features of what Bodansky, Brunnée and Rajamani call the 'second constitutional phase' of the climate regime (2005–2016)[561] was the evolution of the notion of CBDR. By 2005 China surpassed the US as the single largest emitter of CO_2.[562] This landmark development was also a reminder to the international community that an effective climate regime would

556 Beyerlin and Marauhn, *International environmental law*, p. 70.

557 Rajamani, "Ambition and Differentiation in the 2015 Paris Agreement", p. 494.

558 Durban platform, para. 2.

559 Rajamani, "The Durban platform for enhanced action and the future of the climate regime", p. 507 set seqq.

560 Viñuales, "The Paris climate agreement: an initial examination", p. 11.

561 See Bodansky, Brunnée, and Rajamani, *International climate change law*, p. 108 et seqq.

562 World Resource Institute's (WRI), 'CAIT Climate Data Explorer', available at http://cait.wri.org .

eventually have to move away from a focus on developed States and their emissions to a more holistic approach which also considers developing States' emissions. There was a stable consensus that most obligations and responsibilities of States in the climate regime are subject to differentiation. Only few obligations, such as those on reporting or those concerning scientific exchange applied unreservedly to all parties. Even among developed countries, Kyoto entailed differentiations between their mitigation commitments.[563]

A key question is what effect this evolution, the re-framing and re-formulation has had. Did it bring about new forms of interpretation ensuring its applicability in the future or has the process in fact deprived CBDR of its core, leaving it a hollowed-out remnant of the 1990s- version of differentiation?

Some scholars have suggested that while it is recognized that commitments of States vary, the same cannot be said about the evolution of commitments when differences change. Different arguments can be made for this point. An originalist argument could build on the UNFCCC-interpretation of CBDR(RC) and say that either the norm must keep insisting on the allocation of roles made there or be replaced by another. Another argument could be made that given the historical responsibilities of developed countries as defined in the UNFCCC, the differentiation should be kept. Finally, it could be argued that the differentiation along the lines of developed / developing countries is the linchpin inextricably linked to the concept of CBDR and could not be softened without weakening the concept itself. Others invoke, as a contrary indication, the inherent dynamic of CBDR: A norm concept that builds on the assumption that differentiation is necessary due to and along existing differences in capabilities, inevitably changes when those very differences do. Or, in more practice-oriented terms: Differentiated commitments of States in the climate regime should evolve as the recognized differences building their basis diminish.[564]

There is much to be said for the latter view, i.e., that differential treatment should be reviewed and can be changed while leaving its core intact. Differentiation in the climate regime has been introduced because real differences exist that are relevant for the efforts by the States being differentiated. When differences change, shift or vanish altogether, the logical consequence is for differentiation to change, react or be reduced. If differential treatment reflects existing differences and does not change given differences changing, it ceases to serve its purpose

563 Kyoto Protocol, Annex B.

564 cf. International Law Association, Legal Principles Relating to Climate Change (2014), p. 17 et seq.

to address inequalities.[565] Moreover, the historical responsibilities, while often invoked rhetorically, have never become a part of CBDR as used in the climate regime and can thus not be used as an argumentative tool in the interest of an originalist interpretation.

'Taking the Lead' Revis(it)ed

As indicated earlier[566], the Paris negotiations almost collapsed over the question whether Art. 4(4) would state that "Developed country Parties **should** continue taking the lead [...]"[567] or instead "Developed country Parties **shall** continue taking the lead [...]".[568] This would have turned a re-iteration of the respective formulation of the UNFCCC (Art. 3(1)) into a legal valorisation of the developed countries' obligations. The dramatic last-minute changes were an echo and the climax of this issue being contentious to varying degrees through the negotiations of the post-Kyoto regime. In the Cancun negotiations, a formula was introduced which links the taking the lead-approach to the historical contributions of industrialized countries, stating that owing to "historical responsibility, developed country Parties must take the lead in combating climate change and the adverse effects thereof".[569] Notably, Brazil had been pushing for an inclusion of this historical approach.[570] With this debate in turn resembling the one during the negotiations for the UNFCCC, this instance shows one of the pitfalls accompanying the process of re-shaping CBDR. A legal valorisation of developed countries' commitments could have had the potential to reinforce the original core of the concept while reducing the element of exclusivity in the allocation of burdens. Without such valorisation, this process only further underscores a tendency of legality's limitation in both the overall regime and one of its key norm concepts, at least with regard to the 'differentiation' dimension of CBDR.

---

565 As in, Rajamani, *Differential treatment in international environmental law*, p. 173, who even argues that in this constellation continuing differentiation could even perpetuate inequalities instead of addressing them.

566 See already section I.3.

567 Emphasis added.

568 Emphasis added.

569 Cancun outcome, Addendum Part Two: Action taken by the Conference of the Parties at its sixteenth session, UN Doc. FCCC/CP/2010/7/Add.1 para. 35.

570 International Law Association, Legal Principles Relating to Climate Change (2014) p. 16, with further references.

(c) Conclusion

Accounts of how CBDR's normative quality and legal status have developed throughout its process of re-framing vary considerably in scholarship and state practice. Some hold that CBDR finds wide-ranging support in state practice on many different levels or attribute "considerable legal gravitas"[571] to it. Others have taken a more cautious position, submitting that CBDR – in its function as a legal principle rather than a legal rule[572] – has steering effects on norm developments and hence the potential to gain the status of a principle of customary international law, without having done so yet, due to ambivalent attitudes of States.[573] In a similar vein, CBDR has been argued to be the overarching principle guiding the development of the climate regime, which, while not containing a defined legal obligation, forms the basis for the interpretation of existing obligations and the elaboration of future obligations within the regime.[574]

Differentiation or differentiated responsibility as such and in general is widely accepted among States in treaties and state practice. This is shown by instruments over a long period, from the Stockholm Declaration and the 1981 Abidjan Convention and – with broad to nearly universal participation – the 1985 Vienna Convention, the Montreal Protocol, the CBD as well as the various instruments and COP decisions under the UNFCCC.[575] In the climate context, the original version of CBDR has been steadily declining in terms of support in state practice of the climate negotiations since the Kyoto Protocol. The process of re-framing the lines along which differentiation is applied has given rise to a great variety of implementation specificities and formulations of CBDR. Because of this mixed picture, state practice on CBDR itself is equally inconclusive.[576] This uncertainty has arguably even grown during the negotiation process that led from the 2007 Bali Action Plan and the Copenhagen Accord to the Paris Agreement. It has become clear that the classical approach, as used in the UNFCCC and Kyoto, is no longer the only perspective on CBDR. The new forms of differentiation beyond the developed/developing countries line must go through the process of gaining acceptance by States. This might happen in the future and CBDR, given its

571 Ibid., p. 13.

572 Beyerlin, "Different Types Of Norms in IEL", p. 437.

573 Beyerlin and Marauhn, *International environmental law*, p. 70.

574 Rajamani, *Differential treatment in international environmental law*, p. 159 et seq.; Brunnée and Toope, *Legitimacy and legality in international law*, p. 165 et seq.

575 Sands, *Principles of international environmental law*, p. 287 et seq.

576 Ibid., p. 287.

historic linkage to the climate regime and its normative potential, could come to be what it was expected in some scholarship of the 1990s: The norm that every future legal regime must be consistent with to be in line with the UNFCCC.[577]

While the argument can be made that the obligation to co-operate underpins large parts of the efforts of the climate change regime[578], a review of its concretised forms reveals that it is almost exclusively the procedural aspects of co-operation that can be said to have gained the status of hard legal norms in the climate regime. The UNFCCC thus builds a framework of specifications of the co-operation principle aiming at technical co-operation, scientific exchange and other similar proceduralised expressions of the co-operation principle. It is in this sense that 'co-operation' has rightly been called a rather vague obligation of conduct.[579] The substantial notion of co-operation's primary function has been rightly identified as addressing existing gaps in international law and promoting the development of international law, including treaty making.[580]

The fact that CBDR has re-emerged with the Paris Agreement after States could not agree on a way of using it in the Durban negotiations shows that CBDR "has become unavoidable in climate change negotiations."[581] While the differentiation- dimension of CBDR has significantly changed, the same cannot be said about the 'common' dimension. The latter, as the 'co-operation' principle, has taken various procedural forms, while its substantial dimension serves as a political frame, but not as a legal norm. Whether the re-framing of CBDR's differentiation dimension between the Kyoto Protocol and the Paris Agreement has hollowed the principle will be seen over time. If the evolving dynamic interpretation of changing capabilities dissolving the clear lines between developed and developing countries finds sound acceptance in state practice, then CBDR could indeed prove 'unavoidable' and continuously play an important role in the climate regime. In the endeavor of forming new consensus in state practice, the clarity of its content might be even more problematic than the uncertainty concerning the precise legal status. For the time being, CBDR exemplifies

---

577 Alan E. Boyle, "Some Reflections on the Relationship of Treaties and Soft Law", *International & Comparative Law Quarterly* 48, no. 4 (1999), p. 908, discussing the overall role of the convention principles, but pointing to CBDR as the primary example.

578 International Law Association, Legal Principles Relating to Climate Change (2014), p. 27 with further reference.

579 Dupuy and Viñuales, *International environmental law*, p. 66.

580 International Law Association, Legal Principles Relating to Climate Change (2014), p. 30.

581 Viñuales, "The Paris climate agreement: an initial examination", p. 11.

two things: First, it shows how value-laden norms are indeed objects of constant change. Such change is not necessarily to its detriment but can potentially be an element of improvement. Such improvement in turn is not necessarily connected to a densification of its legal status or impact. Second and interconnected, CBRD shows that even the most prominent value-related norm concept in the climate regime calls for restraint in assuming far-reaching legal effects.

3. Intra-generational and Inter-generational Equity: Bringing Justice into the Equation

"Equitable approaches", Dinah Shelton noted, "are not only based in morality and a sense of justice, but may also foster more effective action on issues of common concern and more effective implementation of norms". The ICJ has called 'equity' a legal concept directly emanating from the idea of justice, which the Court is bound to apply as a general principle of law in achieving equitable or just solutions for its cases.[582] The principle or concept of equity is potentially broad and powerful in its ethical implications. It is also arguably the most clearly value-laden concept existing in international discourses in general and regarding climate change. Used and applied in legal contexts, however, it contains numerous ambiguities and requires careful differentiation. While some versions of equity are as old as common law systems, the concept has found specific translations into IEL and climate law, embodying specific value considerations transcending the inner-state realm. It is also gaining importance in international instruments parallel to the historical developments analyzed above. Hence, it is considered as a community value in the climate regime for this analyzis.

(a) Conception, Development and Expectations in the 1990s

Equity is a multifaceted concept, with each of its various shapes building on different legal and philosophical traditions. According to a general meaning, derived from the Roman law concept of 'aequitas', equity refers to what is fair and reasonable in the administration of justice.[583] Another important, but narrower and more technical meaning of equity found expression in Art. 38(2) of the ICJ Statute, which authorizes the Court to decide a case '*ex aequo et bono*' instead of

582 *Case Concerning the Continental Shelf* (Tunisia v. Libya), Judgment, I.C.J. Rep. 1982, p. 18, para. 71.

583 Francesco Francioni, "Equity in International Law", in *MPEPIL*, ed. Rüdiger Wolfrum (Oxford University Press, 2013), para. 1.

on the basis of existing legal norms, in case the parties agree hereto.[584] A third meaning, seeing the 'maxims of equity' as a system of general legal principles to apply to avoid the injustices of the law's strict application, is – as a specificity of Anglo-American law – limited in its analytical value for international law and will therefore be disregarded here.[585] In modern history, the use of equity in international law dates to the inception of the League of Nations and the jurisprudence of the Permanent Court of International Justice (PCIJ). Although Art. 38 (2) was not proposed by the International Committee of Jurists preparing the draft, it was nonetheless included by the Sub-Committee of the Third Committee of the Assembly of the League of Nations. Considerations, however, can also be found in the works of the committee, which contemplated the inclusion of equity based on one member deeming it too strict and potentially unjust if the Court were forced to consider only law without possible recourse to equity.[586] Under the PCIJ, the predominant view on equity was that of a set of principles potentially facilitating fair dispute solutions within the application of existing legal norms.[587] The legal status of equity is as debated as its contours are manifold. Regarding equity in the broader sense, its application '*contra legem*' has not had significant effect – for instance, Art. 38(2) of the ICJ statute has never been applied by the Court as the explicit basis for ruling on a case.[588] The court did, however, refer to "equitable principles"[589] in some cases when filling gaps in existing laws (use *praeter legem*).[590]

The need to balance the conflicting interests of different States or groups has led to the frequent inclusion of 'equity' itself and expressions of it in treaties and soft law instruments.[591] Among the arguably most prominent usages have been those in IEL. The UNCLOS includes, inter alia, references to "equitable and efficient utilization" (of the oceans resources) or "equitable solutions" for

584 Ibid.; Pellet, "Article 38", para. 157 et seq.
585 As in, Francioni, "Equity in International Law", para. 1.
586 Pellet, "Article 38", para. 152 with further reference.
587 Francioni, "Equity in International Law", para. 10.
588 Dinah Shelton, "Equity", in *The Oxford handbook of international environmental law*, ed. Daniel Bodansky, Jutta Brunnée, and Ellen Hey (OUP, 2008)p. 646; Pellet, "Article 38", para. 167.
589 See, e.g., *North sea continental shelf case* (Federal Republic of Germany v. Netherlands), I.C.J. Rep. 1969, p. 3, paras. 47, 85.
590 Shelton, "Equity", p. 646.
591 Francioni, "Equity in International Law", para. 22.

problems surrounding the continental shelf.[592] Explanations for equity's prominence in this field are varying. The two most salient reasons are (i) that IEL is often concerned with limits on the use of existing and exhaustible resources and (ii) that many treaty regimes in IEL allocate burdens and costs in the effort of reducing pollution. In both modes of action, the fair attribution of limits, costs and obligations is as accepted as an abstract goal as it is contentious in its concrete meaning.[593] Analytically, 'equity' can be distinguished in its substantial and its procedural dimension. Along that line, Thomas Franck sees equity as a part of fairness – with the procedural aspect of reaching decisions through the "right process" and the substantive dimension of distributive justice.[594] Equity also relates to law by providing an individualized form of justice – a conception which is rooted in the Aristotelian understanding of the limits of positive law.[595]

In the UNFCCC regime, the notion of equity is not defined in the Convention. However, the usage of the concept focused on two substantial forms of equity: During the negotiations for the Convention, the developing States in particular advocated for the inclusion of equity. In a statement on behalf of the G77 and China, the representative of Ghana pointed out that "[a]ll States have an obligation to protect the climate for the benefit of present and future generations of mankind on the basis of **intra-generational as well as inter-generational equity**."[596] Intra-generational equity is concerned with the assurance of justice among human beings that are alive today. In the field of environmental protection, this has been understood as the responsibility of States and the international community to fairly allocate and regulate resources. The goal in this context is to ensure the equitable sharing of benefits, costs and degradation effects. Furthermore, it is an application of the idea of distributive justice.[597]

Inter-generational equity is based on the notion that those human beings alive today have a right to use the earth and its natural resources to meet their own needs, but also special obligations as custodians of the planet to maintain its

592 UNCLOS, Preamble and Arts. 74, 83; See as well Arts. 82(4), 140, 155(2), 160(2),173(2) for references to other equitable solutions.

593 Shelton, "Equity", p. 652.

594 Thomas M. Franck, *Fairness in international law and institutions* (Clarendon Press, 1995), p. 7 et seqq.

595 Shelton, "Equity", p. 641.

596 Joint statement of the Group of 77, made by the Chairman (Ghana) at the fourth session of the IGNC for a Framework Convention on Climate Change, A/AC.237/WG.I/L.8 (19 Dec 1991.), para. 2(d), emphasis added.

597 Shelton, "Equity", p. 642.

integrity in the interest of following generations, whose lives will also be dependent on the earth's resources. This notion has a certain tradition in international law. In this vein, present generations are trustees for future generations.[598] This assumption of present generations owing duties regarding the environment to yet unborn generations became popular in the late 1980s, with d'Amato noting that it has become "[a] common assumption underlying nearly every book or essay on the global environment".[599] It has also met conceptual criticism from its inception. One of its focal points was the projection of future human beings to which obligations should be owed. Moral philosopher Derek Parfit pointed to what he called the "future individuals paradox"[600]: With interventions in environmental processes, he posited, one would change the pre-conditions for human life in such a way that it would alter the yet unborn individuals' conditions of conception, birth and identity. In some constellations, this could lead to the effect that environmental intervention causes those individuals to not be born at all or under completely different circumstances. The resulting variety of possible outcomes and effects of actions taken today, in his view, complicates the determination of the moral responsibilities to future generations.[601] While Parfit's point was not to discard *all* moral considerations of future human beings, his argument does point to a conceptual pitfall of inter-generational equity. Determining *concrete* obligations vis-à-vis individuals with rights mirroring such obligations, by traditional legal standards, needs *concrete* individuals affected by the compliance or non-compliance with such obligations. Hence, if inter-generational equity is to be based on the idea of future generations individual (and thus *concrete)* rights, then the contingency of those individuals' existence itself poses a conceptual challenge.

Although the concepts have their respective and largely different emphases, 'equity' in the climate context is directly linked to those of CBDR and sustainable development. While CBDR predominantly highlights considerations of intra-generational equity, sustainable development focusses on inter-generational

598 Ibid., p. 643; Edith Brown Weiss, "Intergenerational Equity", in *MPEPIL*, ed. Rüdiger Wolfrum (Oxford University Press, 2013), para. 20, 6.

599 Anthony D'Amato, "Do We Owe a Duty to Future Generations to Preserve the Global Environment?", *AJIL* 84, no. 1 (1990), p. 190.

600 Derek Parfit, "Future generations: Further problems", *Philosophy & Public Affairs* 11, no. 2 (1982), p. 113.

601 Ibid., p. 115 et seqq.

equity as well.[602] Emphasizing it from a different perspective, inter-generational equity has been said to be the foundation of the concept of sustainable development.[603] Especially in relation to CBDR, equity – encompassing a range of visions of justice – is the much broader concept, whereas CBDR is mainly confined to burden-sharing within the UNFCCC regime.[604] The relation of equity and sustainable development, with inter-generational equity being the interface, has been highlighted in the Brundtland report, stating inter-generational equity as principle 2, which reads "States shall conserve and use the environment and natural resources for the benefit of present and future generations". In the commission's work, both aspects of equity can be traced to sustainable development defined as "development that meets the needs of the present without compromising the ability of future generations to meet their own needs".[605] The interconnection between the two aspects of equity is further highlighted by the report submitting that inter-generational equity logically extents to intra-generational equity. Indeed, the two aspects complement, but also logically limit each other. Resources that are used for the benefit of present generations are often lost for future generations, yet likewise, resources that are saved for future generations cannot be used to ensure and advance equitable distribution among present generation.

The open formulation of equity in the framework convention does not, at first sight, clarify the way in which the principle is to be understood within this framework. As for the legal status of equity, as used in the early phase of the climate regime itself, the situation is different. Of course, the procedural dimension of equity plays an important role in the UNFCCC regime as well – but it rather finds different and more specific expressions. The pivotal question therefore is whether any substantial aspects of equity have gained a significant legal status and produced legal obligations. The principle was, in non-binding language, included in the operational Art. 3 of the UNFCCC, where it reads that State Parties "should protect the climate system for the benefit of present and future

602 Bodansky, Brunnée, and Rajamani, *International climate change law*, p. 54; the respective implications for the CBDR concept and sustainable development are discussed in sections II.2. and II.4. This section is restricted to the implications of equity as such.

603 Brown Weiss, "Intergenerational Equity", para. 5.

604 International Law Association, Legal Principles Relating to Climate Change (2014), p. 10.

605 World Commission on Environment and Development, *Our common future*, chapter II, para. 1.

generations of humankind, **on the basis of equity**".[606] Equity hence is made a basis of burden-sharing concerning climate protection, suggesting that both are required to address the *inter*-generational as well as the *intra*-generational effects of climate change.[607] Furthermore, Art. 4 (2)(a) formulates that Annex II-countries should, in designing their climate change mitigation policies, consider the "need for **equitable and appropriate contributions** by each of these Parties to the global effort regarding that objective".[608] Art. 11(2) entails an application of equity in binding language, holding that "[t]he financial mechanism shall have an **equitable and balanced representation** of all Parties within a transparent system of governance."[609] The Berlin Mandate leading to the Kyoto Protocol, cited Art. 3, para. 1 – and only para. 1 – of the Convention.[610] The Kyoto Protocol itself also only took recourse on the principle indirectly.[611]

Equity is broader in scope and content than CBDR, especially as it arguably contains a certain vision of justice.[612] Equity therefore finds one of its most concrete expressions in the UNFCCC regime through CBDR. Conceptually, inter-generational equity has been rightly analyzed "to surmount the threshold of normativity and can therefore be considered a principle", which, if used in a MEA, can give "meaningful legal guidance".[613] The idea of present generations holding the earth in trust for future generations has a considerable tradition in international agreements, dating back to the late 19th century, where it was referred to by the US in the *Pacific Fur Seals Arbitration* and found entrance into instruments like the 1946 Whaling Convention or the 1972 World Heritage Convention.[614]

---

606 UNFCCC, Art. 3, para. 1, emphasis added.

607 International Law Association, Legal Principles Relating to Climate Change (2014), p. 10.

608 Emphasis added.

609 Emphasis added.

610 Berlin mandate, Section I., para. 1(a).

611 Eriika Melkas, "Sovereignty and Equity within the Framework of the Climate Regime", *Review of European, Comparative & International Environmental Law* 11, no. 2 (2002), p. 125 with a further analysis on the indirect references to equity made in the context of the Kyoto Protocol.

612 International Law Association, Legal Principles Relating to Climate Change (2014), p. 10.

613 Beyerlin, "Different Types Of Norms in IEL", p. 446.

614 Sands, Principles of international environmental law, p. 256, with further references and examples that "[o]ther, more recent treaties have sought to preserve particular

One of the few examples for inter-generational equity being referred to in considerable legal practice on the national level was the *Minors Oposa* case before the Philippine Supreme Court in 1993.[615] An environmental activist, Antonio Oposa, together with the 'Philippine Ecological Network', filed a lawsuit on behalf of a group of children, among them his own, to stop the destruction of rain forests in the country. The group based their claims in the constitutional right to a "balanced and healthful" ecology and the right to self-preservation and self-perpetuation. They also raised inter-generational equity in their claim. The Court ruled in favor of the plaintiffs by reversing the original trial court's decision to dismiss the case. It ruled, *inter alia*, that the plaintiffs had standing to represent their yet unborn posterity, that they had adequately asserted a right to a balanced and healthful ecology and that the issues raised were justiciable. Some of the ruling's findings have gained prominence in the debate on equity, such as the court finding a form of inter-generational equity acceptable as the legal basis for a class action:

> "We find no difficulty in ruling that they can, for themselves, for others of their generation and for the succeeding generations, file a class suit. Their personality to sue on behalf of the succeeding generations can only be based on the concept of **intergenerational responsibility** insofar as the right to a balanced and healthful ecology is concerned."[616]

While the case was celebrated by some as a ground-breaking case making inter-generational equity manageable and applicable and "likely to become something of a landmark in the jurisprudence of sustainable development"[617], others pointed to the limited legal impact inter-generational equity really had on the decision.[618]

---

natural resources and other environmental assets for the benefit of present and future generations."

615 "The Philippines: Supreme Court Decision in Minors Oposa v. Secretary of the Department of Environment and Natural Resources (DENR) ", *International Legal Materials* 33, no. 1 (1994), pp. 173–206.

616 Ibid., p. 185, emphasis added.

617 Ben Boer, "The Rise of Environmental Law in the Asian Region", *University of Richmond Law Review* 5 (1999), p. 1537.

618 Dante B. Gatmaytan, "The Illusion of Intergenerational Equity: Oposa v. Factoran as Pyrrhic Victory", *Georgetown International Environmental Law Review* 15, no. 3 (2003), p. 459 et seq., especially p. 460, pointing out that " […] invoking the rights of future generations – while intellectually titillating, is ultimately useless in the resolution of the case. The Philippine Supreme Court would have decided Oposa exactly the same way had the children filed the case solely on their own behalf. In cases involving the protection of the environment, the distinction between present and

Hence, equity in the broader sense is a principle aiming at balancing conflicting interests.[619] In the climate change and environmental context, its usage in the UNFCCC, its concretization in the Kyoto Protocol and its application in cases like the *Minors Oposa* case, also made equity a symbol for high hopes of fundamental changes in the normative underpinning of the international legal regime. At the height of trends toward value-orientation and legalization in the early 2000s, Melkas for instance suggested that equity "should be used to define and delimit sovereignty".[620]

(b) Further Development: Post-Kyoto Until Today

In scholarly discourse, especially inter-generational equity was quickly seen as an emerging norm of customary international law.[621] The subsequent state practice under the Convention, however, is not particularly yielding in terms of evidence for the customary status of concrete elements of equity. Even though equity has been frequently included in submissions under the UNFCCC process, cases of the meaning being concretised into legally applicable forms are barely discernible.

In the Copenhagen Accord, equity is referred to twice, once connected to sustainable development.[622] The Cancun Agreement speaks of the aim to ensure

---

future generations is inconsequential – we cannot protect the rights of future generations without protecting the rights of the present."

619 Dupuy and Viñuales, *International environmental law*, p. 77, categorizing equity as a 'balance-principle'.

620 Melkas, "Sovereignty and Equity within the Framework of the Climate Regime", p. 128.

621 D'Amato, "Do We Owe a Duty to Future Generations to Preserve the Global Environment?", p. 190.

622 Copenhagen Accord, para. 1, reads "[...]To achieve the ultimate objective of the Convention to stabilize greenhouse gas concentration in the atmosphere at a level that would prevent dangerous anthropogenic interference with the climate system, we shall, recognizing the scientific view that the increase in global temperature should be below 2 degrees Celsius, **on the basis of equity** and in the context of sustainable development, enhance our long-term cooperative action to combat climate change."; para. 2 reads "We agree that deep cuts in global emissions are required according to science, and as documented by the IPCC Fourth Assessment Report with a view to reduce global emissions so as to hold the increase in global temperature below 2 degrees Celsius, and take action to meet this objective consistent with science and **on the basis of equity**. [...] [emphases added].

"equitable access to sustainable development".[623] In the Paris Agreement, intergenerational equity is mentioned in the preamble of the COP decision adopting the Agreement, but not in the text itself. Equity without specification is used in the preamble (para. 4) alongside CBDR as the only two convention principles explicitly invoked. The provision is mirrored in the operational part of the Agreement by Art. 2 (2), which reads:

> *"This Agreement will be implemented to reflect equity and the principle of common but differentiated responsibilities and respective capabilities, in the light of different national circumstances."*

Equity is referred to for a second time in the operational part in Art. 14 (1), which elaborates what the Agreement calls the "global stocktake", i.e., the periodical assessment of the implementation efforts on the Agreement and the collective progress towards achieving the long-term goals of the Paris Agreement. This stocktake shall be done "in a comprehensive and facilitative manner, considering mitigation, adaptation and the means of implementation and support, **and in the light of equity** and the best available science."[624]

(c) Conclusion

As far as the concept of equity is broad and powerful, it is also evasive. The general concept of equity can be described as a normative principle with the potential to provide guidance for more concrete legal norms. In the general procedural dimension, the potential to shape judicial findings may theoretically be immense. Yet, practically there are no apparent indications for a growing importance, which would be dependent on the States' willingness to admit the concept of equity to more frequently play a role in judicial proceedings. In the environmental and climate context, the picture is certainly more diverse, given the different expressions of equity, but similar in result:

An early assessment of equity in the environmental context concluded that it is "particularly suitable for discussions in contexts where there are competing interests which have not hardened into specific rights and duties. This will be true primarily in areas where the law is not highly developed." The concept was analyzed to be potentially fruitful "where it is more important to secure a solution which can be sustained in the future than one based upon a strict

---

623 Cancun outcome, Addendum Part Two: Action taken by the Conference of the Parties at its sixteenth session, UN Doc. FCCC/CP/2010/7/Add.1, para. 6.

624 Emphasis added.

vindication of legal rights and duties which arose in the past."[625] Even 30 years later, a strong case can be made for this assessment's accuracy. The repeated use in the UNFCCC context show that the concept remains important in framing the agreement on both the way on how to peruse the objectives of the Convention and on how to take stock of state parties' actions on climate change. The fact that equity and CBDR – in contrast to other UNFCCC principles – are put in such a prominent position in the Paris Agreement speaks to the continued importance of equity as a pivotal element of burden-sharing determination in the climate regime. That some of the procedural aspects of burden-sharing, financial mechanisms or the global stocktake can be interpreted as concretisations of equity in the field, does not mean that the concept would have developed any more legal force in the climate regime. The rather abstract principle of equity is translated and operationalized through other norms such as CBDR.[626] The same is true for the conceptual specifications of inter- and intra-generational equity. Both can be interpreted to have found some translation into other, mainly procedural aspects of the regime.[627] Yet, according to the view taken here cannot be said to have gained significant substantial legal effect in the field. For instance, where the UNFCCC already refrained from specifying the level to which GHG emissions would have to be stabilized to ensure the living conditions of future generations, no subsequent climate agreement did either. With the Paris Agreement shifting the emphasis to national circumstances and flexibility, it is unlikely that any such specification will take place in the future.

Given the reluctance of States to allow international courts to apply even the basic and traditional notions of equity in their jurisprudence, it is hardly imaginable that there will be a significant advancement in this context. In the case of inter-generational equity, the conceptual difficulties in substantiating the standing in courts exacerbate this unlikelihood. The 1993 case before the Philippine Supreme Court has certainly gained much attention in international debates, but can in hindsight not be said to have set a significant example for international practice. Therefore, even though intra- and inter- generational equity have experienced a relatively stable level of inclusion in the important documents of the climate regime, their development since the 1990s is rather one of

625 Vaughan Lowe, "The Role of Equity in International Law", *Aust. YBIL* 12 (1988)
626 Xolisa Ngwadla, Equitable Access to Sustainable Development: Relevance to Negotiations and Actions on Climate Change, (2013), p. 3.
627 See in the sections on CBDR and Sustainable Development.

stagnation. The high expectations elicited by some in scholarly discourse have not materialized in the legal regime.

4. Sustainable Development: Exemplary Debate About the Legal Status

The concept of sustainable development emerged out of the effort to reconcile the competing values of human development and environmental protection, beginning with the 1972 Stockholm Conference and the 1980 World Conservation Strategy of the International Union for the Conservation of Nature. Sustainable development became an internationally formulated aspiration in the 1987 Brundtland Report and has been significantly shaping the discourse on international climate law and policy ever since. Optimistic accounts were confident that the concept could solve the contradictions between economic, human and environmental concerns, and ultimately propitiate these conflicting concerns.[628] Critical voices suspected that the concept could undermine the autonomy of environmental law as a body of rules and standards designed to restrain and prevent environmentally destructive effects. It was feared that the Rio Conference could constitute "the beginning of the decline of international environmental law as an autonomous branch of international law".[629] Sustainable development is a pertinent example for the various forms of engagement different actors have with a community value-laden norm concept on the international level.

(a) Conception, Development and Expectations in the 1990s

In the early 1990s, sustainable development was called the "buzzword [...] of most of the international political and legal debate on environmental issues since the mid-1980s".[630] In 2002, the ILA in their 'Declaration of Principles of International Law Relating to Sustainable development'[631], noted that "sustainable development is now widely accepted as a global objective and that the concept

628 Edith Brown Weiss, "In Fairness to Future Generations and Sustainable Development", *Am. U. J. Int'l L. & Pol'y* 8, no. 1 (1992), p. 25 et seq.

629 Marc Pallemaerts, "International Environmental Law from Stockholm to Rio: Back to the Future?", *Review of European Community & International Environmental Law* 1, no. 3 (1992), p. 264.

630 Ibid., p. 261.

631 International Law Association, "ILA New Delhi Declaration of Principles of International Law Relating to Sustainable Development, 2 April 2002", *Netherlands International Law Review* XLIX (2002), p. 299 et seqq.

has been amply recognized in various international and national legal instruments, including treaty law and jurisprudence at international and national levels". Indeed, by the time of the ILA declaration, the ideas underlying the concept had already been circulating through the international arena for at least 30 years[632]: In the early 1970s, the UNGA pro-claimed the second UN Development Decade[633] and the 1972 Stockholm Declaration[634] featured in its principle 11 the interdependence of environmental policies and development. The present terminology used is usually said to be coined in the Brundtland Report of 1987[635], which defined sustainable development as "development that meets the needs of the present without compromising on the ability of future generations to meet their own needs".[636] As pointed out in the above, this definition points to the inter-generational dimension of sustainable development and is largely congruent with the debate depicted and contextualized on the principle of inter-generational equity. A second dimension of sustainable development, the 'equitable use' of natural resources, also implies that use by one state must take account of the needs of other States. This too is equivalent with the principle of intragenerational equity.[637] In these respects, reference can be made here to the section on equity.

The greatest leap in the evolution of sustainable development was the Rio Declaration, which uses the term in a total number of 12 out of 27 principles.[638] But instead of further defining the concept, the Declaration outlines various elements of it. The equity considerations mentioned above, however, are only two of the recurring elements of the concept of 'sustainable development' that have become focal points in the debate about the concept's legal status since the

---

632 For a general historical overview, see Ulrich Beyerlin, "Sustainable Development", in *Max Planck Encyclopedia of Public International Law online [MPEPIL]*, ed. Rüdiger Wolfrum (Oxford University Press, 2013), para. 2–8; See also Sands, *Principles of international environmental law*, p. 252 et seqq.

633 See UN Doc. A/Res/25/2626 of 24 October 1970, especially para. 18 which draws a link between the purpose of a human-centered development and the necessity to safeguard the environment.

634 Stockholm Declaration', pp. 3–6.

635 Sands, *Principles of international environmental law*, p. 252.

636 World Commission on Environment and Development, *Our common future*, chapter 2, para. 1; On the link between Sustainable Development and inter-generational equity, see already section II.3.

637 Sands, *Principles of international environmental law*, p. 261 et seq.

638 See especially Arts. 1,4,12,20,21,22.

Rio Declaration. Another is the aim of exploiting natural resources in a manner which is 'sustainable', sometimes referred to as 'the principle of sustainable use'. A third is the ambition to ensure that environmental considerations are integrated into economic and other development policies and programs and that development needs are considered in applying environmental objectives, sometimes discussed as 'the principle of integration'.[639] The aspect of integration expresses the bracket function of sustainable development, linking environmental concerns like climate change to other fields of international law and politics like economic and development law and other policy fields. It is in this vein, that the conciliation between economic and environmental concerns has been called the primary function of sustainable development.[640]

The 1992 Rio Declaration called upon the international community to further develop international law in the field of sustainable development. As it has rightly been pointed out, this must mean that in the understanding of those drafting the Declaration, there was international law in the field before.[641] For a certain period of time, the concept experienced a remarkable proliferation in form of references in international treaties, not only in MEAs like the UNFCC or the CBD[642], but also in other fields like economic law[643]: The sustainable use dimension was included in an 1985 agreement concluded by the Association of South East Asian Nations (ASEAN), which required parties to adopt a standard of "sustainable utilisation of harvested natural resources […] with a view to attaining the goal of sustainable development."[644] The 1994 World Trade Organization (WTO) Agreement, in its preamble, connects trade and economic development to social criteria like living standards and an "optimal use of the world's resources **in accordance with the objective of sustainable development**, seeking both to protect and preserve the environment and to enhance the means for doing so in

639 Sands, *Principles of international environmental law*, p. 253.

640 Dupuy and Viñuales, *International environmental law*, p. 53, p. 80 et seq., in who's terminology Sustainable Development in general is a 'balance concept'.

641 Sands, *Principles of international environmental law*, p. 259.

642 Preamble, Art. 1,8,11,12,16,17,18, in the CBD, 'sustainable use' is defined as "the use of components of biological diversity in a way and at a rate that does not lead to the long-term decline of biological diversity, thereby maintaining its potential to meet the needs and aspirations of present and future generations" (Art. 2).

643 For an extensive review, see Sands, *Principles of international environmental law*, p. 258 et seq., including examples like the 1989 Lomé IV convention.

644 ASEAN Agreement on the Conservation of Nature and Natural Resources (9 Jul 1985), Art. 1.

a manner consistent with their respective needs and concerns at different levels of economic development".[645]

Those two aspects of (i) protecting the environment and (ii) integrating this into the individual strategies for economic development arguably are the most prominent ones in the UNFCCC, where it introduces sustainable development explicitly and not its equity-dimensions. Art. 3(4) reads:

> *"The Parties have a right to, and should, promote **sustainable development**. Policies and measures to protect the climate system against human-induced change should be appropriate for the specific conditions of each Party and should be integrated with national development programmes, **taking into account that economic development is essential for adopting measures to address climate change**."*

Much like the concept itself, this version was intended to be a bridge between very different ambitions for what sustainable development was supposed to entail in the Convention: In the negotiations, developing countries had pressed for the inclusion of a 'right to development' as an 'inalienable human right' and furthermore, that all peoples would have an equal right to reasonable living standards. Some developed countries had wished to include a principle that States have a duty to aim at sustainable development. Both proposals met different degrees of resistance by some delegations. The idea of a 'right to development' met the long-standing objections of the US to such a right. The US representatives argued that it is too vague and feared that developing countries could be building financial demands on it. The other proposal, in turn, was rejected by many developing countries fearing that the duty to aim at sustainable development could turn into new forms of conditionality on financial assistance and impede their development ambitions. The formulation in the Convention that all parties both have the right to and should promote sustainable development, bridges the conflict of the 'right to development'. On the one hand, a 'right' is recognized in this formulation, but only one 'to promote' sustainable development, on the other hand, the Convention states that parties 'should' promote sustainable development, which falls short of the envisaged 'duty' to do so.[646]With these provisions neutralizing the respective efforts to equip the Convention's version of sustainable development with more normative force, the aspects of sustainable use and the integration of environmental and development concerns remain the most influential in the Convention.

---

645 Marrakesh Agreement Establishing the World Trade Organization, 15 Apr 1994, 1867 U.N.T.S. 154 [hereinafter WTO Agreement], preamble, para. 1. (Emphasis added).

646 Bodansky, "UNFCCC commentary", p. 504 with further reference.

The Kyoto Protocol followed up the Convention in referring to sustainable development. In its Art. 2, it provides that Annex I-States "shall" implement further policies and co-operate with other parties to achieve the Protocol's quantified emission reduction commitments and to promote sustainable development. It further refers to sustainable development in general with its Art. 10, where all parties, not only Annex I countries are called upon to continue advancing the implementation of their commitments under Art. 4 UNFCCC in order to achieve sustainable development. This connection is then linked to the general obligations of all parties on reporting, policy program formulation and co-operation. Art. 12 mentions sustainable development aiming at non-Annex I-countries, establishing the 'clean development' mechanism, whose purpose is assisting those countries in achieving sustainable development. Examples for the sustainable use- dimension in the Protocol are promotion of sustainable forest management practices (Art. 2(1)(a)(ii)) and the promotion of sustainable forms of agriculture (Art. 2(1)(a)(iii)).

A much-cited event in the evolution of the role of sustainable development in international law is the *Gabčíkovo-Nagymaros Project* case before the ICJ in 1997.[647] The case was concerned with a lengthy dispute between Hungary and Slovakia over the construction and operation of dams on the Danube river. The facts of the case were the following: Hungary and Czechoslovakia had signed a treaty for the building of dam structures in Slovakia and Hungary to produce electric power, flood control and improve navigation on the Danube in 1977. In 1989, Hungary had suspended and then later abandoned completing the project alleging that it entailed grave risks to the Hungarian environment and the water supply of Budapest. Slovakia (as successor to Czechoslovakia) denied these allegations and insisted that Hungary carry out its treaty obligations. It planned and subsequently put into operation an alternative project only on Slovak territory, whose operation had effects on Hungary's access to the Danube's water. The ICJ found both States in breach of their legal obligations and called upon them to carry out their respective duties under the relevant treaty while taking account of the situation that had developed since 1989.[648] In the key passage for the matter at hand, the Court employed the concept of sustainable development, in particular its dimension of integration:

647 *Gabčíkovo-Nagymaros Project* (Hungary v Slovakia), Judgment, I.C.J. Rep. 1997 p. 7 [hereinafter *Gabčíkovo-Nagymaros Project*].

648 I.C.J., Press release No. 97/10, 25 Sep 1997, available at https://www.icj-cij.org/files/case-related/92/092-19970925-PRE-01-00-EN.pdf .

"The Court is mindful that, in the field of environmental protection, vigilance and prevention are required on account of the often irreversible character of damage to the environment and of the limitations inherent in the very mechanism of reparation of this type of damage. Throughout the ages, mankind has, for economic and other reasons, constantly interfered with nature. In the past, this was often done without consideration of the effects upon the environment. Owing to new scientific insights and to a growing awareness of the risks for mankind - for present and future generations - of pursuit of such interventions at an unconsidered and unabated pace, new norms and standards have been developed, set forth in a great number of instruments during the last two decades. Such new norms have to be taken into consideration, and such new standards given proper weight, not only when States contemplate new activities but also when continuing with activities begun in the past. ***This need to reconcile economic development with protection of the environment is aptly expressed in the concept of sustainable development.***"[649]

From this statement, the consequence for the case was that the parties "together should look afresh at the effects on the environment of the operation of the Gabčíkovo power plant" and would have to "find a satisfactory solution" distribution of the released water.

The vice-president of the ICJ, Judge Weeramantry of Sri Lanka, delivered a separate opinion along with his vote joining the majority of the Court, which he used to further elaborate his position on the normative power of sustainable development and its value implications. He found that "the principle of sustainable development [...] is an integral part of modern international law. It is clearly of the utmost importance, both in this case and more generally."[650] Citing a broad range of instruments, many of which have been discussed above, he concludes that "[t]he concept of sustainable development is thus a principle accepted not merely by the developing countries, but one which rests on a basis of worldwide acceptance" and hence, he sees the concept as "a part of modern international law by reason not only of its inescapable logical necessity, but also by reason of its wide and general acceptance by the global community." Being based on components coming from "well-established areas of international law – human rights, state responsibility, environmental law, economic and industrial law, equity, territorial sovereignty, abuse of rights, good neighbourliness – to mention a few", the concept would have "a significant role to play in the resolution of environmentally related disputes" as it offers an important principle for the resolution of tensions between two established rights. It reaffirms in the arena of international

649 *Gabčíkovo-Nagymaros Project*, para. 140, emphasis added.

650 *Gabčíkovo-Nagymaros Project* (Hungary v. Slovakia), Separate Opinion Judge Weeramantry, p. 86.

law that there must be both development and environmental protection, and that neither of these rights can be neglected."[651]

In legal scholarship, the majority decision as well as the separate opinion were widely received. For some, the majority judgment itself indicated that sustainable development, confirmed now by the ICJ, "has a legal function".[652] While it is hardly contradictable that in this case, the Court referred to sustainable development and assigned to it a certain argumentative function in formulating a legal solution to a case at hand, it does not necessarily follow that the Court also aimed at assigning a legal status to sustainable development. Furthermore, both the Court and Judge Weeramantry seem to draw upon the integration-dimension of sustainable development in their argumentation. It is debatable whether the court would have needed sustainable development to justify taking different aspects of the parties' interest into account when making the decision. For the question of whether beyond the integration-dimension, sustainable development also has considerable and legally applicable *substantive* effects, the *'Shrimp-Turtle'* case of the WTO Appellate Body was a notable contribution from the realm of jurisprudence. This case was brought forward by India, Malaysia, Pakistan and Thailand against the US. The appellate and panel reports were adopted in 1998. The Body refers to the Marrakech Decision of Ministers that established a permanent committee on trade and environment and noted that the WTO Agreement, in its preamble, acknowledges "the objective of" sustainable development. Furthermore, the Appellate Body understands that sustainable development "has been generally accepted as integrating economic and social development and environmental protection."[653] The concept is also invoked in the assessment of the US conservation measures regarding sea turtles as an exhaustible natural resource and the implementation of such measures into practice. In an early interpretation of the case's engagement, it was submitted that between the lines, the concept of sustainable development was invoked to extend the jurisdictional scope of Article XX(g) of the General Agreement on Tariffs and Trade (GATT), with the consequence of sustainable development having a significant substantive element.[654]

---

651 Ibid., p. 91 et seq.

652 Sands, *Principles of international environmental law*, p. 254.

653 Nancy L. Perkins, "World Trade Organization: United States – Import Prohibition Of Certain Shrimp and Shrimp Products", *International Legal Materials* 38, no. 1 (1999), p. 155 (para. 129 and reference 107).

654 Philippe Sands, "International Courts and the Application of the Concept of 'Sustainable Development'", *Max Planck Yearbook of United Nations Law* 3 (1999), p. 400.

(b) Further Development: Post-Kyoto Until Today

The Copenhagen Accord, aside from connecting equity and sustainable development as elaborated above, refers to the latter when acknowledging "that social and economic development and poverty eradication are the first and overriding priorities of developing countries and that a low-emission development strategy **is indispensable to sustainable development**."[655] Lastly, it puts the mitigation action of non-Annex I countries to the Convention into "the context of" sustainable development (para.5).

The Paris Agreement uses the concept both in its preamble[656] and in its operative part. In Art. 2, formulating the goal and objectives of the agreement, it puts them in "the context of sustainable development and efforts to eradicate poverty". Likewise, the obligations for States in Art. 4 are placed "in the context of sustainable development and efforts to eradicate poverty". Furthermore, the cooperative approaches in Art. 6 are linked to sustainable development through the promotion of "sustainable development and environmental integrity" (Art. 6(1)). Here, sustainable development is even used in obligatory language, stating that "[p]arties shall, where engaging on a voluntary basis in cooperative approaches that involve the use of internationally transferred mitigation outcomes towards nationally determined contributions, promote sustainable development and ensure environmental integrity and transparency [...]" (Art. 6(2)). The respective mechanism is established "to promote the mitigation of greenhouse gas emissions while fostering sustainable development" (Art. 6(4)(a)). Other references to sustainable development include connections to the "global goal on adaptation of enhancing adaptive capacity, strengthening resilience and reducing vulnerability to climate change (Art. 7), to 'loss and damage' (Art. 8) and finally to the agreement that "[a]ccelerating, encouraging and enabling innovation is critical for an effective, long-term global response to climate change and promoting economic growth and sustainable development" (Art. 10(5)).

The legal status of sustainable development remains disputed. While some scholars have submitted that "there can be little doubt that the concept of 'sustainable development' has entered the corpus of international customary law, requiring different streams of international law to be treated in an integrated

---

655 Copenhagen Accord, para. 2.

656 Paris Agreement, Preamble, para. 8, reads "Emphasizing the intrinsic relationship that climate change actions, responses and impacts have with equitable access to sustainable development and eradication of poverty".

manner"[657], for others "much speaks in favour of the assumption that sustainable development remains below the threshold of normative quality [...] for ascribing the quality of a (legal) principle to it."[658]

(c) Conclusion

Sustainable development has remained one of the guiding concepts of the climate regime due to its stable level of invocation in the instruments under the UNFCCC, including the Paris Agreement. These examples from state practice indicate a relatively stable acceptance by States for the concept to serve as a rhetorical bridge between the environmental ambitions pursued under the climate regime and the development needs of many state parties. As the negotiation history of the Convention shows, a central conflict between different normative ambitions of sustainable development was resolved early on, leaving a limited normative space for the concept. Arguably, this was critical in the States acceptance to enter the Convention.

The legal ramifications of the concept, however, have barely become more clearly defined in the legal practice since the height of its proliferation in the 1990s. The reference to the concept in Judge Weeramantry's separate opinion certainly deserved the wide-ranging reception for its contribution to the scholarly debate. Nevertheless, with his being a *separate* opinion it cannot be counted as if the ICJ had put its authority behind sustainable development defining it as a legal principle. Much can be said for the nuanced analyzes differentiating between the dimensions of the concept, regarding both their actual and their potential effect in international law. The dimension of 'sustainable use' has the conceptual potential to be the basis for legal rules and has been translated as such, albeit rudimentarily, into the Kyoto Protocol. The bracket function of sustainable development aiming at environmental and other aspects – primarily developmental ones – to be treated in an integrated manner is not only a noble, but also a perfectly rational ambition, given the interconnections between climate change, poverty, human and economic development. Used within the scope of the existing sources of international law, however, this ambition cannot be more than a – very useful – political reminder for policy makers and a normative resource for advocacy in their respective fields. In comparison to the height of expectations after the WTO Appellate Body's and the ICJ's engagement with sustainable

657 Sands, *Principles of international environmental law*, p. 254.
658 Beyerlin, "Different Types Of Norms in IEL", p. 444 et seq.

development, the concept experienced a downward trajectory. The conclusion remains accurate that sustainable development exercises a shaping influence on the interpretation and application of certain legal norms, in treaty and in customary law, yet does so without being legally binding or clearly defined.[659]

5. Precaution and Prevention: Proceduralising Community Values

The principles of precaution and prevention are clearly distinct, but at the same time interwoven and hard to consistently analyze separately. In literature, they are therefore more often viewed and treated in conjunction with each other.[660] According to an early description, while prevention is "directed to situations of harm and risks that are known or knowable and are backed by strong scientific evidence, the precautionary principle operates in advance of this".[661] Both principles are in turn connected to specific aspects of the co-operation between States. Reinforced by the principle of precaution, the principle of prevention serves as a legal basis for States to co-operate both in terms of further enhancing scientific findings relating to climate change and in joint efforts based on such findings. It also extends to taking appropriate measures to identify the harms and risks that are knowable, as mentioned in the above quotation.[662]

(a) Conception, Development and Expectations in the 1990s

The precautionary principle – or precautionary *approach* as some States and scholars prefer to call it[663] – is designed to guide the decision-making of States

659 Vaughan Lowe, "Sustainable Development and Unsustainable Arguments", in *International law and sustainable development: Past achievements and future challenges*, ed. Alan E. Boyle and David Freestone (Oxford University Press, 1999), p. 31.

660 Harald Hohmann, *Precautionary legal duties and principles of modern international environmental law* (Graham&Trotman / Martinus Nijhoff, 1994), p. 10; In comparison to German environmental law, it has been noted that international environmental law does not contain the differentiation between the two concepts, see Eckard Rehbinder, *Das Vorsorgeprinzip im internationalen Vergleich* (Werner-Verlag, 1991).

661 David Freestone, "The Precautionary Principle", in *International law and global climate change*, ed. Robin Churchill and David Freestone (Graham&Trotman / Martinus Nijhoff, 1991), p. 31.

662 International Law Commission, "Draft Articles on the Prevention of Transboundary Harm", p. 154.

663 Sands, *Principles of international environmental law*, p. 268.

towards the goal of an environmentally sustainable policy.[664] Its core characteristic is the idea of bringing States to act on environmental challenges even given scientific uncertainty about the possible damage. [665] Two ideas are arguably at the foundation of the principle: Firstly, the idea of a need for decision makers to anticipate harm before it occurs, and secondly, the idea of proportionality and feasibility of the action to be taken.[666]

The notion of precaution began to play a role in international legal development during the 1980s, after having been introduced in some national legal orders, most prominently the one of the – then west – German Federal Republic of Germany: Here, the so-called 'Vorsorgeprinzip' had been a part of environmental law since the beginning of the 1970s.[667] There is no unique or universally accepted formulation of this principle.[668] The most accepted formulation is widely held to be the one in principle 15 of the 1992 Rio Declaration. [669]Here it reads:

> *Where there are threats of serious or irreversible damage, lack of full scientific certainty shall not be used as a reason for postponing cost-effective measures to prevent environmental degradation.*[670]

In climate law, the prevention principle was included in the preamble of the UNFCCC[671], the precautionary principle in Art. 3 of the Convention, but only after controversial debates. The main conflict was whether the element of 'cost-effectiveness' should be included, signifying the introduction of economic considerations in an otherwise ecological context.[672] Consequentially, in the UNFCCC

---

664 Meinhard Schröder, "Precautionary Approach/Principle", in *MPEPIL*, ed. Rüdiger Wolfrum (Oxford University Press, 2014), para. 1.

665 Ibid., para. 2.

666 Andrew Jordan and Timothy O'Riordan, "The Precautionary Principle: A Legal and Policy History", in *The precautionary principle: Protecting public health, the environment and the future of our children*, ed. Marco Martuzzi and Joel A. Tickner (World Health Organization, 2004), p. 34.

667 Sands, *Principles of international environmental law*, p. 267.

668 Anne van Aaken, "Is International Law Conducive To Preventing Looming Disasters?", *Global Policy* 7 (2016), p. 86; For different formulations, *see Schröder, "Precautionary Approach/Principle"*, paras. 3–5.

669 Dupuy and Viñuales, *International environmental law*, p. 63; Sands, *Principles of international environmental law*, p. 268; Schröder, "Precautionary Approach/Principle", para. 14, all with further references.

670 Rio Declaration, principle 15.

671 UNFCCC, Preamble, para. 8.

672 Bodansky, "UNFCCC commentary", p. 503 with further reference.

version of referencing the precautionary principle, its application is limited by the requirement of a threat of "serious or irreversible damage" and by linking it – as in the Rio Declaration as well – to "cost-effective" measures.[673] Although it has been argued that climate change is outside the scope of the traditional concept of transboundary pollution[674], there is little evidence in the practices of bodies like the ILC, international courts or state practice that would support the view that more complex phenomena of environmental change should not be covered by a general duty to prevent harm.[675] The application to climate change is supported by both large parts of the scientific community and state practice: The UNFCCC preamble came to quote principle two of the Rio Declaration in its entirety.[676] In the Kyoto Protocol, there was only an indirect allusion to the principle as its preamble states that the parties are "[b]eing guided by Article 3 of the Convention".

In the context of climate change law, prevention and precaution are examples for the growing importance attributed to future emissions, while current emissions remain the reference point for regulations.[677] One of the main difficulties with the principle is an "extreme variety of interpretations"[678], which leaves various ambiguities despite seemingly broad support in the international community.[679] Consequentially, the principle is difficult to apply in a coherent manner.[680] In addition, the conceptual framing of the principle is debated. Some authors have defined it as an "action-oriented rule" as defined in the Rio Declaration, with requirements like the one to perform EIAs being a special manifestation of

673 Art. 3 (3) UNFCCC; see also Sands, *Principles of international environmental law*, p. 271.

674 Harald Hohmann, *Präventive Rechtspflichten und-prinzipien des modernen Umweltvölkerrechts. Zum Stand des Umweltvölkerrechts zwischen Umweltnutzung und Umweltschutz* (Duncker & Humblot, 1992),p. 374 et seq.; Meinhard Schröder, "Klimaschutz als Problem des internationalen Rechts", *Jahrbuch des Umwelt-und Technikrechts* (1993), p. 196.

675 As in, Roda Verheyen, *Climate change damage and international law: Prevention duties and state responsibility* (Martinus Nijhoff Publishers, 2005), p. 167.

676 UNFCCC, Preamble, para. 8.

677 International Law Association, Legal Principles Relating to Climate Change (2014), p. 16.

678 Schröder, "Precautionary Approach/Principle", para. 9.

679 Sands, *Principles of international environmental law*, p. 272.

680 Daniel Bodansky, "Deconstructing the Precautionary Principle", in *Bringing New Law to Ocean Waters*, ed. David D. Caron and Harry N. Scheiber (Leiden: Brill [online], 2004), p. 381 et seq.

it.[681] In its strongest possible reading, the principle would lead to a shift in the burden of proof: from this perspective, it states that if an action or policy has a suspected risk of causing harm to the public or the environment, in the absence of scientific consensus that there is no harm to be expected, the burden of proof is with those taking an action.[682]

The linkage between the concepts is seen in the practice of States and regional organizations. In EU environmental policy, the EU Commissions' communication on the precautionary principle submits that "precautionary measures should be maintained as long as the scientific data are inadequate, imprecise or inconclusive and as long as the risk is considered too high to be imposed on society. The measures may have to be modified or abolished by a particular deadline, in the light of new scientific findings. However, this is not always linked to the time factor, but to the development of scientific knowledge".[683] The prevention principle as it developed is also connected to, but distinct from, the no-harm principle. The modern understandings of both are rooted in Principle 21 of the Stockholm Declaration.[684] One conceptual difference is their strategic goals: While the no-harm principle is rather concerned with the determination of liability for damage that has already been caused, the prevention principle is focused on an obligation to prevent environmental damage in general. Especially in environmental contexts, where damages are often irreversible, the development of the principle gained traction.[685]

By the late 1990s and the early 2000s, there was already considerable support in international law both for 'preventive action' (Stockholm Declaration, principles 6, 7, 15, 18 and 24) as well as 'precaution' (Rio Declaration principle 15). The precautionary principle has also been introduced into various international treaties.[686] Apart from the non-binding Rio Declaration, the most notable examples are the 1993 Agreement on the Application of Sanitary and

681 Beyerlin, "Different Types Of Norms in IEL", p. 440 et seq., although he admits that the rule is still in need of specification.

682 van Aaken, "Is International Law Conducive To Preventing Looming Disasters?", p. 86; Sands, *Principles of international environmental law*, p. 273.

683 European Commission, 'Communication from the Commission on the precautionary principle', EUR-Lex no. COM/2000/0001 final.

684 See also part C, section I.1., and section II.6 of this part.

685 Dupuy and Viñuales, *International environmental law*, p. 58.

686 For a more extensive overview, see Schröder, "Precautionary Approach/Principle", para 14.

Phytosanitary Measures, the 1995 UN Fish Stocks Agreement[687], the 2000 Stockholm Convention on Persistent Organic Pollutants[688] and the 2000 Cartagena Protocol on Biosafety to the CBD.[689]

As in various regional and national legal orders, precaution was prominently introduced into the law of the EU, where Art. 191 (2) of the Treaty on the Function of the EU (TFEU) states that "Union policy on the environment shall aim at a high level of protection taking into account the diversity of situations in the various regions of the Union. It shall be based on the precautionary principle and on the principles that preventive action should be taken, that environmental damage should as a priority be rectified at source and that the polluter should pay".[690] The Government of New Zealand has introduced the principle into the national legal order.[691] Germany employs the principle in its technical impact assessment and as a guiding principle for its environmental policy.[692] However, whether the precautionary principle has gained the status of customary international law is a matter of ongoing debate. While some authors claim that the precautionary principle is now so widely adopted that it has developed into an enforceable norm of customary international law, others disagree, arguing that the practice on precaution lacks the consistency, clarity and uniformity to

---

687 Agreement for the Implementation of the Provisions of the United Nations Convention on the Law of the Sea of 10 December 1982 relating to the Conservation and Management of Straddling Fish Stocks and Highly Migratory Fish Stocks

688 UNTS, vol. 2256, p. 119.

689 Convention on Biological Diversity, 2226 UNTS 208, reprinted in (2000) 39 ILM 1027, Art. 1.

690 See also Communication From The Commission on the Precautionary Principle COM(2000) 1, 2 February 2000.

691 See Department of Conservation, New Zealand Coastal Policy Statement, 4 Nov 2010, especially 'Guidance note on policy 3', available at https://www.doc.govt.nz/Documents/conservation/marine-and-coastal/coastal-management/guidance/policy-3.pdf.

692 There is no uniform environmental code in Germany, but a variety of laws on different aspects of the environment. The Federal government declared the precautionary principle to be a guiding principle of its environmental policy for the first time in 1976, see German Bundestag, 'Drucksache' 7/5684; It finds expression in Article 5 para. 1 no. 2 of the Federal Immission Control Act (Bundes-Immissionsschutzgesetz) and the special precautionary duty in Article 5 para. 2 of the Federal Water Act (Wasserhaushaltsgesetz).

support the claim that it is a clear and binding norm.[693] A closer assessment of the principle's reception in adjudication practice shows a divided case law.[694]

In international jurisprudence, the ICJ first was called upon to engage with the precautionary principle in the 1995 *Nuclear Test* case[695], but the majority chose not to. New Zealand thought France was in breach of international law and an ICJ ruling of 1974[696] through their nuclear tests conducted in 1995. In its petition to the court, New Zealand invoked the principle as a widely accepted principle of international law, claiming that the burden of proof would have shifted to France concerning the proposed tests and their potential to cause environmental damage.[697] France disputed this position in the proceedings and called the status of the principle uncertain.[698] The ICJ itself refrained from any direct reference to the precautionary principle in its decision not to allow New Zealand to reopen the 1974 case. Only two dissenting judges considered the precautionary approach to be a part of the corpus of international law.[699] In the *Gabčíkovo-Nagymaros Project case*, Hungary argued that a previously existing obligation not to cause damage to the territory of another state had evolved into an *erga omnes* obligation of prevention of damage following from the precautionary principle. The Court declined to override the treaty obligations of the parties[700] and did not engage in detail with the precautionary principle.[701]

---

693 For an overview, see Jonathan B. Wiener, "Precaution", in *The Oxford handbook of international environmental law*, ed. Daniel Bodansky, Jutta Brunnée, and Ellen Hey (OUP, 2007), p. 601; For an affirmative position on the customary nature in general, see Beyerlin, "Different Types Of Norms in IEL", p. 440 et seq.; for the perspective rejecting the customary nature, see Jonathan B. Wiener and Michael D. Rogers, "Comparing Precaution in the United States and Europe", *Journal of risk research* 5, no. 4 (2002), p. 343.

694 Dupuy and Viñuales, *International environmental law*, p. 63 et seq.

695 Request for an Examination of the Situation in Accordance with paragraph 63 of the Court's Judgment of 20 December 1974 in the Nuclear Tests (New Zealand v. France) case, Order, I.C.J. Rep. 1995, p. 288.

696 *Nuclear Tests* (New Zealand v. France), Judgment, I.C.J. Rep. 1974, p. 457.

697 Aide-mémoire of New Zealand, para. 38; Verbatim record 1995/20, p. 20 et seq., 36 et seq.

698 Verbatim record 1995/20,

699 See the Dissenting opinions of Judge Weeramantry (para. 342 et seq.) and ad hoc Judge Palmer (para. 412.).

700 Gabčíkovo-Nagymaros Project, para. 115.

701 Judge Weeramantry, in his separate opinion famous for discussing sustainable development (see section II.4 above), also did not engage with the substantial aspects of precaution in detail.

As for the principle of prevention, it is widely seen as a "part of the corpus of international law relating to the environment".[702] Having a significantly longer tradition than the precautionary principle, it has been endorsed by the *Trail Smelter* decision, *the Corfu Channel* judgment[703] and the ILC, e.g. in its work on Transboundary Harm in 2001.[704] In the reading of the ILC, in order for the prevention principle to be invoked, the degree of harm should be foreseeable and the State must know or should have known that the activity concerned bears the risk of significant harm.[705]

The precautionary principle has attracted much scholarly attention and there were high expectations concerning its potential role in IEL and climate law. Arguably, this was due to its normative potential to dictate action in the absence of absolute scientific certainty about a given risk. At the beginning of the 1990s, advocates of the precautionary principle optimistically forecasted that it "could become **the** fundamental principle of environmental protection policy and law."[706]

(b) Further Development: Post-Kyoto Until Today

The post-Kyoto development of the precautionary principle and that of prevention has risen both principles to considerable importance given their inclusion in legal instruments, policies and court decisions. But moreover, it shows that this importance is primarily due to the translation of both principles into more concrete and largely procedural forms.

In more recent international adjudication, some decisions stand out. The WTO Dispute Settlement Body (DSB) had to engage with the substantive legal status of the precautionary principle and was reluctant regarding its legal status, noting in 2006 that "there has, to date, been no authoritative decision by an international court or tribunal which recognizes the precautionary principle as a principle of general or customary international law." While recognizing the

702 Legality of the Threat or Use of Nuclear Weapons (Advisory opinion) I.C.J. Rep 1996, p. 226, 242, para. 29; confirmed in Gabčíkovo-Nagymaros Project.

703 Corfu Channel, para. 22.

704 International Law Commission, "Draft Articles on the Prevention of Transboundary Harm", p. 148 et seq.

705 Ibid., para. 155.

706 James Cameron and Juli Abouchar, "The Precautionary Principle: A Fundamental Principle of Law and Policy for the Protection of the Global Environment", *BC Int'l & Comp. L. Rev.* 14, no. 1 (1991), p. 27. [Emphasis added].

numerous provisions of international instruments explicitly or implicitly applying it, the DSB holds that "the debate over whether the precautionary principle constitutes a recognized principle of general or customary international law is still ongoing."[707] The ICJ, some 13 years after the second *Nuclear Test case*, had the opportunity to clarify its stance on precaution and prevention in a case that has quickly become an important reference in IEL. In the *Pulp Mills* case, the core procedural aspect of the precautionary principle was a matter of intensive debate. Argentina argued that the precautionary principle was recognized by customary international law, including the shift in the burden of proof.[708] Uruguay, in turn, argued that the precautionary principle was not applicable to the case at hand.[709] While implicitly acknowledging the principle itself, Uruguay held that its actions were in compliance with the precautionary principle as stated in Principle 15 of the Rio Declaration, if this were applicable.[710] The Court did not side with Argentina in its interpretation of the principle, but rather with the interpretation by Uruguay. It held that "while a precautionary approach may be relevant in the interpretation and application of the provisions of the Statute, it does not follow that it operates as a reversal of the burden of proof."[711] The decision was met with criticism, partially because of its engagement with the principles of prevention and precaution. There was also criticism within the Court itself: Judges Simma and Al-Khasawneh criticized the reluctance of the Court to accept new approaches to attain scientific evidence.[712] Judge Trindade in his separate opinion criticized that "the ICJ did not acknowledge, nor affirmed, the existence of those principles, nor elaborated on them, thus missing a unique occasion for their consolidation in the present domain of contemporary international law."[713] Insisting on the existence and applicability of these principles and

---

707 WTO, European Communities – Measures affecting the approval and marketing of biotech products [Panel Report], WT/DS291/R, WT/DS292/R, WT/DS293/R, 29 Sep 2006, para. 7.88.

708 Pulp Mills, para. 160.

709 Pulp Mills, Counter-Memorial of Uruguay, para. 4.79 et seqq.

710 Ibid., para. 4.82.

711 ICJ case concerning the Pulp Mills on the River Uruguay [Argentina v Uruguay], para. 164.

712 See Dissenting Opinion of Judge Simma and Al-Khasawneh in the ICJ Case Pulp Mills on the River Uruguay [Argentina v Uruguay], Judgment of 20 April 2010, paras. 3 and 24.

713 See Separate Opinion of Judge Trindade in the ICJ Case Pulp Mills on the River Uruguay [Argentina v Uruguay], Judgment of 20 April 2010, para. 113.

their importance for IEL, he noted that "[t]he Court had a unique occasion [...] to assert the applicability of the preventive as well as the precautionary principles; it unfortunately preferred not to do so, for reasons which go beyond, and escape, my comprehension."

The concepts of both prevention and precaution, are thus important examples for the trend to put a greater emphasis on the procedural aspects of international environmental and climate law. It has been argued that the due diligence standard has emerged as a potential bridging concept between harm prevention and the duty to take precautionary measures, including to avert harm to the global commons.[714] The ITLOS Seabed Chamber has significantly contributed to this aspect of interconnectedness in an advisory opinion from 2012. The contextual nature of the due diligence standard, it held, would mean that the standard could change over time.[715] The obligation to conduct environmental impact assessments is directly linked to this development and one of its main procedural elements, besides consultation and negotiations.[716] Regarding the legal status of the interconnected aspects of the precautionary principle and due diligence standards, the ITLOS Seabed Chamber held that the precautionary approach is "an integral part of the due diligence obligation of sponsoring States", applicable even outside the scope of the specific obligations in a concrete case.[717] On a regional level, the precautionary principle has primarily played a role in European Courts. The EU Courts have applied the principle, e.g., in cases C-180/96 United Kingdom v Commission [1998], C-236/01 Monsanto v Italy [2003] and E–3/00 EFTA Surveillance Authority v Norway [2001]. The European Court of Human Rights (ECtHR) acknowledged "the importance of the precautionary principle (enshrined for the first time in the Rio Declaration), which 'was intended to

---

714 Jutta Brunnée, "International Environmental Law and Community Interests – Procedural Aspects", in *Community interests across international law*, ed. Eyal Benvenisti and Georg Nolte (Oxford University Press, 2018), p. 154 et seq. and 174 et seq.

715 International Tribunal for the Law of the Sea (ITLOS) (Seabed Chamber), Responsibilities and Obligations of States Sponsoring Persons and Entities with Respect to Activities in the Area (Advisory Opinion), ITLOS Case No. 17, 1 February 2011.

716 See Beyerlin, "Different Types Of Norms in IEL", p. 439 et seq.; International Law Association, Legal Principles Relating to Climate Change (2014) p. 23; Brunnée, "Procedural Aspects", p. 154.

717 Responsibilities and Obligations of States Sponsoring Persons and Entities with Respect to Activities in the Area (Advisory Opinion), Seabed Chamber, ITLOS Case No 17, ITLOS Rep. 2011, p. 10, para. 131.

apply in order to ensure a level of high protection of health, the safety of consumers and the environment in all community activities"".[718]

In the post-Kyoto climate instruments, neither prevention nor precaution were prominently included. The Copenhagen Accord only indirectly referred to the Convention principles[719], while the Bali Action Plan and the Durban Platform Agreement did not mention them at all. In the Paris Agreement, where other principles of the Convention have been explicitly highlighted, precaution was, along with inter-generation equity, among the UNFCCC principles *not* explicitly restated in Art. 2 defining the objective and goal. Here too, the precautionary principle is only indirectly mentioned, when the preamble states that the agreement is "[i]n pursuit of the objective of the Convention, and being guided by its principles".[720]

(c) Conclusion

The principles of prevention and precaution have gained significant traction in international environmental policy over the last decades. They have been further developed in various instruments and found specifications like the EIA, which has gained such a broad acceptance by States that it "may now be considered a requirement under general international law to undertake [...] where there is a risk that the proposed industrial activity may have a significant adverse impact in a transboundary context."[721] Nevertheless, the ICJ, the ITLOS, the EU Courts, and the WTO Appellate Body have all been reluctant to accept explicitly that the precautionary principle has customary law status.

Arguably, this reluctance is primarily due to two interconnected features of these principles: First, they do not dictate specific regulatory measures or a specific outcome but are rather action-oriented. Second, the substance of both, but especially the precautionary principle, is more vague than the procedural specifications both principles yielded. This divergence can be looked at from two perspectives: From the negative one, it could be argued that the procedural aspects are merely a disguise for the substantive weakness of the principles. From a more positive perspective, the procedural aspects could eventually foster both

---

718 ECtHR, Tatar v. Romania, App. No. 67021/01, Judgment (27 Jan 2009, Final 6 Jul 2009), para. 120.

719 Copenhagen Accord, preamble.

720 Paris Agreement, preamble, para. 3.

721 *Case concerning Pulp Mills on the River Uruguay* (Argentina v. Uruguay), Judgment, I.C.J. Rep. 2010, p. 14, 55, para. 204.

a political and legal development capable of demarcating the substantive side, especially under instruments like the Paris Agreement, which put significant emphasis on procedural co-operation.[722] Nevertheless, precaution and prevention still have the potential to create obligations for States, should courts decide to pursue that course of action. Their second potential is decisive for the inclusion of more and newer scientific evidence in the international arena.[723]

The fact that the precautionary principle was not restated in the Paris Agreement, can be read in two different ways. Either States wanted to exclude the principle to weaken the agreement, taking out a norm that is deemed (or feared) to have an increasing normative and practical potential if further elaborated, e.g., in court decisions. Or – to the more positive interpretation – it could be assumed that climate change has become so established as a universally acknowledged risk that it is no longer a matter of precaution to pursue action against climate change, but rather only a matter of prevention.[724] The precautionary principle thus shares with many other principles both its potential and its limitations. Its flexibility and interconnection with other norm concepts impart its capacity to cover a wide range of situations, circumstances, possible obligations and actions. At the same time, it remains difficult for the principle to overcome the threshold of being transformed from a soft law norm into hard law provisions.[725] Furthermore, the precautionary principle in particular also shares a fate with many of the other norms discussed here, as it did not rise to the defining role that some thought it would have during the 1990s.

6. No-Harm Rule: Bilateralist Version of Community Obligations with Remaining Importance

Within this context, a final concept to discuss is the no-ham rule. At the outset, the no-harm rule seems to precede all community value considerations in international environmental and climate law and is firmly based in classical bilateralist international law. However, the no-harm rule remains the concept with the broadest acceptance in the international community. By application, it has also developed interconnections with the thread of community value orientation in post-1990 developments of international law such as the Rio Declaration. As one

722 As in, Brunnée, "Procedural Aspects", p. 165 et seq., 174 et seq.

723 van Aaken, "Is International Law Conducive To Preventing Looming Disasters?", p. 86

724 Viñuales, "The Paris climate agreement: an initial examination", p. 11 apparently leans towards this latter interpretation, without however being explicit about it.

725 Schröder, "Precautionary Approach/Principle", para. 11.

of the firmest principles in IEL, it exercises an influence on the climate regime, both substantially and by means of its procedural translations.

(a) Conception, Development and Expectations in the 1990s

In the 19th century understanding of absolute territorial sovereignty, States were free to engage in any environmentally degrading activity within their territory, regardless of the transboundary effects such activities had on other States. This so-called 'Harmon Doctrine' was all pre-modern international law had to say regarding the environment. This remained so until developments like the *Island of Palmas* case[726] and the previously discussed *Trail Smelter* arbitration case. In the latter case, this law was finally made obsolete by stating that no state has the right to use or allow the use of its territory in a way that causes transboundary harm to another state. The dogmatic roots of 'no-harm' are disputed, with opinions on its provenience ranging from ancient Roman law to US constitutional law as well as early international laws finding that the abusive use of sovereignty is prohibited. It is, however, best characterized as a compromise between the territorial sovereignty of one state and the territorial integrity of another, while ultimately favoring territorial integrity over territorial sovereignty.[727] It combines the prohibition of causing harm with the preventive dimension of calling upon States to take measures in advance to control sources of potential harm. Hence, it can be conceptually understood as a predominantly substantive principle concerned with prevention, which explains its importance in treaty practice and jurisprudence.[728] But the principle also requires procedural co-operation from States, with this requirement complementing its substantial meaning.[729]

With the inclusion of the 'no-harm' rule in Principle 21 of the 1972 Stockholm Declaration, the norm entered one of the first documents of modern environmental law. This emerging field was thus discernibly developed around the aim

726 Reports of international arbitral awards, Island of Palmas case (Netherlands, USA), 4 April 1928, VOLUME II pp. 829–871, available at http://legal.un.org/riaa/cases/vol_II/829-871.pdf, especially p. 839, where it reads *"This right [territorial sovereignty] has as corollary a duty: the obligation to protect within the territory the rights of other States, in particular their right to integrity and inviolability in peace and in war, together with the rights which each State may claim for its nationals in foreign territory."*

727 Beyerlin and Marauhn, *International environmental law*, p. 39 et seq.

728 Dupuy and Viñuales, *International environmental law*, p. 56 et seq.

729 Beyerlin and Marauhn, *International environmental law*, p. 41. Regarding the specific manifestations of the procedural requirements of 'no harm', see also section II.,5.

to balance sovereign interests.[730] In the Stockholm version, however, the concept applied not only to the territory of other States, but also to "areas beyond the limits of national jurisdiction" (Principle 21) more generally. Thus, it was also extended to the environment in common areas such as Antarctica, the High Seas or the Seabed.[731]

The responsibility of States not to cause transboundary harm found confirmation in the 1992 Rio Declaration where principle 2 reiterates the Stockholm Declaration in stating that

> *"[s]tates have, in accordance with the Charter of the United Nations and the principles of international law, the sovereign right to exploit their own resources pursuant to their own environmental and developmental policies, and the responsibility to ensure that activities within their jurisdiction or control do not cause damage to the environment of other States or of areas beyond the limits of national jurisdiction."*

This version, adding that States can exploit pursuing their environmental and developmental policies, reflects the efforts to better balance environmental and development concerns.[732] One of the most important substantial legal ramification of 'no harm' is the establishment of state responsibility for harm inflicted.[733] As follows, one of the key challenges in the conceptual extension of 'no harm' to climate change concerns the intersection with state responsibility for damages through climate change. Regarding traditionally conceived transboundary harm, the attribution of a certain harmful effect to a specific behavior is relatively simple – one only needs to think of the *Trail Smelter* case and the fumes which were clearly emerging from an easily identified source. In the case of damages through climate change, which are mostly conveyed through changes in the atmosphere and indirect effects such as rising sea levels or droughts, the attribution of one given effect to a given activity is more difficult.

The notion that States are responsible for transboundary harm has been confirmed through numerous MEAs, court decisions and other international instruments. Aside from those already mentioned, it finds application in Art. 3 of the CBD, which introduces Stockholm Principle 21 as the sole 'principle' of the convention. As a consequence of its wide-ranging proliferation, the 'no-harm' rule is regarded by most scholars as part of customary international law. This position is further collaborated by the ICJ: The Court found, in its advisory opinion on

730 Bodansky, Brunnée, and Rajamani, *International climate change law*, p. 40.
731 Beyerlin and Marauhn, *International environmental law*, p. 39.
732 Bodansky, Brunnée, and Rajamani, *International climate change law*, p. 40 et seq.
733 Beyerlin and Marauhn, *International environmental law*, p. 41 and 45 et seq.

nuclear weapons, that the "[g]eneral obligation of States to ensure that activities within their jurisdiction and control respect the environment of other States or of areas beyond national control is now part of the **corpus of international law relating to the environment**".[734] The Court repeated this conclusion in the *Gabčíkovo-Nagymaros* case in 1997, however, without specifying what legal character it ascribed to the obligation.[735]

(b) Further Development: Post-Kyoto Until Today

Drawing from the above, the Court did not specify whether this 'general obligation' was considered to be part of customary law or seen as a general principle of law until 2010, when the Court clarified that it considers the obligation to be part of customary international law.[736] Nevertheless, conceptually the 'no harm' rule remains the most fundamental framing for the obligations States have regarding the effects their climate change inducing activities may cause other States and common areas.

(c) Conclusion

The 'no-harm' concept is the longest standing rule of IEL. As a part of customary international law, as supported practically unanimously in scholarship and evidenced by the numerous treaties, covenants and court decisions, the rule finds extension to the context of climate change. This extension, however, remains challenging as the mechanism of attribution elaborated in the application of this rule is difficult. In need of procedural translation in the context of climate change, the 'no harm' rule is an exemplary conclusion of this chapter: The development of the no-harm rule itself could be called one of the first turns towards community value orientation within the means of classical, bilateralist international law. That is, it stands for the turning away from absolute sovereignty towards a basic notion of other-regardingness in international law, also in the field of the use of resources. In this regard, it depicts a turn towards community values. But arguably, the broad acceptance for the rule among States is due to the fact that the 'no harm' rule remains firmly based in bilateralist international law.

---

734 *Legality of the Threat or Use of Nuclear Weapons* (Advisory opinion), I.C.J. Rep. 1996, pp. 226, 242, para. 29.

735 Gabčíkovo-Nagymaros Project, para. 53.

736 Case concerning Pulp Mills on the River Uruguay (Argentina v Uruguay), Judgment, I.C.J. Rep. 2010, pp. 14, 55, para. 101.

7. Interim Conclusion: Relatively Stable, but Largely Extra-legal Community Value Orientation in the Climate Regime

The analysis of whether, or in how far, community value related norm concepts play an important role in the climate change regime offers mixed results. Nonetheless, some common denominators can be determined. While overall, there is a relatively stable level of inclusion of such norms in the key instruments of the regime and an apparently broad acceptance on the political level, the legal effect of community value related norms is limited. Only where concepts have the potential to be translated into procedural norms, does there seem to be prospects of them finding legal application.

The UNFCCC stood out in the mass of MEAs in the prominence it accorded to its principles, even including them in an operative article. The subsequent practice under the regime, especially regarding the key instruments (Kyoto Protocol, Copenhagen Accord, Paris Agreement), includes slightly varying, but overall, stably recurring references to the principles of the Convention and the community values comprised in them. Beyond that, the treaty practice reveals little legally substantial development of those values and principles. Moreover, very few norms can be said to have gained the status of legal norms under customary international law. The clearest (and largely undisputed) example is the linkage between the sovereign right of States to exploit their resources and the no-harm rule as expressed in Principle 21 of the Stockholm Declaration and Principle 2 of the Rio Declaration.[737] It is argued here that it is no coincidence that this element, which is the most stable of those discussed here, is also the one most firmly based in classical and bilateralist international law and the one with the longest tradition, dating back to the 1972 Stockholm Conference. This reconnection of community values to state sovereignty has apparently allowed for this element to gain such sustainable acceptance.

Several reasons can be invoked for the fact that the legal status, meaning and application of many of the community value related norms discussed above remain unclear. The simplest of them is their short time of existence. The period since the 1990s, or even the one since the 1970s, is relatively short compared to the timespan over which many legal norms with a solid basis as customary rules or even general principles of law have developed. Another is the constantly evolving practice under the climate regime. In part, this evolving practice is the entire purpose of the UNFCCC regime, which aims at keeping States in constant

737 As in, Sands, *Principles of international environmental law*, p. 232.

interaction to work on solutions to climate change. As exemplified best in the case of CBDR, this constant practice brings with it recurring opportunities to re-open debates about the meaning of different norm concepts and their re-interpretation. While having this possibility of shaping and re-shaping norms seems to make States more prone to accept the presence of the norm concepts, it also limits the concepts clarity and practical applicability. This, in turn, is linked to a pivotal common denominator, which is a fundamental phenomenon that has been lingering since the early inclusion of community value related norm concepts in the field:

The 'Normative Language' Problem Reloaded

The question whether the concept of sustainable development has risen to a status of customary international law caused vivid scholarly debate in the 1990s which is still relevant today. While some, like Sands[738], argued that it indeed has, others like *Lowe* disagreed. One of Lowe's arguments against the customary law status deserves special attention here: He makes the point that the main impediment for norm concepts like sustainable development to gain customary status is what he called the "normative language problem".[739] He develops his argument starting from the *North Sea Continental Shelf* case, where the ICJ in its analysis on the customary nature of a norm, had posited that

> *"it would in the first place be necessary that the provision concerned should, at all events potentially, be of a fundamentally norm-creating character such as could be regarded as forming the basis of a general rule of law."*[740]

Lowe holds that normativity, "by definition, must express itself in normative terms: it must be possible to phrase a norm in normative language. But it is by no means clear that the components of Sustainable Development can be so phrased."[741] Against this backdrop, he argues that 'sustainable development' can at best be a "name for a set of norms"[742], but not a norm itself. He does, however, not conclude that sustainable development lacks any kind of normativity

---

738 Ibid., p. 254, confirming a position taken earlier; cf. also Pierre-Marie Dupuy, "Où en est le droit international de l'environnement à la fin du siècle?", *Revue générale de droit international public* 101 (1997), p. 886.

739 Lowe, "Sustainable Development and Unsustainable Arguments", p. 26 et seqq.

740 *North Sea Continental Shelf* (Germany v Denmark) (Judgment), ICJ Rep. 1969, p. 3, 41 et. seq.

741 Lowe, "Sustainable Development and Unsustainable Arguments", p. 26.

742 Ibid.

but argues that its development can be characterized as that of a 'meta-principle' having "a kind of interstitial normativity, pushing and pulling the boundaries of true primary norms when they threaten to overlap or conflict with each other".[743] It is in this indirect sense he ascribes "real normative force"[744] to sustainable development.

Lowe's line of argumentation points to a more general phenomenon regarding normative concepts like the ones discussed above. Especially for the concepts of 'common concern', CBDR, sustainable development, and, to a certain extent, 'equity', their substantive implications are difficult to phrase in a language sufficiently normative to be applicable by courts. Their *potential* substantive implications are manifold. They all are complex structures, conceived and developed to give expression to the numerous ethical, political and economic considerations. The downside of this complexity being accommodated in singular norm concepts is their necessary vagueness and difficulty to express any obligation sufficiently clear to exercise a legal function. In the cases of other concepts, a slightly different perspective presents itself. The co-operation aspect of CBDR, the burden-sharing aspect of equity, the various implications of the prevention principle and the no-harm rule which remains at the center of IEL all seem to have gained a more secure footing in international law. This is insofar as they experienced a translation into more procedural norms. The most salient examples are the translation of the prevention principle into the procedural requirement of conducting EIAs or the translation of the alleged 'principle of co-operation' into procedurally manageable norms. This later is expressed though requirements like engaging in research-sharing or regular assessments of progress in climate policy programs.

The UNFCCC regime, in this vein, has created a framework for the application of the idea of 'international co-operation' for the gradual development and implementation of the international legal and governance framework on climate change. Providing an underpinning for this institutional framework is the primary achievement of the idea of 'co-operation' in the climate context. This relatively solid set of procedural norms has come to be a characteristic feature of the climate regime.[745] The substantive norms to which the procedural norms

743 Ibid., p. 31.; Lowe puts *sustainable development* in his category of 'modifying norms', which he regards as designed to regulate the relationships between other primary norms. The term 'modifying norms' in Lowe's use is equipollent to that of 'interstitial norms', cf. p. 33.

744 Ibid., p. 33.

745 As in, Brunnée and Toope, *Legitimacy and legality in international law*, p. 176.

could be applied meanwhile remain underdeveloped. Whether they can be further developed will be answered in the continuing practice. Where they do develop, strong indications say that they will do so beyond the realm of classically applicable legal norms.

III. Putting Community Values into Legal Practice: Prospects and Problems

Having identified tendencies of 'decline' in the structural role of law in the climate regime and, conversely, a rather stable development of the community value underpinnings in the international climate change regime, the ensuing question is whether the resulting gap in the role of the law is or could be filled on other levels. Therefore, an overview on recent trends in climate litigation on the national and regional level (1.) as well as an assessment of the prospects for the further engagement of international courts, primarily the ICJ (2.) shall conclude the empirical part of this study.

1. Advancing Community Values in Domestic Courts?

'Can climate litigation save the world?' asked the British newspaper The Guardian in March 2018.[746] Despite its melodramatic tone, the article makes an important point: In recent years, climate litigation on the national and regional level has had a growing influence as a platform for advocating political action on climate change. This is connected to a considerable proliferation in climate legislation since the 1990s. A 2017 study concluded that there are today over 1,200 climate change or climate change-relevant laws worldwide, which means that today three out of four countries have specific climate legislation. This is a twentyfold increase since 1997, when about 60 climate laws were in place.[747] Consequentially, the 'Climate Change Litigation of the World'[748] dataset includes over 250

746 Damian Carrington, "Can Climate Litigation Save the World?", *The Guardian*, 20 March.

747 Michal Nachmany et al., Global trends in climate change legislation and litigation: 2017 update, (2017) p. 5, finding a further reflection of the stable ground existing in climate change laws in the fact that the rate at which new laws are passed has decreased from over 100 new laws per year in 2009–13 to around 40 new laws in 2016, and p. 10, in each case with further reference.

748 The database is accessible online: http://www.lse.ac.uk/GranthamInstitute/climate-change-laws-of-the-world/; for the US data, see http://wordpress2.ei.columbia.edu/climate-change-litigation/us-climate-change-litigation/.

court cases in which climate change is a relevant factor across 25 jurisdictions for which data exists. A staggering number as the dataset even excludes the US.[749]

In some instances, petitions by NGOs or individuals against governments and companies were successful. In other cases, despite not producing the result envisaged by the claimants, court proceedings have fostered engagement with the legal dimension of certain features of the climate regime. This section discusses two of the prominent trends of climate litigation connected to the norms and policies analyzed above. These are, namely, the strategy of using commitments made by States under international instruments to foster governmental actions on the national level (a) and efforts to fill the gaps in legal responsibility for climate change impacts on the national or regional level (b).

(a) Using Legislative and Policy Commitments in Substantiating Legal Claims

The climate litigation trend most directly connected to the community values related norm concepts analyzed above is the strategy to refer to the commitments made by States on the international level to substantiate claims in national courts. A salient example in recent practice was the *Urgenda* case in the Netherlands.

In 2012, the Dutch *Urgenda Foundation*, together with several co-plaintiffs, initiated proceedings against the Dutch government, claiming that the government had not been doing enough to prevent hazardous climate change. In the words of one of the leading attorneys on the case

> *"[...] it was a conscious decision to bring tort law to bear against a national government rather than against the fossil fuel sector. In contrast to companies, national governments have made quite explicit statements – in the context of the United Nations Framework Convention on Climate Change (UNFCCC) and its annual climate change conferences – regarding the danger of climate change and what should be done about it. They have consistently done so based on the scientific findings of the UN's Intergovernmental Panel on Climate Change (IPCC)."*[750]

The notion that developed countries "should take the lead in combating climate change and the adverse effects thereof" (Art. 3 (1) UNFCCC), analyzed above and shown to be of limited legal acceptance in the final phase of negotiations for

749 Nachmany et al., Global trends in climate change legislation and litigation: 2017 update (2017), p. 13. In the US, there have been over 600 court cases.

750 Roger Cox, "A Climate Change Litigation Precedent: Urgenda Foundation v The State of the Netherlands", *Journal of Energy & Natural Resources Law* 34, no. 2 (2016), p. 145.

the Paris Agreement[751], was crucial in this case. It exemplifies what role the principles of the climate regime can play in legal procedures: As the *Urgenda* Foundation has emphasized in their own case material, the plaintiffs essentially built their case upon the principles and commitments made by the Dutch government under the UNFCCC regime.[752] The *Urgenda case* is the first in which regular citizens, through an NGO, have held their government accountable for taking insufficient action to safe civilians from climate change. On the 24th of June 2015, the District Court of The Hague ruled that the Dutch government must reduce its emissions by at least 25 % by the end of 2020 (compared to 1990 levels). In its ruling, the court, while insisting that the considered international legal norms do not entitle private citizens or organizations, did accept the premise that such commitments and principles had to be taken into account in determining the state's legal duty under national law.[753] The decision, if upheld, would mean that the Dutch government is forced by national tort law in conjunction with the relevant international norms, to take more effective action on climate change. In September 2015, despite calls from top scientists, lawyers, citizens, companies and the almost 900 co-plaintiffs, the Dutch government decided to appeal the verdict. Urgenda subsequently filed a cross-appeal. It argued that the court should not only take into consideration international legal norms relevant to the issue, but additionally should also explicitly base the state's legal duties in human rights provisions, especially those under the European Convention of Human Rights (ECHR)."[754]

The Hague Court of Appeal rendered its judgment on the 9th of October 2018 and upheld the 2015 decision of the District Court. The Court ruled that failure to reduce greenhouse gas emissions would amount to a violation of the rights of Dutch citizens. The Court of Appeal based its ruling on the State's legal duty

751 See section II.,2. above.

752 Cf. Urgenda Foundation, Translation Summons Urgenda Foundation v. Kingdom of the Netherlands (2014), para. 177 et seqq., available at http://www.urgenda.nl/wp-content/uploads/Translation-Summons-in-case-Urgenda-v-Dutch-State-v.25.06.10.pdf.

753 Cox, "A climate change litigation precedent: Urgenda Foundation v The State of the Netherlands", p. 155 et seq. with an English translation of the relevant subsection 4.43 of the decision.

754 Urgenda Foundation, The Hague Court of Appeal, 18 April 2017, Case number 200.178.245, Respondent's Notice on Appeal Including Notive of Cross-Appeal, p. 182 et seqq., available at https://www.urgenda.nl/wp-content/uploads/Urgenda-notice-on-appeal-21112017.pdf.

to ensure the protection of the life (Art. 2) as well as the private life, family life, home and correspondence (Art. 8) of citizens as enshrined in the ECHR.[755] In January 2019, the Dutch Government filed an appeal before the Dutch Supreme Court in a final attempt to overturn the Court of Appeal's decision. Challenging many aspects of the Court of Appeal's line of reasoning, the Government submitted that the Court of Appeal did not sufficiently take into account the wide margin of appreciation states have in determining how to fulfill their legal duties under the ECHR.[756] On the 20th of December 2019, the Dutch Supreme Court upheld the Court of Appeal's decision, including the line of reasoning directly referring to Articles 2 and 8 of the ECHR.[757] Moreover, the Supreme Court rejected the government's line of defence that given the global nature of climate change and the multiplicity of its causes, Dutch emission reductions could not solve the problem of climate change. The court found that accepting the above assertion as a defence, *"would mean that a country could easily evade its partial responsibility by pointing out other countries or its own small share."*[758]

There were early indications that the *Urgenda* case would serve as a blueprint for similar efforts in other (European) countries. The *Urgenda* case had been filed and argued before the entry into force and even the adoption of the Paris Agreement, so that the plaintiffs did not include the commitments that the Dutch government later made under it. After the Agreement's entry into force, a case in Switzerland resembled the *Urgenda* line of argumentation, only now fortified with the Paris Agreement as an additional source. The group of petitioners, the "Union of Swiss senior women" grounded their claims in their constitutional right to life[759], the sustainability principle[760] and the precautionary

755 Gerechtshof Den Haag, 9 October 2018, case number 200.178.245/01, ECLI:NL:GHDHA:2018:2591; an English translation of the decision (ECLI:NL:GHDHA:2018:2610) is available at https://uitspraken.rechtspraak.nl/inziendocument?id=ECLI:NL:GHDHA:2018:2610.

756 The Government's Appeal to the Supreme Court (in dutch only) is available at http://climatecasechart.com/climate-change-litigation/wp-content/uploads/sites/16/non-us-case-documents/2019/20190108_2015-HAZA-C0900456689_appeal-1.pdf.

757 Hoge Raad, 20 December 2019, case number 19/00135, ECLI:NL:HR:2019:2006; an English translation of the decision (ECLI:NL:HR:2019:2007) is available at http://climatecasechart.com/climate-change-litigation/wp-content/uploads/sites/16/non-us-case-documents/2020/20200113_2015-HAZA-C0900456689_judgment.pdf.

758 Ibid., para. 5.7.7.

759 Articles 10 of the Swiss constitution of 18 Apr 1999, as of 01 Jan 2018, see https://www.admin.ch/opc/de/classified-compilation/19995395/index.html.

760 Article 73 of the Swiss constitution.

principle[761], as well as Art. 2 (Right to life) and 8 (Right to respect for private and family life) of the European Convention on Human Rights (ECHR).[762] Regarding their right to life, they specifically argued that as elderly people they would be especially vulnerable to and affected by heat waves resulting from climate change. Their petition asked that the legislature and the responsible government branches be required to develop policies ensuring that GHG emissions would be cut by 25 % by the year of 2020 and by 50 % by 2050, in comparison to the 1990 levels. The argument includes the assumption that current policies are incapable of pursuing those targets set by the government's commitments on the international level and renewed by the Paris Agreement.[763] The Federal Department of Environment, Transport, Energy and Communications declined the petition in May 2017 arguing that the plaintiffs had no appropriate standing. In 2018, the Federal Administrative Court ("Bundesverwaltungsgericht") rejected the appeal by the plaintiffs, following the Government's line of reasoning that – in comparison with other citizens – the plaintiffs are not specifically affected by climate change to an extent that would give them appropriate standing before the court.[764] The decision was later upheld by the Federal Court ("Bundesgericht").[765] An appeal is now pending at the ECtHR.[766]

One of the latest examples of a climate litigation case referring to the Dutch *Urgenda* case, was decided upon by the German Federal Constitutional Court ("Bundesverfassungsgericht") in March 2021.[767] Numerous individuals as well as

---

761 Article 74 of the Swiss constitution.

762 Union of Swiss Senior Women for Climate Protection v. Swiss Federal Council [Verein KlimaSeniorinnen Schweiz v. Bundesrat], at para. 1(a) (led 25 Oct 2016), https://perma. cc/3LGB-3V7H.

763 Union of Swiss Senior Women for Climate Protection v. Swiss Federal Council [Verein KlimaSeniorinnen Schweiz v. Bundesrat], para. 60.

764 Bundesverwaltungsgericht, 27 November 2018, case number A-2992/2017, especially para. 7.4.3., available (in German) at https://www.bvger.ch/dam/bvger/de/dokumente/2018/12/Urteil%20A-2992-2017.pdf.download.pdf/A-2992-2017_WEB.pdf.

765 Bundesgericht, 5 May 2020, case number 1C 37/2019, available (in German) at https://entscheide.weblaw.ch/cache.php?link=05.05.2020_1c_37-2019&sel_lang=de.

766 See Greenpeace, European Court of Human Rights greenlights Swiss seniors' climate case, Press release, 26 March 2021, available at https://www.greenpeace.org/international/press-release/47031/european-court-of-human-rights-greenlights-swiss-seniors-climate-case/.

767 Bundesverfassungsgericht, Order of the First Senate of 24 March 2021, case number 1 BvR 2656/18 (ECLI:DE:BVerfG:2021:rs20210324.1bvr265618), an English translation of the decision is available at http://www.bverfg.de/e/rs20210324_1bvr265618en.html.

two environmental associations had brought the case before the court, claiming the unconstitutionality of the Federal Climate Change Act of the 12th of December 2019 ("Bundes-Klimaschutzgesetz").

With the Federal Climate Change Act, the German government had sought to implement the States' obligations under the Paris Agreement as well as the commitment to the long-term goal of greenhouse gas neutrality by 2050. Pursuant to para. 3(1) of the Act, GHG emissions must be gradually reduced by at least 55 % relative to 1990 levels by the target year of 2030. Paragraph 4(1) third sentence of the Act in conjunction with its Annex 2 sets out the annual allowable emission amounts for various sectors in line with the reduction quota for the target year 2030. Provisions applicable beyond 2030 are not contained in the Act. Rather, para. 4(6) KSG provides that in the year 2025, the government must set annually decreasing emission amounts for periods after the year 2030 by means of ordinances.[768]

Through their constitutional complaints, the plaintiffs primarily claimed that the state, in enacting para. 3(1) and para. 4(1) of the Federal Climate Change Act, has failed to introduce a legal framework that is sufficient for reducing emissions and fulfilling the goals of the Paris Agreement. While primarily – and in accordance with the Courts Jurisdiction – focusing their reasoning on provisions in the German Constitution ("Grundgesetz"), the plaintiffs also made reference to a wide range of international norms, including the preamble of the UNFCCC.[769]

The Court discarded the constitutional complaints of the two environmental associations arguing they have no standing to invoke the individual rights in questions. The Court also found that it cannot be ascertained that duties of protection arising from the right to life (Art. 2) and the right to property (Art. 14) of the German Constitution are violated due to the risks posed by climate change. This, the Court argued, was primarily due to the leeway afforded to the legislator in fulfilling these duties of protection.[770]

However, the Court did find that the legal mechanism under para. 3(1) and para. 4(1) of the Federal Climate Act outlined above, amount to a violation of

---

768 The original version of the Act was published in BGBl. I 2019, p. 2513.

769 The statement of claim of one group of plaintiffs is available (in German only) at https://www.greenpeace.de/sites/www.greenpeace.de/files/publications/verfassungsbeschwerde_final_fuer_web.pdf; see especially p. 24 et seqq. for references to the international legal instruments.

770 Bundesverfassungsgericht, Order of the First Senate of 24 March 2021, case number 1 BvR 2656/18 (ECLI:DE:BVerfG:2021:rs20210324.1bvr265618), para. 151 et seqq.

fundamental rights. In the Court's view, the two provisions specifying emission amounts until 2030 *"significantly narrow the emission possibilities available after 2030"* and thereby *"create disproportionate risks that freedom protected by fundamental rights will be impaired in the future"*: The Constitution would under certain conditions impose obligations to safeguard fundamental freedoms and rights over time and across generations. Hence, as *"intertemporal guarantees of freedom"*, fundamental rights would protect individuals against having emission reduction burdens *"unilaterally offloaded onto the future"*.[771] In this regard, the Court concludes that the legislator should have taken precautionary steps to ensure a transition to climate neutrality that respects freedom. The lack of such steps thus far would make the Act unconstitutional.[772]

The Court thus found that only one aspect of the Federal Government's climate policy is violating the constitution, which was considerably less than the plaintiffs had claimed. But the Court did define – for the first time in this degree of clarity – the constitutional requirements for the State's response to climate change.

The Court also made clear that the global nature of climate change, and the fact that the German state alone is incapable of halting climate change, does not rule out the possibility of a duty of protection arising from fundamental rights. In this regard, the decision echoed the Dutch *Urgenda* judgment.[773] Moreover, while not explicitly invoking the principle of inter-generational equity, the judgment developed a blueprint for future decisions on the impact of legislative actions on future generations. Both aspects are likely to shape the future legal response to climate change policies in Germany and may influence legal actions in other countries as well.

Another court case that serves as a final example of legislative and policy commitments being put into practice is from the Netherlands. The key particularity in this case was that the defendant was not a state, but a private corporation, namely, the Royal Dutch Shell (RDS) – the top holding company of the Shell group. In *Milieudefensie v Royal Dutch Shell*, a case was brought by public class action by *Milieudefensie* – the Dutch Branch of Friends of the Earth International – on behalf of itself, many individual claimants and six other NGOs.

Much like the *Urgenda* case, the claims brought before the court were primarily based on Dutch national (tort) law, but indirectly included references to

---

771 Ibid., para. 183.
772 Ibid., para. 251 et seqq.
773 Ibid., para. 149.

multiple international legal instruments as well as soft law norms. And like in the *Urgenda* case, so to did the Judgment by the District Court of The Hague.[774] Having established the – largely undisputed – impact of Shell's activities on the climate and the environment, the case revolved primarily around the question whether or not RDS had an obligation to reduce GHG emissions of the Shell group's energy portfolio.[775] The Court found that RDS has indeed an obligation to reduce the Shell group's emissions by 45 % by the end of 2030 relative to 2019 by influencing the corporate policy accordingly.[776] It moreover found that RDS is currently violating this obligation and, therefore, granted the claimed order for compliance with the emission reduction obligations.[777]

The Court grounded it's reasoning for the emission reduction obligations of a private corporation in the 'standard of care' in Dutch tort law. It further drew the interpretation of this from international law and the commitments made by the state on the international level.[778] Explicitly in line with the *Urgenda* case, the court i.a. referred to Articles 2 and 8 of the ECHR.[779] The court even included the mentioning of non-party stakeholders in the Paris Agreement in its assessment of the legal framework and the determination of the extent of RDS's emission reduction obligations.[780] This indirect application of international legal norms on climate change in determining the obligations of a private corporation as well as the extent of such obligations as found by the court, make the judgment a remarkable example of climate change litigation. Given that RDS has announced the intention to appeal the decision[781], its legal impact remains to be determined.

774 Rechtbank Den Haag, 26 May 2021, case number C/09/571932 / HA ZA 19-379, ECLI:NL:RBDHA:2021:5337, an English translation of the decision (ECLI:NL:RBDHA:2021:5339) is available at https://uitspraken.rechtspraak.nl/inziendocument?id=ECLI:NL:RBDHA:2021:5339.

775 Ibid., para. 4.1.1. et seqq.

776 Ibid., para. 4.1.4 and para. 4.4.55.

777 Ibid., para. 4.5.3.

778 Ibid., para. 4.4.1. et seqq.

779 Ibid., para. 4.4.9. et seq.

780 Ibid., para. 2.4.7. and 4.4.26. et seqq.

781 Shell, Shell Response to Climate Case verdict, Press release, 26 May 2021, available at https://www.shell.nl/media/persberichten/media-releases-2021/reactie-shell-op-uitspraak-klimaatzaak.html#english.

(b) Establishing Links Between Emissions and Impacts

Another salient trend can be discerned regarding climate change related international law being put into practice. This is, namely, to pursue cases meant to establish a causal relationship between emissions produced by a given actor, and the environmental damages arising from these. A case in point is *Lliuya v. RWE* in Germany[782]: Saúl Luciano Lliuya, a Peruvian farmer who lives in Huaraz, Peru, filed claims at the regional court ("Landgericht") of Essen, Germany. The claim was filed in November 2015 against RWE – a large German electricity producer – for declaratory judgment and damages. The claim concerned mountain glaciers which were melting near Mr. Lliuya's hometown. Specifically, a glacial lake located above Huaraz, had experienced a substantial volumetric increase since 1975, which had then accelerated since 2003. This presented an acute threat to the city of Huaraz. The suit was based on the claim that the company had knowingly contributed to climate change by its considerable GHG emissions. Therefore, RWE should bear some measure of responsibility for melting the mountain glaciers.

Mr. Lliuya's attorneys presented several legal theories in support of his claim. They acknowledged that RWE was only one contributor to the emissions responsible for climate change and thus for the adverse effect in question, the lake's growth. However, they asked the court to order RWE to reimburse Mr. Lliuya for a portion of the costs he and the Huaraz authorities had incurred to establish flood protections. That portion was calculated at the exact amount of 0.47 % of the costs, which is the same percentage as their estimate of RWE's annual contribution to global GHG emissions. The regional court in Essen declined Mr. Lliuya's request for declaratory judgment and injunctive relief in its order of the 15th of December 2016.[783] It argued that the plaintiff had failed to establish a linear causal chain considering the complexities of the causal relationship between particular GHG emissions and particular impacts.[784] Moreover, the court stressed, relying on an established line of reasoning in German civil jurisprudence, that the establishment of a clear causal link would be hindered by the excessive number of contributions to the damaging phenomenon.[785]

---

782 For a brief English summary, see http://climatecasechart.com/non-us-case/lliuya-v-rwe-ag/.

783 Landgericht Essen, 15 December 2016 – case number 2 O 285/15.

784 Ibid., para. 40 – 46.

785 Ibid., para. 44, („Bei einem solchen Übermaß an Kausalitätsbeiträgen können einzelne Schäden und Beeinträchtigungen ihren Verursachern nicht individuell zugeordnet werden").

What makes the case remarkable is that in the appeal, Mr. Lliuya has been more successful. On the 30th of November 2017, the Higher Regional Court ("Oberlandesgericht") Hamm, found the case to be well enough founded to be admissible.[786] Arguing that according to German civil law, even someone acting lawfully can potentially be held liable for harm to the property of others, the court found that further evidence should be gathered, especially through expert witness testimony. Here again, the concrete prospects of the case and claim are still unclear. The successful appeal only means that Mr. Lliuya has another opportunity to make his case. However, the fact that a Higher Regional Court regards the case as well founded and admissible is a major step in the effort to close an important accountability gap for climate change related damage.

What the case examples show is that efforts of strategic litigation in the field of climate change are seeing a growing willingness by courts to admit such cases. Especially in the field regarding the responsibility of private actors, where the law on the international level remains underdeveloped and is likely to remain as such, procedures like the one against RWE could set an example. Ultimately, making it expensive for companies not to adapt more climate change- aware policies. At the same time, however, the limits of such legal proceedings must not be forgotten. With their limited effect, exercised only on one specific actor, the long way from one sympathetic judge or court on a lower level to an enforceable court order, they cannot replace national legislation, let alone an effective international regulation.

2. Advancing Community Values in International Courts?

Finally, there is the remaining question of what role international adjudication could play in addressing the gap between the reduced role of law and the level of community value commitments.

(a) The International Court of Justice

First and foremost, the above question concerns the ICJ, which has a rather difficult standing in the climate regime by design to start with: In Art. 14, the UNFCCC contains a jurisdictional clause by which state parties, upon ratification, can indicate whether they accept the jurisdiction of the ICJ (Art. 14, para. 2(a))

786 Oberlandesgericht Hamm, Az. 5 U 15/17; Press release on the Court ordering evidence to be taken, 30 Nov 2017, available at https://www.justiz.nrw/JM/Presse/presse_weitere/PresseOLGs/archiv/2017_02_Archiv/30_11_2017_/index.php (German only).

or arbitration proceedings (Art. 14, para. 2(b)). Of the 195 state parties, only the Netherlands has opted in to the ICJ-jurisdiction.[787] The clause has therefore been of no practical use.

This is one of the major reasons why the debate about the possible contributions of the ICJ has largely been focusing on the instrument of an advisory opinion. An advisory opinion by the court can, according to Art. 96 (a) of the UN Charter, be requested by the UNGA or the Security Council on any legal question. Other UN organs or specialized agency also have a right to request an advisory opinion, but this being limited to the "legal questions arising within the scope of their activities" (Art. 96 (b)). Mirroring this right to request and pursuant to Art. 65 et seqq. of the ICJ statute, the court can give an advisory opinion on any legal question put before it.

In 1990, it was submitted that "[t]he goal of an advisory opinion or a case submitted by special agreement would be a declaration of law aimed at creating a structure for a new regime of global environmental protection. The new regime should make preventative action a priority, but should also provide for liability and compensation for the consequences of global warming." The respective authors hoped that "[t]he Court might even be persuaded to support a declaration of law with a ruling that the activities revealed by the evidence as causing global warming should be ceased, limited, controlled, or compensated. The Court might even address how the cost of any urgent remedial actions should be allocated among particular [S]tates or international organizations funded by [S]tates."[788] Some 22 years of climate regime development later, an attempt was made to fulfill at least parts of these ambitions. In 2012, the small, low-lying island- State of Palau started an initiative to bring the UNGA to ask the Court for an advisory opinion on international law and climate change. Especially, Palau sought to have the Court clarify the responsibilities of States under international law to ensure that GHG emissions under their jurisdiction do not cause damages to other States.[789] The effort by Palau was part of a campaign founded in 2011,

787 https://treaties.un.org/Pages/ViewDetailsIII.aspx?src=TREATY&mtdsg_no=XXVII-7&chapter=27&Temp=mtdsg3&clang=_en.

788 Zaelke and Cameron, "Global Warming and Climate Change – An Overview of the International Legal Process", p. 271.

789 UN, Press Conference on Request for International Court of Justice Advisory Opinion on Climate Change, 3 Feb 2012, available at https://www.un.org/press/en/2012/120203_ICJ.doc.htm.

involving practitioners, lawyers and academics.[790] Despite high hopes for the initiative, it did not lead to an advisory opinion by the Court. For the request to take place, a corresponding resolution would need at least a simple majority in the UNGA (Art. 18 et seqq. of the UN Charter). The issue has thus far not been put to a vote by the UNGA.[791]

Since 2012, the Paris Agreement has given new urgency to the question of legal obligations in the climate regime. This, in turn, also raises the question of the prospects of another attempt to obtain an advisory opinion from the ICJ.[792] There are indications that the chances for the Court to provide a 'helpful' opinion in the years to come could be better than in 2012. One such indication is the still growing public awareness for climate change. The Paris Agreement, its ramifications in public debates and extensive media coverage have contributed to this. Before the Paris Conference, the Encyclical letter of Pope Francis discussed earlier accelerated the public reception of climate change. While not decisive for judicial decisions, it is not completely unrealistic that this could have a certain influence on judges. A further indicator is the proliferation of court practice on the national and regional level, including the cases discussed earlier in this chapter. The legal questions raised and/or operated with by the courts involved could provoke a further motivation for some of these questions being clarified on the international level.

The ICJ's track record of politically contentious issues is ambivalent: In the 1996 *Nuclear Weapons opinion*, a reference to IEL[793] was made, but the Court did not conclude on the unlawfulness of the use of nuclear weapons. The "unhappy conclusion", as one commentator noted, that "you might be acting lawfully in extinguishing others if you yourself face extinction"[794] is not an indication

790 Douglas A. Kysar, "Climate Change and the International Court of Justice", *Yale Law School Public Law Research Paper* 315 (2013), p. ii.

791 According to Yale law school professor Douglas Kysar, who was involved with Palaus bid for an advisory opinion, the US government exerted what Kysar calls "significant diplomatic pressure to stop the resolution reaching the floor for a vote.", see Fred Pearce, "Should Polluting Nations Be Liable for Climate Damages?," Yale Environment 360 – Published at the Yale School of Forestry & Environmental Studies, https://e360.yale.edu/features/should_polluting_nations_be_liable_for_climate_damages.2013.

792 For a broad evaluation of the question, see Sands, "Climate Change and the Rule of Law", p. 27 et seq.

793 Legality of the Threat of Use of Nuclear Weapons, para. 29.

794 Sands, "Climate Change and the Rule of Law", p. 20, citing from the Advisory opinion the Court stating that "it cannot conclude definitively whether the threat of use of nuclear weapons would be lawful or unlawful in an extreme circumstance of self-defence,

that the Court would draw bold conclusions on the legal implications of climate change. In its 1999 advisory opinion on the Kosovo, it showed similar restraint concerning the politically contentious questions of a State declaring independence. On the other hand, the Court delivered an opinion on the Jerusalem Wall that has been received as surprisingly robust.[795] On environmental concerns, the 2014 decision that the Court had jurisdiction to review the whaling programs of Japan alongside the requirements of the 1946 Whaling Convention showed that the Court's reluctance is not without exceptions.[796] Overall, much can be said for the numerous accounts of the ICJ being rather cautious in its stance on progressive normative developments.[797] In recent years, cases like *Georgia v. Russia*[798] or the case between the Marshall Islands and India on nuclear disarmament[799] seem to confirm the Court's reluctance to engage in politically sensitive issues.

The possible contributions of the Court to the field of climate change are wide ranging. An important conceivable contribution would be if the Court would be ready to settle the scientific discourse with judicial authority: It could to give the – still often challenged – basic scientific insights about climate change the authority of a judicial determination of the facts.[800] Another area for clarification by the ICJ would be the more general obligations of States under the climate regime, which is the most important overlap with the subject of this study. As

in which the very survival of a State would be at stake" in the view of "the current state of international law, and of the elements of fact at its disposal", *Legality of the Threat of Use of Nuclear Weapons*, para. 105.

795 Malcolm D. Evans and Susan C. Breau, "Legal Consequences of the Construction of a Wall in the Occupied Palestinian Territory: Advisory Opinion, 9 July 2004", *ICLQ* 54, no. 4 (2005), p. 1003 et seqq.; critically, Michla Pomerance, "The ICJ's Advisory Jurisdiction and the Crumbling Wall between the Political and the Judicial", *AJIL* 99, no. 1 (2005), p. 26 et seqq., favorably, Iain Scobbie, "Words my Mother Never Taught Me – "In Defense of the International Court"", *AJIL* 99, no. 1 (2005), p. 76 et seqq.

796 *Whaling in the Antarctic* (Australia v. Japan: New Zealand intervening), Judgment, I.C.J. Rep. 2014, p. 226.

797 See, e.g., Hernández, "A reluctant guardian", p. 27 et seqq. with further reference and examples.

798 Application of the International Convention on the Elimination of All Forms of Racial Discrimination (Georgia v. Russian Federation), Preliminary Objections, Judgment, I.C.J. Rep. 2011, p. 70.

799 Obligations concerning Negotiations relating to Cessation of the Nuclear Arms Race and to Nuclear Disarmament (Marshall Islands v. India), Jurisdiction and Admissibility, Judgment, I.C.J. Rep. 2016, p. 255.

800 Sands, "Climate Change and the Rule of Law", p. 29.

elaborated above, many of the community value related norms remain unclear in their substance and, as such, are volatile in their acceptance by States. Hence, these norms are unlikely to gain further status under customary international law. Similarly, obligations, which are more general than norms, remain "crushingly vague [in] nature".[801] The Court could elaborate its stance on the '(well below) 2-degree goal' and the legal status of the overall objective of the climate regime more than 25 years into its practice. Finally, the court could elaborate on the relationship between the UNFCCC provisions and the existing international law on state responsibility.

It remains unclear whether the Court will get the opportunity to make such contributions to the field. Moreover, it remains uncertain whether the ICJ would use such an opportunity in the way many in favor of a new initiative are hoping for. The Court could also remain vague on important issues instead of delivering clarity. It could come to a similar conclusion as the present study that the substantive obligations stemming from the many community value related norms remain largely limited. In short, there are many ways in which an advisory opinion could halt norm development in the field. Especially, the Court could do so in the interest of not risking to reduce acceptance by States in times when not only parts of international law, but also the ICJ itself could come under political challenge.

(b) Other International Bodies

Apart from the ICJ, other international bodies are potentially capable of contributing to the further development of international law regarding community values and the climate regime. On the international level, the ITLOS is a potential candidate. For instance, its 2012 seabed chamber advisory opinion contributed to the development of the role of due diligence, the application of state responsibility and the role of *erga omnes* obligations in the field of the Law of the Sea.[802] Given the Law of the Sea's intersections with climate change in the areas of sea related pollution or the implications of rising sea levels, the Court could find various ways to contribute to the field if called upon. Further contribution could be made by regional courts with high reach and influence, especially human rights courts like the ECtHR or the European Court of Justice (ECJ). From the ECtHR, some decisions of the past could be cited as having laid the grounds for further

801 Ibid., p. 28.
802 Brunnée, "Procedural Aspects", p. 162.

human rights based jurisdiction relevant to the field of climate change.[803] But for all these efforts, similar limitations as discussed above on political cautiousness apply to the ICJ. Moreover, limits of reach and influence also apply for these courts. The ITLOS cannot exercise the same influence as the ICJ and regional courts are limited in the number of States any findings would apply to.

3. Climate Change Advocacy by NGOs

Finally in this context, the role of non-State actors, especially NGOs, should be considered. In particular in the 1990s, some argued that a valorisation and broader inclusion of NGOs could lead to a democratization of international relations.[804] Others have inversely focused their criticism on the NGOs, pointing to difficulties in overcoming their lack of legitimacy and transparency.[805] In the climate change context, NGOs gained significant influence in the late 1980s and early 1990s, and began exerting political influence on climate summits and negotiations.[806] According to the UNFCCC, the number of admissions of observer organizations has risen from 176 NGOs and 21 intergovernmental organizations

---

803 See *Lopez Ostra v. Spain*, App no. 16798/90, judgment 9 Dec 1994, para 51, where the Court noted that "severe environmental pollution may affect individuals' well-being and prevent them from enjoying their homes in such a way as to affect their private and family life adversely", signifying a potential violation of Art. 8 ECHR; see also *Taşkin and others v. Turkey*, App no. 46117/99, judgment 30 Mar 2005, where the court confirmed the obligation of States to conduct proper studies before allowing an activity which could cause environmental damage and making such studies publicly available. See furthermore, *Budayeva and Others v. Russia*, App no. 15339/02, judgment 29 Sep 2008, where the court found a violation of the right to life (Art. 2 ECHR) in a case where the authorities did not take preventive action when they were aware of an increased risk of large-scale damages.

804 Laura Macdonald, "Globalising Civil Society: Interpreting International NGOs in Central America", *Millennium* 23, no. 2 (1994), p. 267 et seqq.; Vikram K. Chand, "Democratisation from the Outside in: NGO and International Efforts to Promote Open Elections", *Third World Quarterly* 18, no. 3 (1997), p. 543 et seqq.

805 For an analysis of this line of NGO criticism and its merits, see Steve Charnovitz, "Nongovernmental Organizations and International Law", *AJIL* 100, no. 2 (2006) p. 363 et seqq.

806 Ronnie D. Lipschutz and Corina McKendry, "Social Movements and Global Civil Society", in *The Oxford handbook of climate change and society*, ed. John S. Dryzek, Richard B. Norgaard, and David Schlosberg (Oxford University Press, 2012), p. 370 et seq.

(IGOs) at COP 1 to 2133 NGOs and 126 IGOs at COP 23.[807] The Climate Action Network (CAN), an organization on its own as well as an international alliance of environmental groups, is an important example. Founded in 1989, it brings together over 1300 NGOs in more than 120 countries.[808]

In recent years, various social movements have added to the political pressure on governments to tackle climate change and to fulfill the commitments made on the international level. Salient examples are organizations like 'Fridays for Future' and 'Extinction Rebellion'.

'Fridays for Future' (also known as 'School Strike for Climate') was initiated by Swedish student Greta Thunberg who, in August 2018, went to protest in front of the Swedish parliament during school hours. Within months, her example was followed by more than one million students in over 110 countries.[809] Organized regionally, but also rather loosely, the movement advocates for more ambitious climate policies, especially in the interest of future generations who will be most affected by the effects of climate change.[810] Aside from setting up strikes, members of 'Fridays for Future' also engage in other forms of political – and judicial – activism. A leading representative of the German branch of the organisation, for instance, was part of the group of plaintiffs bringing the above-mentioned[811] case before the German Constitutional Court.[812] 'Extinction Rebellion' was founded in the United Kingdom in 2018, bringing together activists from multiple existing initiatives as well as scientists from a wide range of disciplines. Organized as a decentralized grassroots movement, 'Extinction Rebellion' engages in non-violent civil disobedience tactics – e.g. blocking five bridges across the river Thames in London in November 2018 – to draw further political attention to climate change and environmental degradation.[813] Both

807 UNFCCC, Statistics on Admission, Non-Party Stakeholders, available at: https://unfccc.int/process-and-meetings/parties-non-party-stakeholders/non-party-stakeholders/statistics-on-non-party-stakeholders/statistics-on-admission.

808 Climate Action Network, About, available at: http://www.climatenetwork.org/about/about-can.

809 BBC online, "School strike for climate: Protests staged around the world", 24 May 2019.

810 For a mission statement from the organisation itself, see https://fridaysforfuture.org/what-we-do/who-we-are/.

811 See already section D.III.1.

812 For an overview of the plaintiffs, see https://germanwatch.org/en/constitutional-complaint.

813 Matthew Taylor and Damien Gayle, "Dozens Arrested After Climate Protest Blocks Five London Bridges", *The Guardian*, 17 Nov 2018.

organizations, as different as they are in their approach and methods, show a growing willingness among civil societies to push for more effective political and legal action on climate change as well as an increasingly effective assemblage of international activist networks.

Recent examples from state practice have given causes for doubts, however, about the prospects of a broader role of NGOs in international relations: In the last years, a growing number of countries have implemented increasingly restrictive legislation on NGOs, including Russia[814], China[815] and India[816], European States like Hungary[817] or Poland[818] and South American countries like

814 In July 2012, Russia enacted the 'foreign agent' law ('On Amendments to Legislative Acts of the Russian Federation regarding the Regulation of the Activities of Non-profit Organisations Performing the Functions of a Foreign Agent'), requiring organisations receiving foreign funding to register with the public authorities as foreign agents. Moreover, organisations marked as 'foreign agents' are required to indicate this mark on every publication or oral statement they make available. Organisations marked as foreign agents are also under closer supervision, including a duty to submit more frequent reports and to undertake an annual mandatory auditing; See http://www.venice.coe.int/webforms/documents/default.aspx?pdffile=CDL-AD(2014)025-e, para 47.

815 In December 2016, China for the first time adopted a coherent piece legislation on foreign NGO activities that came into force in January 2017 (The "Overseas NGO Management Law".).

816 In 2010, the Foreign Contribution Regulation Act (FCRA) was enacted by the Indian Parliament. The country has been criticised, e.g. as summarized in a review by the Office of the United Nations High Commissioner for Human Rights, which cites allegations that the "FCRA had been used to disproportionately target and harass NGOs and activists critical of governmental priorities and policies, including Greenpeace, Lawyers Collective, and Sabrang Trust.", see A/HRC/WG.6/27/IND/3, para. 56.

817 Hungary implemented a legislation resembling the Russian 'foreign agents law' called the 'Law on the transparency of organizations funded from abroad', adopted on 13 June 2017, for an English translation of the most relevant sections of the law, see European Commission for Democracy through Law (Venice Commission), Hungary – Law on the Transparency of Organisations receiving support from abroad – adopted 13 June 2017, (2017) http://www.venice.coe.int/webforms/documents/default.aspx?pdffile=CDL-REF(2017)031-e.

818 Poland has introduced a bill indirectly dealing with foreign funding: The recently established 'National Freedom Institute-Center for the Development of Civil Society' – a government-related institution – will be responsible for assigning public funds, inter alia, from the European Union to Polish NGOs, see Claudia Ciobanu and Wojciech Kość, Warsaw grabs purse strings of Polish NGOs, Politico, 8 December 2017, available at https://www.politico.eu/article/pis-polish-ngos-fear-the-governments-embrace/; For the Polish original of the draft law setting up the institute,

Venezuela.[819] They either introduce new forms of restrictions, like in the cases of Hungary and Poland, or concretized pre-existing ones, like in the cases of Russia and China. Arguably, these are not only coincidental examples of certain governments acting restrictively on NGOs, but part of larger trend: A 2013 empirical study found that world-wide, out of 98 countries examined, 51 either prohibit (12) or restrict (39) NGO funding from abroad.[820] While NGO restrictions are often aimed primarily at Human Rights advocacy groups and organizations active in fields that are politically more controversial than climate change, examples such as the Indian regulation show that climate change-oriented groups are affected by this trend to the same extent.

Hence, while there are certainly examples of organizations being accepted as observing members in international fora, it seems reasonable to conclude that for the foreseeable future, the number of States with little interest in a more prominent role for NGOs in international relations remain the majority. Not only does this trend further exemplify a countermovement against the trend of the 1990s, it also has direct consequences for the idea of an international community. If the role of NGOs was central in the conception of a more community oriented and representative international realm, their restricted role begs the question of where the aspired representation of a broader range of actors should come from. A representation of individuals or non-state actors on the international realm more effective or more normatively grounded than the state thus remains unavailable.

This does not mean that there are no reasonable ways to include non-state actors and broaden the perspective of international relations and legal norms to

---

see Seyjm Rzeczypospolitej Polskiej, Druk Nr. 1713, available at http://orka.sejm.gov.pl/Druki8ka.nsf/0/C57CFC456352A1B5C1258155005FF00E/%24File/1713.pdf; For an English translation of the draft law, see Organisation for Security and Cooperation in Europe (OSCE), Annex to OSCE/ODIHR Opinion on the Draft Act of Poland on the National Freedom Institute – Center for the Development of Civil Society, Opinion-No.: NGO-POL/303/2017.

819 The Government passed the 'Defence of Political Sovereignty and National Self Determination Law' in 2010. The law does not concern all NGOs indiscriminately, but specifically aims at NGOs with a political purpose as well as political parties; See http://www.icnl.org/research/library/files/Venezuela/Leysober.pdf (text in spanish); http://www2.ula.ve/cja/images/stories/cja/ley_ong.pdf (Official Explanation of the law in spanish).

820 Darin Christensen and Jeremy M. Weinstein, "Defunding Dissent: Restrictions on Aid to NGOs", *Journal of Democracy* 24, no. 2 (2013), p. 80.

take individuals into account. The field of climate change is a good example for non-state actors – not only NGOs, but especially cities and other entities – filling important governance gaps and enhancing political processes.[821]

The considerations outlined above should be kept in mind when considering the further role of community structures. These considerations, in this field and more generally, exemplify the inherent limits of a systemically state-centered international legal system in accommodating a trend towards community value orientation.

4. Interim Conclusion

The assessment of the recent practice and future prospects of advancing community values in the climate regime by means of adjudication further confirms the analyzes of the historical evolution of the climate regime and the development of individual norm concepts comprising community values.

Recent trends in climate litigation show how the principles and commitments of States on the international level can serve as an important source of arguments for actors on the national and regional level, such as non-state organizations pursuing climate advocacy by legal means. Even norm concepts which have not gained substantive legal status on the international level can be influential, if not decisive, in such procedures. This shows how such norms can exercise judicial effect beyond their intrinsic limits. They show how far-reaching normative conceptions like the operationalized principles of the UNFCCC can be. This trend of using international commitments as a resource in legal proceedings could even be accelerated by the Paris Agreement. Putting the States back in control and making climate progress yet again more dependent on national implementation policies could indeed motivate more actors in climate litigation to focus on those policies in national courts. Therefore, the switch to a 'bottom-up' approach could go hand in hand with the trend of States being held accountable on the national level. In this field, future challenges include the strengthening of the legal basis on the various national levels. While there are indications that low-income countries are increasingly active on climate change litigation, and thus broadening the legal basis for climate action worldwide, there is low progress in other areas such

821 On the role of cities in this context, see Helmut P. Aust, "The Shifting Role of Cities in the Global Climate Change Regime: From Paris to Pittsburgh and Back?", *Review of European, Comparative & International Environmental Law* (2018), especially p. 5 et seqq.

as the inclusion of climate concerns in national development policies. This latter having only been realized by about 40 % of countries.[822]

Finally, the scope of application of the above-mentioned (national) laws and court proceedings is also their inherent and most relevant limitation for the matter at hand: These laws and cases are often a mixture of national civil and public law, only substantiated with international norms. By means of national legislation and national or regional jurisprudence, the desire to combat climate change can certainly be fostered; important contributions can be made, further awareness can be raised, and some national policies could be (positively) influenced. Notwithstanding the above, efforts at this level cannot, by design, replace action at the international level. That is not least because a rights-based approach to foster climate action, let alone based on and including community values, includes the risk of working only in States with a dense web of legislation and a stable court system based on the rule of law. Given how limited the number of States fulfilling such criteria will remain in the foreseeable future, climate litigation, to respond to The Guardian's question cited at the beginning of this section, will not 'save the world'.

What remains is the potential future contributions of international courts, which at this point necessarily remains speculative. But the factors that could incline the ICJ to deliver an advisory opinion fostering climate change law and the status of community values in the field also need to be juxtaposed with indications in the opposite direction. The historical reluctance of the Court to step into politically contentious questions is not without foundation. The ICJ, like the entire system of international law, depends on the continuing acceptance by States. Recent elections to the Court have shown that even the composition of the bench itself has become more politicized in recent years.[823] While the changes in the Court certainly could have the effect of classically developed countries exercising less influence in it, making the ICJ more perceptive to concepts such as equity or sustainable development, another effect is more likely: An increased caution by the Court, i.e. a tendency to refrain from fostering the development of international law beyond the sovereign decision by States to do so by treaty or custom, in order not to antagonise any group of States. As for other fora, the considerations

---

822 Nachmany et al., Global trends in climate change legislation and litigation: 2017 update (2017), p. 5.

823 On the failed re-election of British Judge Sir Christopher Greenwood, see Owen Bowcott, "No British Judge on World Court for First Time in Its 71-Year History", *The Guardian*, 20 Nov 2017.

for the ICJ also apply to a large extent to other court systems like ITLOS or even the ECtHR, which has been facing its own challenges in terms of acceptance. Finally, there is indication that the practices of the Security Council will remain the same in terms of not further pursuing climate change as a security issue or assuming law-making functions. This is consistent with the changing approach in the climate regime to (re-)attribute such responsibilities to the national level.

Hence, it is posited here, that in the foreseeable future the assessed gap between the community value-underpinning of the climate regime and the role of the law in their realization will not be closed by judicial action, on neither the national and regional level, nor on the international one.

IV. Conclusion Part D: Elements of Both 'Rise' and 'Decline' – Community Values and Legal Form Parting Ways in International Climate Law

Looking at community values in international climate change law, it becomes clear that the question of 'rise' or 'decline' is not a straightforward one. While a limited tendency of 'rise' in the set of politically accepted community values is discernible, a tendency of 'decline' presents itself concerning the role of the law. The gap in legal implementation between the two findings is further confirmed by recent trends in climate change and community value related judicial practice.

Tracing the developments of international climate change law historically has shown an overall shift from a strong emphasis on multilateralism, legal bindingness and value-underpinning in the 1990s towards a more informalised regime re-emphasizing national circumstances and flexibility. The period between the conclusion of the UNFCCC and the Kyoto Protocol is the peak of the climate regime overlapping with the progressive developments in the international law of the 1990s. The Kyoto Protocol translated these developments into comparatively wide-ranging legal obligations, which seems to have overstretched States' willingness to accept such a high level of legal bindingness at the international level. After the slow but steady demise of the Kyoto Protocol, a shift in emphasis is recognizable nearly from the start of the negotiations for the post-Kyoto-period. As of latest after the Copenhagen conference – which despite already being cautious, failed to produce a legally binding instrument capable of replacing the Kyoto Protocol – this shift gained the critical traction to bring about the much-discussed change from a 'top-down' to a 'bottom-up' approach in the climate regime. While – shaped from the debates in many democratic cultures – the notion of a 'bottom-up' approach is positively connoted standing for enhanced participation and legitimacy, in international law this move away from a 'top-down' approach signifies a lower level of legal bindingness and an overall reduced role of the law exercising its classical functions. At a first glance, this development is a clear-cut example of 'decline' as defined at the outset of this study.

This indication of 'decline', however, needs to be juxtaposed with the results of analyzing the various norm concepts identified as comprising community values to complete the perspective on the interconnection between community values and the structural challenges for international law. Here, a two-fold picture is discernable: On the one hand, there is a relatively stable overall level of inclusion of community value related norm concepts in the climate regime since the beginning of the 1990s. References to sustainable development have survived the changing regulatory approach, CBDR seems to have proven indispensable to climate negotiations and the notion of 'common concern' regularly resurfaces in important documents and debates at the international level. Discernibly, this stable acceptance by States for these concepts to be included is due to the important functions that they serve. Sustainable development has had a bridging function between the interests of developed and developing countries and has remained sufficiently vague ever since the UNFCCC negotiations for States not to fear negative legal effects from it. On the other hand, the 'common concern' notion is the counterexample for what happens when States begin to be anxious about potentially growing legal ramifications. Here, the deliberations in the Sixth Committee regarding the ILC reports on the protection of the atmosphere show such a high level of objection and concern raised by States that any debate about a customary legal status for the concept can be seen as settled for the foreseeable future. This case can serve as an example for what happens when the lines between legal and non-legal norms are blurred and how States will react to the consequential legal uncertainty. Inversely, this example also shows that where the development of such norm concepts does not cross the line of States feeling compelled to halt such normative developments, community value related norms can exercise a largely positive function. They can help build a stable consensus on the objectives of the regime and contribute to the ties that bind the massively diverse interests together. In this vein, even elements like the overall objective of the climate regime or the ambition to develop a 'shared vision' (Bali Action Plan) should not too easily be dismissed as irrelevant political rhetoric, as they help to provide a common reference frame for fostering political action.[824] In this

824 As in Brunnée and Toope, *Legitimacy and legality in international law*, p. 177, counting the 'shared vision' as an example for the development of *shared understandings* in the climate regime which can build the basis for further commitments.

limited sense, a 'rise' can be identified in the continuing value-underpinning of multilateralism in the climate regime.

These positive effects on state behavior in political terms, especially in IEL and climate law can, to a certain extent, mitigate the uncertainty caused by these norm concepts.[825] But the fierce debates on the 'common concern' concept and the tendencies they uncover in state practice contradict the often-drawn conclusion that international law has moved in a direction where these norms' capacity to influence policy decisions has become more important than their legal status.[826] This shows why the 'rise' in community values is limited as predominantly political, but also that the 'decline' of law does not mean that States no longer are mindful of the law's potential influence.

A similar conclusion can be drawn regarding the influence of community values on state sovereignty. States can be influenced by a value laden system like the climate regime, yet be insistent on their interest-based, sovereign flexibility. Meanwhile, good prospects for the norm concepts discussed to gain substantive legal status are to be found only where primarily procedural aspects are concerned. Indeed, the procedural side is the second way in which community value considerations can exercise a positive effect. Procedural requirements can fill gaps when substantive requirements lack specificity or when States are reluctant to invoke them. This is especially the case in the framework of treaty-based regimes like the UNFCCC, but goes beyond these regimes as well. For instance, procedural translations of community value considerations contribute to stabilizing ongoing practice between States which can strengthen the overall resilience of a legal regime in terms of acceptance.[827] Such a procedural implementation can serve as a technical bridge between the realm of classical international law. At the same time, they provide the necessary delimitation between the realm of law and substantive normatively ambitious concepts with little prospects to gain acceptance among States.

Finally, there is the influence of community values in climate law being put into practice by actors at levels other than the international realm, primarily by national and regional courts. Ultimately, the tendencies described there support

825 As in Beyerlin, "Different Types Of Norms in IEL", p. 447.
826 Ibid., who seems to arrive at just that conclusion, writing "Indeed [...] whether or not a given norm is a 'principle' and, thus, a norm with the capacity to guide decisions and the interpretations or application of existing rules may be more important to its potential impact than whether it is legally binding or not."
827 As in, Brunnée, "Procedural Aspects", p. 155.

the dialectical view deduced from the two other sections on historical evolution and substantive norm concept development. On the one hand, cases in which national courts recur to commitments made within the frame of norm concepts, such as CBDR, to substantiate decisions are good examples for the above-mentioned effect, specifically, of community value related norms exercising influence beyond the limits of the law. Here, non-state actors use these norms as an argumentative resource, ultimately influencing a court decision, which can then become influential on the governmental action of the state concerned. On the other hand, these instrumentally positive effects cannot detract from the fact that there is a growing gap between what international law itself does and can do in these fields and what the respective ambitions were in the period of the 1990s.

Part E: Conclusion

The conclusion of this study summarizes the key findings and issues in the preceding parts. Bringing these findings together, it supports the overall arguments regarding both the specific developments in the international legal regime on climate change showing elements of both 'rise' and 'decline' and highlights the implications which follow for the overall development of international law.

I. Summary of Findings

At the outset of this thesis, current challenges to the international legal order densified after the Cold War were chosen as the backdrop to the following analysis. The aim of the study was to contribute to the 'closer look' identified as necessary in order to see whether the international law developed after 1990 is on the 'rise' or in 'decline'. The following elements were identified as key in elaborating the overall perspective of 'rise or decline': the element of legal bindingness, the emphasis on multilateralism and the underpinning of the two with notions of values transcending the realm of state interests. Having identified the international climate change regime as a case in point for the emerging of community values and their grown importance in international law, especially after 1990, the study scrutinized its structural and conceptual development, as well as the implementation efforts in adjudication.

Against the backdrop of existing scholarly accounts on both the notion of 'international community' and the role of values in international law, the conceptual framework of the thesis was developed to focus on the three main areas of tension between the notion of community values and the structures of classical international law: The community itself, the idea of universalized values and the role of legal bindingness. In conjunction with the criteria for 'rise' and 'decline', this lens was applied on the structural and the community value-related conceptual development of the climate regime as well as such values' practical implementation. After delineating the historical background of the modern climate regime and the considerations making climate change a concise example for a matter of community values, the study turned to its main empirical part.

The historical background of climate change law and its interconnections as matter of community values makes it a relevant field to study international law's ability to organize, structure and regulate political action.

The main empirical part of this study identified a gap between a relatively stable level of acceptance for community value concepts in the field of climate change policy, but a tendency of 'decline' of legal form in the climate regime. The structural analysis of the regime's development has shown a steady trend from a strong and combined emphasis on multilateralism, legal bindingness and value-underpinning in the 1990s, towards a more informalised regime re-emphasizing national circumstances and flexibility is discernible up to the Paris Agreement. While this might foster political acceptance of the regime and leave the political commitment to many community value norms intact, it is nonetheless an overall shift indicating a 'decline' of international law as understood in the framework of this thesis.

The conceptual perspective on community value related norm concepts playing an important role in the climate regime offers a mixed picture, with some common denominators. While overall, there is a relatively stable level of inclusion of such norms in the key instruments of the regime and an apparently broad acceptance on a political level, the legal effect of community value related norms is very limited. Only where concepts could be translated into procedural norms, do there seem to be prospects of them finding legal application. This is rather stagnation than a 'decline' in comparison to the actual developments of the 1990s, but can be considered a 'decline' in comparison to some scholarly and political aspirations during that period.

Analyzing recent trends in climate change related adjudication practice, this gap between community value norms and their legal implementation is further confirmed. While some trends indicate implementation efforts on the national and regional level, none of them can be identified as promising effects comparable to a strong legal implementation on the international level. Similarly, possible action in international courts, especially an advisory opinion of the ICJ, could contribute to the legal development of the field, but cannot be expected to make up for the lack in legal substance brought about by the 'decline' identified.

Overall, when looking at community values in international climate change law, it becomes clear that the question of 'rise' or 'decline' is not a straightforward one. While a certain stability in the set of politically accepted community values is discernible, a tendency of 'decline' presents itself concerning the role of the law.

II. Prospects of Conceivable Reactions from Practice and Scholarship

A pertinent question remains about how responses to this finding could be envisioned, both in practice and in scholarship. As pointed to at the outset of this study, the issue of community value implementation through law is highly connected to the conceptual work surrounding the progressive international law development of the 1990s.

Considering the relationship between the emergence of community values and the development of the overall climate change regime, this section shall evaluate the conceivable ways forward in dealing with the structural and conceptual pitfalls of community values in international law. First, a further densification of international law including an expanding legal implementation will be discussed (1.). Then, as second conceivable way forward, a significant reduction of international law's ambition and the abandonment of the aspiration to accommodate community values in international law is evaluated (2.). Finally, the author suggests as a middle ground between the two, an approach combining the further proceduralisation of the community aspects of international law and an understanding of community values as 'meta'-norms in international law (3.).

1. More Law? The Plea for a Further Densification of International Law

A first reaction to tendencies of 'decline' in the structural importance of law could be the attempt to rectify the deficiencies of international law insofar as they are taken to be a problem. In recent international law scholarship, a "fortification of the power of international law" has both been predicted and declared necessary.[828] That is, the author argues, the expected changes in globalization, economic development, demography, technology and democracy would broaden the domain of international law. Consequentially, a more powerful and extensive international legal system – a "stronger version of international law" – would be needed to cope with these changes. This increased demand for legal responses to the growing complexities of international relations could be met by States providing greater legislative, adjudicative and executive authority to international organizations or the international legal system in general.[829] Consequentially,

828 Joel P. Trachtman, *The future of international law: Global government* (Cambridge University Press, 2013), p. 2.

829 Ibid., p. 253.

there should and would be a steady move from international governance to international government, meaning more formal rules and organisation.[830] Such pleas for more formal law and a fortification of international law fostering social causes are directly linked to the role and influence of community values in international law, as scrutinized in this study: If the proposed solution is to be an extension of formal law, hence a move from soft law to hard law, this would presumably also extend to many of the community value provisions analyzed in the case of climate change law.

Taking this thought further, the consequence would be a steady increase of the legal ramifications of community values. But, as the preceding case analysis shows, States are continuously reluctant to allow any such development. To some extent there is even a renewed reticence by at least a significant number of States to give community values a more prominent role in international law. Given this political reality which is likely to continue in the foreseeable future, the question remains how the idea of a fortification of international law applied to community values could look like. In absence of a realistic perspective to persuade the States to act differently, only a recourse to other actors seems plausible. International Courts are the most apparent example. But as shown for the example of climate change, significant progress in this regard by means of international adjudication is not very likely, even in a field as prominent in the international debate as climate change. Moreover, litigation on levels other than the international do not seem promising in this pursuit.

Hence, further contemplations about what could bring about a change towards more international law with more community values quickly lead back to larger meta-concepts like the constitutionalisation hypothesis. This would include a further move towards the reliance on sources of legitimacy for international law other than state consent. The exploration of such sources lies beyond the limits of this thesis. As for the current state of international law, it is submitted here that a fortification of international law regarding community values, in the sense of exceeding the material legal status of such norms, should not be the way forward. The results of the foregoing analysis suggest that the acceptance for such developments would not only be limited but could trigger further counter-reactions by States in forms of active efforts to limit the influence of such norms and the actors pursuing their implementation. Herein also lies the reason why the reliance on customary law in fostering community values should be handled

830 Ibid., p. 8.

with care.[831] Recent practice suggests that States are reluctant in accepting far-reaching value-laden norms gaining traction in customary international law.

2. Less Law? 'Back to the Roots' or 'Elements of Classical International Law Revisited'

"Know your limits. This familiar adage is not an inspirational rallying cry or a recipe for bold action. It serves better as the motto for the tortoise than the hare."[832] This scholarly remark was made in the context of discussing the Paris Agreement's comparatively modest legal character and acclaiming it as "a firmer foundation on which to build than its more ambitious predecessor, the Kyoto Protocol".[833] The Paris Agreement, in this reading, makes up in modest, technical effectiveness what it lacks in legal bindingness and ambitiousness. The apparent firm basis that the Agreement has in the acceptance by a large number of States, which exceeds initial expectations, seems to support the argument. The remark also speaks to a broader trend in international law scholarship which sees in the retreat of international law to its classical and less ambitious functions the appropriate legal answer to the social changes and political frictions of recent years. This could potentially lead to a more polycentric or non-polar world order.[834]

Many of the positions arguing for a return to more classical elements of international law share the assumption that international law must, by design, fail in realizing the common interest of the international community, let alone humanity.[835] As accurately summarized by Allot, that is because international law orders a "world fit for governments" – an "unsociety ruled by a collective of self-conceived sovereigns whose authority is derived neither from the totality of international society nor from the people but from the intermediating state systems".[836] Consequentially, the trends of the 1990s and early 2000s – often summarized as a mixture of more value-orientation, a broader range of actors and a wider range of subjects regulated by international law – are deemed to

831 Simma, "From bilateralism to community interest ", p. 324, already noting that "I myself at least have reached the conclusion that law-making by way of custom is hardly capable of accommodating community interest in a genuine sense".

832 Bodansky, "A New Hope?", p. 288.

833 Ibid., p. 289.

834 Krieger and Nolte, "The International Rule of Law – Rise or Decline? Points of Departure ", p. 6 et seq.

835 Brunnée, "Common Areas, Common Heritage, and Common Concern", p. 552.

836 Allott, *Eunomia: new order for a new world*, p. 249.

be responsible for the pressure the international legal system has come under by conflicting with the pre-conditions of the 'world fit for governments'. This explanation for phenomena often discussed under headers like 'backlash' then commonly leads to the conclusions that States are to be given (back) more control and that the role of non-state actors should be reduced. Furthermore, it is concluded that international courts should be more cautious in assuming jurisdiction over cases and in finding norms to have customary legal status. In short, States ought to be put 'back in the driver's seat'.

Against the backdrop of this study's results, there is reason to uphold a twofold perspective on this group of suggestions. Firstly, these arguments have some merit given the relationship between community values and international law. As discernible in the case study of the climate regime, the growing influence of the former on the latter has created tensions, at times even negatively impacting the state's willingness to further engage in the climate regime. Not by coincidence, the recent multilateral success – the Paris Agreement – came at the expense of loosening the legal bindingness of a legal framework deeply coined by its underpinning with community value related norms and principles. Thus, to point out the necessary mindfulness for the States' position and the limits of bilateralist international law accommodating community values is a valid point.

Conversely, neither scholarship nor practice should succumb to the temptation of 'throwing the child out with the bath water'. To put it in less conventional terms, the well-known image of the swinging pendulum can help in understanding and avoiding a conceivable overreaction. In a 1950 article, Austrian American jurist Josef Kunz applied this image to the perceptions of public international law comparing the 1920s to the late 1940s. He argued that in the 'Geneva spirit' of the 1920s, "legal arguments were at the core of every debate", which then lead to a period of discrepancy between this optimism and the sobering political circumstances during the 1930s.[837] With the adoption of the UN Charter system after World War II, in Kunz' view, the pendulum swung from an overestimation to an underestimation of the law's capacity, noting that "if the most undiplomatic

837 Josef L. Kunz, "The Swing of the Pendulum: From Overestimation to Underestimation of International Law", *AJIL* 44, no. 1 (1950), p. 137 et seq.; in a paragraph that could also have been written looking from today's perspective on the 1990s, he wrote: "[T]he more 'collective security' was shown to be non-existent, the more the utopian writers emphasized it. The more the facts were in contradiction to their writings, the more lyrical they grew. The confusion between lex lata and lex ferenda, the mistaking of often contradictory trends and tendencies for new rules of international law already established […] grew worse".

language, bitterness, invectives and political propaganda constitute realism, then there is plenty of realism".[838]

With all due caution in the use of historical analogies – especially to a period as turbulent as that between the two World Wars – both observations share a striking resemblance with the more recent developments in international law and, in particular, legal scholarship. In the 1990s, observations like that of the 'Geneva spirit' could be made, as there is 'plenty of realism' in today's world politics. From the many lessons to be learned from history, the one pertinent here is that neither *over*estimation nor *under*estimation are, by definition, *accurate* estimations. Hence, as much as the community value orientation of the 1990s can rightly be analyzed to have played a role in the creation of today's tensions, it should neither be discredited nor too easily abandoned. A careful analysis of a concrete pattern of applying and implementing community value norms shows that such an implementation can have positive effects, such as providing normative underpinning and fostering interaction between States and other actors under the umbrella of a legal framework. In insisting upon the necessary boundaries between the realm of hard law and that of often extra-legal value considerations, these positive effects should not be neglected.

3. Other Law! A Move Towards 'Proceduralisation' and Community Values as Meta-norms

Finally, a third perspective might strike a balance between the two, namely the perspective discussed here under the header of 'proceduralisation', while regarding community values as meta-norms. More accurately, these are different groups of scholarships from which it is posited here that by a common denominator can be drawn together.

As pointed out in section II of this part, it is key for any conception of international relations to accommodate the diverging interests of States or groups of States. This diversity of positions is not only a necessity, but also a desirable feature of the international community. The reservations expressed in (I.) towards a substantial fortification of international law implementing community values are directly linked to this thought. But, as Hurrell submitted, notwithstanding the positive aspects of diversity, "it is intellectually vacuous to celebrate difference and diversity in a closely integrated world without confronting the need to specify the general global principles and procedures by which interaction

838 Ibid., p. 139.

necessarily and unavoidably has to be regulated."[839] Following this, the pertinent question should not be whether community values should play a role in international law and international relations, but how a reasonable implementation should look like.

There are many ways in which community values can be implemented legally – from hard, substantial rules, to hard procedural rules with more flexible substance up to principles only providing the frame which is then filled by soft law rules. The examples of community value norms from climate law indicate that hard rules implementing community values have prospects of being accepted by the States only in rare cases. The reason can often be attributed to one of the following; they are overstretching the States' willingness to accept limitations to sovereignty, the contentious inclusion of a broader range of actors through the application of community value norms or that they are too culturally contingent to be accepted as universal.

In the conclusion of Part D (IV.), Lowe's suggestions regarding 'normative language' were discussed with a focus on normative language as a problem. There is, however, a more positive side to this perspective. Describing the evolution of sustainable development, he argues that its development can be characterized as that of a 'meta-principle'. Having emerged as such principle, it would have "a kind of interstitial normativity", meaning that it would be capable of "pushing and pulling the boundaries of true primary norms when they threaten to overlap or conflict with each other".[840] This aspect bears more general insights regarding norm concepts like sustainable development, or community value related norm concepts in general: The indirect sense in which Lowe ascribes "real normative force"[841] to sustainable development, is also fruitful for the more general phenomenon of community value related norm concepts. The perspective seeing them as 'modifying norms' or 'concepts' in Lowe's parlance, or meta-norms in the one chosen here, liberates such norms from the customary international law focus on state practice and opinio iuris, on which they would be entirely depending if one were to search for their influence only in their direct application, e.g., by courts, alongside any traditionally structured rule of international

---

839 Hurrell, *On global order*, p. 298.

840 Lowe, "Sustainable Development and Unsustainable Arguments", p. 31; Lowe puts *sustainable development* in his category of 'modifying norms', which he regards as designed to regulate the relationships between other primary norms. The term 'modifying norms' in Lowe's use is equipollent to that of 'interstitial norms', cf. p. 33.

841 Ibid., p. 33.

law. Community values can, in this vein, build a prism for actors applying international law to look through. This does not, by any means, prevent the possibility of community value norms also being translated or transformed into primary norms of international law or rules in the classical sense. But this differentiation is both useful and necessary to draw appropriate lines between these realms of normativity and increase the overall acceptance of them.

Both the procedural aspects of international law and the building of 'shared understandings' – interwoven with the notion of community values applied in this study – play an important role in the approach of Brunnée and Toope. Insisting that their 'interactional international law' "is not founded on any presumption of universally shared values", they submit that "it is possible to build procedural law that shapes the parameters of social relations, even with only weak shared values." According to them, what it requires "to begin the process of law-building in international society is a shared understanding that law is needed in a given context".[842] Central to the further development of such understandings, in their approach, is procedural interaction. Over time, the resulting practice "can become more interconnected and value-based, allowing for richer substantive rules."[843] Brunnée has applied this line of thinking on the procedural aspects of 'community interests' in IEL. Especially procedural aspects of treaty regimes, she submitted, are not mere concealments of lacking substantive obligations, but instead serve community interests in their own way. By facilitating continued practice within the regime, they could help cultivate and adapt substantial obligations. Strong procedural elements, she concludes, are "indispensable to the law's capacity to serve community interests."[844]

Drawn together, this results in an approach of proceduralisation and regarding community values as meta-norms in international law, which seems to be the most promising approach of the three presented here. The focus on procedure and process allows for community values to be translated into applicable legal rules, even in fields of international law that are either too contentious, or simply too complex to accommodate all contingencies in substantial rules. Regarding community values behind such (procedural) legal rules as meta-norms allows for a precise differentiation between the possible roles of community value norms and an advancement of their acceptance as it avoids the blurring of boundaries between lex late and lex feranda. Climate change is not the only

842 Brunnée and Toope, *Legitimacy and legality in international law*, p. 354 et seq.
843 Ibid., p. 87.
844 Brunnée, "Procedural Aspects", p. 175.

phenomenon that is too complex in structure, levels and number of actors involved for international law to exercise the same role it has had in classical inter-state application, for instance think of the law of diplomatic relations. Especially in aiming at preserving the classical functions of public international law in such areas where it cannot realistically work substantively the same way as it used to, this combination offers a pragmatic way forward. A shift towards framing principles and more proceduralised rules therefore does not necessarily mean a weakening of the international legal framework.

III. Overall Concluding Remark: The Usefulness of Community Values and the Limits of Legal Practice Accommodating Them

Climate change, Ulrich Beck posited, could lead to a revaluation of values, "turning the system of value orientation upside down – […] to a historical new fixed star by which to mobilize solidarities and actions […] because the global climate risk contains a sort of navigation system in the otherwise storm-tossed seas of cultural relativism".[845] Climate change as a phenomenon, in this vein, could alter the ways in which we conceive of certain political questions, problems and interdependencies. Through this, a process of norm creation could unfold that is potentially capable of re-shaping the way in which humankind is assuming responsibility for the effects of the climate change it induced. The question, as Beck remarks, is if "that active, sub-political and political metamorphosis is fast enough to counter the galloping process of climate catastrophes that might throw the entire planet into droughts, floods, chaos, starvation and bloody conflicts."[846]

International climate *law* is a reminder that international law cannot do and accomplish everything. But it is submitted here that such beliefs and aspirations, especially in the 1990s, always were an overestimation of the law – a swing of the pendulum a little too far in a 'positive direction'. But climate law also teaches us why the consequence should not be to let the pendulum swing too far into the opposite direction, explicitly, of international law receding to its basic and minimalistic roots. Theoretical lenses including constructivist perspectives like the 'culture of legality' show how international law can, in a sense, have effects 'beyond itself' – i.e., how it can shape without exercising classically binding

845 Beck, *Metamorphosis*, p. 43 et seq.
846 Ibid., p. 47.

functions. This idealistic side of the spectrum can draw on the insight that lack of ambition barely ever led to discernible progress. Legal instruments can be an important resource for various political as well as legal actors to draw upon in the promotion of community values. Hence, combining classical structures and community values necessarily means that a law including community values will not always function in the exact same way as it did without them. However, if executed prudently, this change does not necessarily indicate a further 'decline' but instead can be an instrument for positive change. Beside the development of proceduralised community value-based norms, e.g., by international courts, more substantial norms can be fostered in their development by civil society actors, businesses, cities and beyond. That such latter fora are rather informal, would signify a further decline of international law and legal form. Certainly, both the developments and the normative conclusions drawn above signify a decline in comparison to many of the expectations regarding international law in the 1990s. But, like submitted at the outset of this study, this notion of decline is not congruent with undesirable. Acknowledging the limits of international law in the context of community values could even strengthen the stability of international law as a regulatory system. The example of climate law shows that the current changes are neither impossible to positively shape nor that they a clear indicators of community value-oriented multilateralism's demise. We see in the field of climate change a roving between different layers of norms and a certain confirmation of those norm theories in international law and international relations scholarship that insist on the dynamic of international norm making and the influence that many different actors have on it. The historical example of the UNFCCC regime shows that there are instances where structurally weaker States have an interest in a principle-based formulation of parts of international agreements.

This, in turn, can only work if the limits of formal law are heeded: If community value-elements are forced into classical legal instruments and sources – often by prematurely insisting on status like general principles of law or customary obligations (*erga omnes*) –, States are likely to be less inclined to accept the legal status of those norms. On a larger scale, this can cause the decline of international law as a regulatory system. In sum, from a normative perspective, the developments analyzed here are rather a transformation than a decline. There is, however, a clearly discernible decline in comparison to the ambition of an international law that can to the same degree accommodate normatively ambitions values and produce substantial legal obligations. "The world community" Villalpando observed, "is not yet ready to change […] an international law centred on the figure of the state as the principal subject, and the preservation of sovereignty continues to be one of the fundamental objectives of the system." "As a consequence", he wrote, "the change which is brought about by the emergence of community interests needs to take into account the fact that the legal system will remain the same."[847] According to the view advanced here, he is right in many regards. This does not mean, however, that there are not ways in which the concept of community values can meaningfully contribute to the development of international law. Whether this is possible or not, is a matter of balance and differentiation.

As made clear when devising the conceptual frame of this study, community values neither introduce values into international law, nor do they necessarily conflict with individual state interests. Sometimes there will be an overlap. But in other instances, they cannot both be fulfilled at the same time.[848] Given the absence of a supranational institution that could reliably and authoritatively resolve conflicts between community values and individual state interests where they arise, the mechanisms to resolve such conflicts need to be found within the existing, bilateralist structures of international law. At the outset of this study, a caveat was made regarding the risk of overestimating one's own time. Mindful of this risk, one can reasonably observe that international law is in currently going through a critical period of its history. One can only urge those entrusted with influence over its further development to exercise it responsibly.

847 Villalpando, "The legal dimension of the international community", p. 414 et seq.
848 Ibid., p. 417.

Bibliography

Abbott, Kenneth W., and Duncan Snidal. "Hard and Soft Law in International Governance." *International Organization* 54, no. 03 (2000): 421–56.

Abbott, Kenneth W., Robert O. Keohane, Andrew Moravcsik, Anne-Marie Slaughter, and Duncan Snidal. "The Concept of Legalization." *International Organization* 54, no. 03 (2000): 401–19.

Adede, Andronico O. "The Treaty System from Stockholm (1972) to Rio de Janeiro (1992)." *Pace Environmental Law Review* 13, no. 1 (1995): 33.

Allott, Philip. *Eunomia: New order for a new world.* Oxford University Press, 1990.

Alter, Karen J. "The Contested Authority and Legitimacy of International Law: The State Strikes Back." *iCourts Working Paper Series* 134 (2018), Available at SSRN: https://ssrn.com/abstract=ct =3204382.

Aquinas, St. Thomas. *St. Thomas Aquinas: Political Writings,* edited by R. W. Dyson. Cambridge Texts in the History of Political Thought ed.: Cambridge University Press, 2002.

Arajärvi, Noora. "The Requisite Rigour in the Identification of Customary International Law – A Look at the Reports of the Special Rapporteur of the International Law Commission." *International Community Law Review* 19, no. 1 (2017): 9–46.

Aust, Helmut P. "The Shifting Role of Cities in the Global Climate Change Regime: From Paris to Pittsburgh and Back?." *Review of European, Comparative & International Environmental Law* (2018): 1–10.

Barrett, Scott. "The Paris Agreement: We Can Do (and Have Done) Better." In *Paris agreement and beyond: International climate change policy post-2020*, edited by Robert N. Stavins and Robert C. Stowe. Cambridge, MA: Harvard Project on Climate Agreements, 2016.

Barry, Brian. "Statism and Nationalism: A Cosmopolitan Critique." *Global Justice* 41 (1999): 12–66.

Bauerschmidt, Jonathan, Bardo Fassbender, Michael Wolfgang Müller, Angelika Siehr, and Christopher Unseld. *Konstitutionalisierung in Zeiten globaler Krisen*. Vol. 1: Nomos, 2015.

Beck, Ulrich. *The metamorphosis of the world.* Polity Press, 2016.

Benhabib, Seyla. "In Defense of Universalism: Yet Again! A Response to Critics of Situating the Self." *New German Critique* 62 (1994): 173–89.

Bernstein, Steven. *The compromise of liberal environmentalism.* Columbia University Press, 2001.

Besson, Samantha, and Jean d'Aspremont. "The Sources of International Law: An introduction." In *The Oxford handbook on the sources of international law*, edited by Samantha Besson, Jean d'Aspremont and Sévrine Knuchel: Oxford University Press, 2017.

Betsill, Michele, Navroz K. Dubash, Matthew Paterson, Harro Van Asselt, Antto Vihma, and Harald Winkler. "Building Productive Links between the UNFCCC and the Broader Global Climate Governance Landscape." *Global Environmental Politics* 15, no. 2 (2015): 1–10.

Beyerlin, Ulrich. "Different Types of Norms in International Environmental Law Policies, Principles, and Rules." In *The Oxford handbook of international environmental law*, edited by Daniel Bodansky, Jutta Brunnée and Ellen Hey: OUP, 2008.

———. "Sustainable Development." In *Max Planck Encyclopedia of Public International Law online [MPEPIL]*, edited by Rüdiger Wolfrum: Oxford University Press, 2013.

Beyerlin, Ulrich, and Thilo Marauhn. *International environmental law*. 1. print ed.: Hart u.a., 2011.

Biniaz, Susan. "Comma but Differentiated Responsibilities: Punctuation and 30 Other Ways Negotiators Have Resolved Issues in the International Climate Change Regime." *Mich. J. Envtl. & Admin. L.* 6 (2016): 37.

———. "I Beg to Differ: Taking Account of National Circumstances under the Paris Agreement, the ICAO Market-Based Measure, and the Montreal Protocol's HFC Amendment." *Sabin Center for Climate Change Law, Columbia Law School* (2017). http://columbiaclimatelaw.com/files/2017/01/Biniaz-2017-01-Taking-Account-of-National-Circumstances.pdf.

Bodansky, Daniel. "Deconstructing the Precautionary Principle." In *Bringing new law to ocean waters*, edited by David D. Caron and Harry N. Scheiber: Leiden: Brill [online], 2004.

———. "Elaborating the Paris Agreement's Rules." In *Paris agreement and beyond: International climate change policy post-2020*, edited by Robert N. Stavins and Robert C. Stowe: Cambridge, MA: Harvard Project on Climate Agreements, 2016.

———. "The History of the Global Climate Change Regime." In *International relations and global climate change*, edited by Urs Luterbacher and Detlef F. Sprinz: MIT Press, 2001.

———. "The Legal Character of the Paris Agreement." *Review of European, Comparative & International Environmental Law* 25, no. 2 (2016): 142–50.

———. "The Paris Climate Change Agreement: A New Hope?." *American Journal of International Law* 110, no. 2 (2016): 288.

———. "The United Nations Framework Convention on Climate Change: A Commentary." *Yale J. Int'l l.* 18 (1993): 451.

———. "What's in a Concept? Global Public Goods, International Law, and Legitimacy." *European Journal of International Law* 23, no. 3 (2012): 651–68.

Bodansky, Daniel, Jutta Brunnée, and Lavanya Rajamani. *International climate change law*. Oxford University Press, 2017.

Bodansky, Daniel, and Lavanya Rajamani. "The Evolution and Governance Architecture of the United Nations Climate Change Regime." In *Global Climate Policy: Actors, Concepts, and Enduring Challenges*, edited by Detlef F. Sprinz and Urs Luterbacher: MIT Press, 2018.

Boer, Ben. "The Rise of Environmental Law in the Asian Region." *University of Richmond Law Review* 5 (1999): 1503.

Bowcott, Owen. "No British Judge on World Court for First Time in Its 71-Year History." *The Guardian*, 20 Nov 2017 2017.

Boyle, Alan E. "International Law and the Protection of the Global Atmosphere: Concepts, Categories and Principles." In *International Law and Global Climate Change*, edited by Robin Churchill and David Freestone: Graham and Trotman, 1991.

———. "Some Reflections on the Relationship of Treaties and Soft Law." *International & Comparative Law Quarterly* 48, no. 4 (1999): 901–13.

Bradley, Curtis A. *International law in the U.S. legal system*. Oxford University Press, 2013.

Brown, Chris, Kirsten Ainley, and Chris Brown. *Understanding international relations*. Palgrave Macmillan, 2009.

Brown Weiss, Edith. "The Coming Water Crisis: A Common Concern of Humankind." *Transnational Environmental Law* 1, no. 1 (2012): 153–68.

———. "In Fairness to Future Generations and Sustainable Development." *Am. U. J. Int'l L. & Pol'y* 8, no. 1 (1992): 19.

———. "Intergenerational Equity." In *MPEPIL*, edited by Rüdiger Wolfrum: Oxford University Press, 2013.

Brunnée, Jutta. "Climate Change, Global Environmental Justice and International Environmental Law." In *Environmental law and justice in context*, edited by Jonas Ebbesson and Phoebe Okowa: Cambridge University Press, 2009.

———. "Common Areas, Common Heritage, and Common Concern." In *The Oxford handbook of international environmental law*, edited by Daniel Bodansky, Jutta Brunnée and Ellen Hey: OUP, 2008.

———. "'Common Interest' – Echoes from an Empty Shell? – Some Thoughts on Common Interest and International Enviornmental Law." *Zeitschrift für ausländisches Öffentliches Recht und Völkerrecht* 49 (1989): 791–808.

———. "International Environmental Law and Community Interests – Procedural Aspects." In *Community interests across international law*, edited by Eyal Benvenisti and Georg Nolte: Oxford University Press, 2018.

———. "The Sources of International Environmental Law: Interactional Law." In *Oxford handbook on the sources of international law*, edited by Samantha Besson and Jean d'Aspremont: Oxford University Press, 2017.

Brunnée, Jutta, and Stephen J. Toope. *Legitimacy and legality in international law: An interactional account*. Cambridge University Press, 2010.

Buzan, Barry. *An introduction to the English school of international relations: The societal approach*. Polity, 2014.

Cameron, James, and Juli Abouchar. "The Precautionary Principle: A Fundamental Principle of Law and Policy for the Protection of the Global Environment." *BC Int'l & Comp. L. Rev.* 14, no. 1 (1991): 1.

Carrington, Damian. "Can Climate Litigation Save the World?" *The Guardian*, 20 March 2018.

Chand, Vikram K. "Democratisation from the Outside in: NGO and International Efforts to Promote Open Elections." *Third World Quarterly* 18, no. 3 (1997): 543–62.

Charnovitz, Steve. "Nongovernmental Organizations and International Law." *AJIL* 100, no. 2 (2006): 348–72.

Chen, Lung-chu. *An introduction to contemporary international law: A policy-oriented perspective*. 3rd ed.: Oxford University Press, 2015.

Chimni, B. S. "International Institutions Today: An Imperial Global State in the Making." *EJIL* 15, no. 1 (2004): 1–37.

Christensen, Darin, and Jeremy M. Weinstein. "Defunding Dissent: Restrictions on Aid to NGOs." *Journal of Democracy* 24, no. 2 (2013): 77–91.

Christoff, Peter. "The Promissory Note: COP 21 and the Paris Climate Agreement." *Environmental Politics* 25, no. 5 (2016): 765–87.

Clark, Pilita. "China Warns Trump against Abandoning Climate Change Deal." *Financial Times*, 11 Nov 2016, 2016.

Claude, Inis L. *Swords into plowshares: The problems and progress of international organization*. 4th ed.: Random House, 1971.

Commission on Environmental Law of IUCN – The World Conservation Union in Cooperation with the International Council of Environmental Law. *Draft international covenant on environment and development*. 3rd ed. Vol. 31, Rev. 2 Environmental Policy and Law Paper IUCN, 2004.

Commission), European Commission for Democracy through Law (Venice. "Hungary - Law on the Transparency of Organisations Receiving Support from Abroad –Adopted 13 June 2017." In *CDL-REF(2017)031*, 2017 http://www.venice.coe.int/webforms/documents/default.aspx?pdffile=CDL-REF(2017)031-e.

Cox, Roger. "A Climate Change Litigation Precedent: Urgenda Foundation v The State of the Netherlands." *Journal of Energy & Natural Resources Law* 34, no. 2 (2016): 143–63.

D'Amato, Anthony. "Do We Owe a Duty to Future Generations to Preserve the Global Environment?." *AJIL* 84, no. 1 (1990): 190–98.

d'Aspremont, Jean. "The Foundations of the International Legal Order." *Finnish Yearbook of International Law* 18 (2007): 219–55.

———. "International Law in Asia: The Limits to the Western Constitutionalist and Liberal Doctrines." *Asian Yearbook of International Law* 13 (2007): 89–111. Available at SSRN: https://ssrn.com/abstract=1266065.

Davison, W. Phillips. "Public Opinion." In *Encyclopædia Britannica online*, edited by Dale H. Hoiberg: Encyclopædia Britannica, inc., 2017.

De Vitoria, Francisco. *Vitoria: Political writings*, edited by Anthony Pagden and Jeremy Lawrence. Cambridge Texts in the History of Political Thought ed.: Cambridge University Press, 1991.

De Wet, Erika. "The Emergence of International and Regional Value Systems as a Manifestation of the Emerging International Constitutional Order." *Leiden Journal of International Law* 19, no. 3 (2006): 611–32.

———. "Entrenching International Values Through Positive Law: The (Limited) Effect of Peremptory Norms." In *A metamorphosis of international law – tracing value changes in the international legal order from the perspectives of legal and political science (Forthcoming)*, edited by Heike Krieger and Andrea Liese: KFG Working Paper Series, No. 25, Berlin Potsdam Research Group "The International Rule of Law – Rise or Decline?", 2019.

De Wet, Erika, and Jure Vidmar, eds. *Hierarchy in international law: The place of human rights*: OUP, 2012.

Deitelhoff, Nicole, and Lisbeth Zimmermann. *Things we lost in the fire: How different types of contestation affect the validity of international norms*. Frankfurt am Main: Hessische Stiftung Friedens- und Konfliktforschung (Ed.), 2013 http://nbn-resolving.de/urn:nbn:de:0168-ssoar-455201.

Delbrück, Jost. "The International Obligation to Cooperate –An Empty Shell or a Hard Law Principle of International Law? – A Critical Look at a Much

Debated Paradigm of Modern International Law." In *Coexistence, cooperation and solidarity – Liber Amicorum Rüdiger Wolfrum*, edited by Holger P. Hestermeyer, Doris König, Nele Matz-Lück, Volker Röben, Anja Seibert-Fohr, Peter-Tobias Stoll and Silja Vöneky: Martinus Nijhoff Publishers, 2012.

Dewar, Helen, and Kevin Sullivan. "Senate Republicans Call Kyoto Pact Dead." *The Washington Post*, 11 Dec 1997, 1997, A37.

Drezner, Daniel W. "The New New World Order." *Foreign Affairs* 86, no. 2 (2007): 34–46.

Drezner, Daniel W. "Why the Trump Administration Hates Multilateral Trade Agreements the Most." *The Washington Post*, 9 Mar 2017, 2017.

Dunne, Timothy. "The Social Construction of International Society." *European Journal of International Relations* 1, no. 3 (1995): 367–89.

Dupuy, Pierre-Marie. "Formation of Customary International Law and General Principles." In *The Oxford handbook of international environmental law*, edited by Daniel Bodansky, Jutta Brunnée and Ellen Hey: Oxford University Press, 2008.

———. "Où en est le droit international de l'environnement à la fin du siècle?." *Revue générale de droit international public* 101 (1997): 873.

———. "Some Reflections on Contemporary International Law and the Appeal to Universal Values: A Response to Martti Koskenniemi." *European Journal of International Law* 16, no. 1 (2005): 131–37.

Dupuy, Pierre-Marie, and Jorge E. Viñuales. *International environmental law: A modern introduction*. Cambridge University Press, 2015.

Dupuy, René-Jean. *La Communauté internationale entre le mythe et l'histoire*. Economica, 1986.

Dworkin, Ronald. "A New Philosophy for International Law." *Philosophy & Public Affairs* 41, no. 1 (2013): 2–30.

———. *Taking rights seriously*. Duckworth, 1977.

Eckersley, Robyn. "Moving Forward in the Climate Negotiations: Multilateralism or Minilateralism?." *Global Environmental Politics* 12, no. 2 (2012): 24–42.

European Commission. "Special Eurobarometer 459 'Climate Change' - Report." In *Survey conducted by TNS political & social at the request of the European Commission, Directorate-General for Climate Action (DG CLIMA)*, 2017 https://ec.europa.eu/clima/sites/clima/files/support/docs/report_2017_en.pdf.

Evans, Malcolm D., and Susan C. Breau. "Legal Consequences of the Construction of a Wall in the Occupied Palestinian Territory: Advisory Opinion, 9 July 2004." *ICLQ* 54, no. 4 (2005): 1003–13.

Falk, Richard A. *Status of law in international society*. Princeton University Press, 1970.

Fallon Jr., Richard H. "Reflections on Dworkin and the two faces of law." *Notre Dame L. Rev.* 67, no. 3 (1991): 553–85.

Fassbender, Bardo. "The United Nations Charter as Constitution of the International Community." *Colum. J. Transnat'l L.* 36 (1998): 529.

Fastenrath, Ulrich. "Relative Normativity in International Law." *EJIL* 4 (1993): 305.

Finnemore, Martha, and Judith Goldstein. "Power Politics in the Contemporary World – Lessons from the Scholarship of Stephen Krasner." In *Back to basics: State power in a contemporary world*, edited by Martha Finnemore and Judith Goldstein: Oxford University Press, 2013.

Finnemore, Martha, and Kathryn Sikkink. "International Norm Dynamics and Political Change." *International Organization* 52, no. 04 (1998): 887–917.

Fitzmaurice, Malgosia. "Responsibility and Climate Change." *German Yearbook of International Law* 53 (2010): 89.

Fleming, James Rodger. *Historical perspectives on climate change*. Oxford University Press, 2005.

Francioni, Francesco. "Equity in International Law." In *MPEPIL*, edited by Rüdiger Wolfrum: Oxford University Press, 2013.

Francis, I. "Laudato Si: On Care for Our Common Home." In *Encyclical Letter of 6 Oct 2015*, 2015.

Franck, Thomas M. *Fairness in international law and institutions*. Clarendon Press, 1995.

Freestone, David. "The Precautionary Principle." In *International law and global climate change*, edited by Robin Churchill and David Freestone: Graham&Trotman / Martinus Nijhoff, 1991.

French, Duncan. "Common Concern, Common Heritage and Other Global(-ising) Concepts: Rhetorical Devices, Legal Principles or a Fundamental Challenge?." In *Research Handbook on Biodiversity and Law*, edited by Michael Bowman, Peter Davies and Edward Goodwin: Edward Elgar, 2016.

French, Duncan, and Lavanya Rajamani. "Climate Change and International Environmental Law: Musings on a Journey to Somewhere." *Journal of Environmental Law* 25, no. 3 (2013): 437–61.

Friedmann, Wolfgang. *The changing structure of international law*. Columbia University Press, 1964.

Friends of the Earth. "Copenhagen: A Disaster for the World's Poorest." *News release*, 17 Dec 2009, 2009, https://www.foei.org/no-category/copenhagen-a-disaster-for-the-worlds-poorest.

Frowein, Jochen. "Konstitutionalisierung des Völkerrechts." *Völkerrecht—Menschenrechte—Verfassungsfragen Deutschlands und Europas* (2004): 173–98.

———. "Obligations Erga Omnes." In *MPEPIL*, edited by Rüdiger Wolfrum: Oxford University Press, 2008.

Gaja, Giorgio. "General Principles of Law." In *MPEPIL*, edited by Rüdiger Wolfrum: Oxford University Press, 2013.

Gardiner, Stephen M. "A Perfect Moral Storm: Climate Change, Intergenerational Ethics and the Problem of Moral Corruption." *Environmental Values* 15 (2006): 397–413.

Gardiner, Stephen Mark. *A perfect moral storm: The ethical tragedy of climate change*. Oxford University Press, 2011.

Gatmaytan, Dante B. "The Illusion of Intergenerational Equity: Oposa v. Factoran as Pyrrhic Victory." *Georgetown International Environmental Law Review* 15, no. 3 (2003): 457.

Gemenne, François. "L'environnement, nouveau facteur de migration?." In *L'enjeu mondial*, edited by François Gemenne: Presses de Sciences Po (PFNSP), 2009.

———. "One Good Reason to Speak of 'climate refugees'." *Forced Migration Review* 49 (2015): 70.

Goldsmith, Jack L., and Eric Posner. *The limits of international law*. Oxford University Press, 2007.

Grote, Rainer. "Westphalian System." In *Max Planck Encyclopedia of Public International Law [MPEPIL]*, edited by Rüdiger Wolfrum: Oxford University Press, 2006.

Grotius, Hugo. *De Jure Belli Ac Pacis Libri Tres*. Translated by Francis W. Kelsey. Edited by James Brown Scott. The Classics of International Law: Grotius, Vol. 2 ed.: William S. Hein & Co., 1995.

Haass, Richard. *A world in disarray: American foreign policy and the crisis of the old order*. Penguin, 2017.

Halman, Loek. "Political Values." In *The Oxford handbook of political behavior*, edited by Russell J. Dalton and Hans-Dieter Klingemann: Oxford University Press, 2007.

Hardin, Garrett. "The Tragedy of the Commons." *Science* 162 (1968): 1243–48.

Harrison, Kathryn, and Lisa McIntosh Sundstrom. "The Comparative Politics of Climate Change." *Global Environmental Politics* 7, no. 4 (2007): 1–18.

Harvey, Fiona. "Paris Climate Change Agreement: The World's Greatest Diplomatic Success." *The Guardian*, 14 Dec 2015, 2015.

Henkin, Louis. *International law: Politics and values*. Nijhoff, 1995.

Hermitte, Marie-Angèle. "La convention sur la diversité biologique." *Annuaire français de droit international* 38 (1992): 844–70.

Hernández, Gleider I. "A Reluctant Guardian: The International Court of Justice and the Concept of 'international community'." *British Yearbook of International Law* 83, no. 1 (2013): 13–60.

Hohmann, Harald. *Präventive Rechtspflichten und-prinzipien des modernen Umweltvölkerrechts. Zum Stand des Umweltvölkerrechts zwischen Umweltnutzung und Umweltschutz*. Duncker & Humblot, 1992.

———. *Precautionary legal duties and principles of modern international environmental law*. Graham&Trotman / Martinus Nijhoff, 1994.

Horn, Laura. "Climate Change and the Future Role of the Concept of the Common Concern of Humankind". *Australian Journal of Environmental Law*, (2015, vol. II): p. 24–56.

Hovi, Jon, Detlef F. Sprinz, and Guri Bang. "Why the United States Did Not Become a Party to the Kyoto Protocol: German, Norwegian, and US Perspectives." *European Journal of International Relations* 18, no. 1 (2012): 129–50.

Hummel, Ralph P., and Camilla Stivers. "Postmodernism, Bureaucracy, and Democracy." In *The Oxford handbook of American bureaucracy*, edited by Robert F. Durant: Oxford University Press, 2010.

Hurrell, Andrew. *On global order: Power, values, and the constitution of international society*. Oxford University Press, 2007.

Hurrell, Andrew, and Sandeep Sengupta. "Emerging Powers, North–South Relations and Global Climate Politics." *International Affairs* 88, no. 3 (2012): 463–84.

Ikenberry, G. John. "The End of Liberal International Order?." *International Affairs* 94, no. 1 (2018): 7–23.

International Institute for Sustainable Development. "Summary of the Resumed Sixth Session of the Conference of the Parties to the UN Framework Convention on Climate Change: 16-27 July 2001." *Earth Negotiations Bulletin* 12, no. 176 (2001).

International Law Association. "Draft Rules of International Law Applicable to Transfrontier Pollution." *Umwelt- und Planungsrecht* 3, no. 1 (1983): 21.

———. "ILA New Delhi Declaration of Principles of International Law Relating to Sustainable Development, 2 April 2002." *Netherlands International Law Review* XLIX (2002): 299–305.

———. "Washington Conference (2014): Legal Principles Relating to Climate Change – Report of the International Law Association's Committee on Legal Principles Relating to Climate Change", 2014.

International Law Commission. "Draft Articles on State Responsibilities – with Commentaries." *Yearbook of the International Law Commission* 2, no. 2 (2001): 31–143.

———. "First report on formation and evidence of customary international law by Michael Wood", 2013.

———. "First report on jus cogens by Dire Tladi", 2016.

———. "First report on Protection of the atmosphere by Shinya Murase", 2014.

———. "Fourth report on Protection of the atmosphere by Shinya Murase", 2017.

———. "Report of the Commission to the General Assembly on the Work of Its Fifty-Third Session, Draft Articles on the Prevention of Transboundary Harm from Hazardous Activities, with Commentaries." *Yearbook of the International Law Commission* 2, no. 2 (2001): 148–70U.N. Doc. A/56/10.

———. "Report of the Commission to the General Assembly on the work of its sixty-eighth session, Draft articles on the protection of persons in the event of disasters", 2016.

———. "Second report on formation and evidence of customary international law by Michael Wood", 2014.

———. "Second report on Protection of the atmosphere by Shinya Murase", 2015.

———. "Third report on formation and evidence of customary international law by Michael Wood", 2015.

———. "Third report on Protection of the atmosphere by Shinya Murase", 2016.

Jacobs, Michael. "High Pressure for Low Emissions: How Civil Society Created the Paris Climate Agreement." *Juncture* 22, no. 4 (2016): 314–23.

Ji, Zou. "Enhancing Climate Mitigation Ambition Successively: The Drivers." In *Paris Agreement and Beyond: International Climate Change Policy Post-2020*, edited by Robert N. Stavins and Robert C. Stowe: Cambridge, MA: Harvard Project on Climate Agreements, 2016.

Joas, Hans. "Die kulturellen Werte Europas – Eine Einleitung." In *Die kulturellen Werte Europas*, edited by Hans Joas and Klaus Wiegandt: Fischer Taschenbuch Verlag, 2005.

Jordan, Andrew, and Timothy O'Riordan. "The Precautionary Principle: A Legal and Policy History." In *The precautionary principle: Protecting public health, the environment and the future of our children*, edited by Marco Martuzzi and Joel A. Tickner: World Health Organization, 2004.

Jouannet, Emmanuelle. "Universalism and Imperialism: The True-False Paradox of International Law?." *European Journal of International Law* 18, no. 3 (2007): 379–407.

Kelsen, Hans. *Principles of international law*, edited by Robert W. Tucker. 2nd ed.: Holt, Rinehart and Winston, 1967.

Kelsen, Hans, and John H. Herz. "Essential Conditions of International Justice." *Proceedings of the American Society of International Law at Its Annual Meeting (1921–1969)* 35 (1941): 70–98.

Keohane, Robert O. "Twenty Years of Institutional Liberalism." *International Relations* 26, no. 2 (2012): 125–38.

Keohane, Robert O., and David G. Victor. "The Regime Complex for Climate Change." *Perspectives on Politics* 9, no. 1 (2011): 7–23.

Kiss, Alexandre. "The Common Concern of Mankind." *Envtl. Pol'y & L.* 27, no. 4 (1997): 244.

Kleinlein, Thomas. "Konstitutionalisierung im Völkerrecht." *Konstruktion und Elemente einer idealistischen Völkerrechtslehre* (2012).

Koskenniemi, M. "International Law in Europe: Between Tradition and Renewal." *European Journal of International Law* 16, no. 1 (2005): 113–24.

Koskenniemi, Martti. *The gentle civilizer of nations: The rise and fall of international law; 1870–1960*. Cambridge University Press, 2007.

———. "Histories of International Law: Dealing with Eurocentrism." *Rechtsgeschichte Legal History – Zeitschrift des Max-Planck-Instituts für europäische Rechtsgeschichte*, no. 19 (2011): 152–76.

———. "Lauterpacht: The Victorian Tradition in International Law." *European Journal of International Law* 8, no. 2 (1997): 215–63.

Krieger, Heike. "Trumping International Law? Implications of the 2016 US Presidential Election for the International Legal Order." *EJIL: Talk! Blog of the European Journal of International Law*, https://www.ejiltalk.org/trumping-international-law-the-implications-of-the-2016-us-presidential-election-for-the-international-legal-order/, 3 January 2017.

———. "Verfassung im Völkerrecht – Konstitutionelle Elemente jenseits des Staates? The Constitutionalization of Public International Law – Constitutional Elements Beyond the State?." In *Verfassung als Ordnungskonzept. Referate und Diskussionen auf der Tagung der Vereinigung der Deutschen Staatsrechtslehrer in Speyer vom 7. bis zum 10. Oktober 2015*, edited by Franz Mayer, Hans M. Heinig, Lothar Michael and others: De Gruyter, 2016.

Krieger, Heike, and Georg Nolte. "The International Rule of Law – Rise or Decline? Points of Departure." *KFG Working Paper Series* 1 (2016), Available at SSRN: https://ssrn.com/abstract=2866940.

Kunz, Josef L. "The Swing of the Pendulum: From Overestimation to Underestimation of International Law." *AJIL* 44, no. 1 (1950): 135–40.

Kysar, Douglas A. "Climate Change and the International Court of Justice." *Yale Law School Public Law Research Paper* 315 (2013).

Lauterpacht, Hersch. *International law: Being the collected papers of Hersch Lauterpacht. International law in general,* edited by Elihu Lauterpacht Vol. 2: Cambridge University Press, 1975.

Lawrence, Peter, and Daryl Wong. "Soft Law in the Paris Climate Agreement: Strength or Weakness?." *Review of European, Comparative & International Environmental Law* 26, no. 3 (2017): 276–86.

Leiserowitz, Anthony, Edward Maibach, Connie Roser-Renouf, Seth Rosenthal, and Matthew Cutler. "Climate Change in the American Mind." In *Yale University and George Mason University. New Haven, CT: Yale Program on Climate Change Communication*, 2017 http://climatecommunication.yale.edu/wp-content/uploads/2017/07/Climate-Change-American-Mind-May-2017.pdf

Leiserowitz, Anthony, and Jagadish Thaker. "Climate Change in the Indian Mind." In *Yale University and George Mason University. New Haven, CT: Yale Program on Climate Change Communication.*, 2012 http://climatecommunication.yale.edu/wp-content/uploads/2016/02/2012_08_Climate-Change-in-the-Indian-Mind.pdf

Leiserowitz, Anthony, Robert Kates, and Thomas Parris. "Sustainability Values, Attitudes and Behaviors: A Review of Multi-national and Global Trends." *Annual Review of Environment and Resources* 31 (2006): 413.

Levin, Kelly, Benjamin Cashore, Steven Bernstein, and Graeme Auld. "Overcoming the Tragedy of Super Wicked Problems: Constraining Our Future Selves to Ameliorate Global Climate Change." *Policy Sciences* 45, no. 2 (2012): 123–52.

life, Coalition on the environment and Jewish. "Jewish Energy Guide, ed. David Krantz." In *Jewish Council for public affairs*, 2014 http://aytzim.org/JewishEnergyGuide-web.pdf.

Lipschutz, Ronnie D., and Corina McKendry. "Social Movements and Global Civil Society." In *The Oxford handbook of climate change and society*, edited by John S. Dryzek, Richard B. Norgaard and David Schlosberg: Oxford University Press, 2012.

Lowe, Vaughan. "The Role of Equity in International Law." *Aust. YBIL* 12 (1988): 54.

———. "Sustainable Development and Unsustainable Arguments." In *International law and sustainable development: Past achievements and future challenges*, edited by Alan E. Boyle and David Freestone: Oxford University Press, 1999.

Lynas, Mark. "How do I know China wrecked the Copenhagen deal? I was in the room." *The Guardian*, 22 Dec 2009, 2009.

Macdonald, Laura. "Globalising Civil Society: Interpreting International NGOs in Central America." *Millennium* 23, no. 2 (1994): 267–85.

McCrudden, Christopher. "Human Rights and Traditional Values." In *Law's Ethical, Global and Theoretical Contexts: Essays in Honour of William Twining*, edited by Abdul Paliwala, Christopher McCrudden and Upendra Baxi: Cambridge University Press, 2015.

McDougal, Myres S., and Harold D. Lasswell. "The Identification and Appraisal of Diverse Systems of Public Order." *American Journal of International Law* 53, no. 1 (1959): 1–29.

McMaster, H. R., and Gary D. Cohn. "America First Doesn't Mean America Alone." *Wall Street Journal*, 30 May 2017, 2017.

Mearsheimer, John J. *The tragedy of great power politics*. WW Norton & Company, 2001.

Mearsheimer, John J. "Structural Realism." In *International Relations Theories: Discipline and Diversity*, edited by Tim Dunne, Milja Kurki and Steve Smith: Oxford University Press, 2007.

Meixler, Eli. "Michael Bloomberg Pledged $4.5 Million to Uphold U.S. Commitment to the Paris Agreement." *TIME*, 23 Apr 2018, 2018.

Melkas, Eriika. "Sovereignty and Equity within the Framework of the Climate Regime." *Review of European, Comparative & International Environmental Law* 11, no. 2 (2002): 115.

Mickelson, Karin. "South, North, International Environmental Law, and International Environmental Lawyers." *YB Int'l Env L.* 11 (2000): 52.

Morgenthau, Hans J., Kenneth W. Thompson, and David Clinton. *Politics among nations: The struggle for power and peace: The struggle for power and peace*. McGraw-Hill Education – Europe, 2005.

Mosler, Hermann. "The International Society as a Legal Community." In *Recueil des Cours*, edited by Académie de Droit International: A. W. Sijthoff, Leyde, 1974.

Nachmany, Michal, Sam Fankhauser, Joana Setzer, and Alina Averchenkova. "Global Trends in Climate Change Legislation and Litigation: 2017 Update." In *Grantham Research Institute on Climate Change and the Environment, May 2017*, 2017.

Ngwadla, Xolisa. "Equitable Access to Sustainable Development: Relevance to Negotiations and Actions on Climate Change." In *Mitigation Action Plans & Scenarios (MAPS) Research Paper Series*, 2013.

O'Connell, Mary Ellen. "The Role of Soft Law in a Global Order." In *Commitment and compliance: The role of non-binding norms in the International Legal System*, edited by Dinah Shelton: Oxford University Press, 2000.

Office of the High Commissioner for Human Rights (OHCHR). "Analytical Study on the Relationship between Human Rights and the Environment." In *UN Doc. A/HRC/19/34*, 2011.

Onufrio, Giuseppe. "The Encyclical: Spirituality and Ethics Join the Climate Debate." *Greenpeace International news blog*, https://www.greenpeace.org/archive-international/en/news/Blogs/makingwaves/the-encyclical-blog/blog/53267/, 18 June 2015.

Orakhelashvili, Alexander. "Natural Law and Justice." In *MPEPIL*, edited by Rüdiger Wolfrum: Oxford University Press, 2007.

Pallemaerts, Marc. "International Environmental Law from Stockholm to Rio: Back to the Future?." *Review of European Community & International Environmental Law* 1, no. 3 (1992): 254–66.

Paradell-Trius, Lluís. "Principles of International Environmental Law: An Overview." *Review of European Community & International Environmental Law* 9, no. 2 (2000): 93–99.

Parfit, Derek. "Future Generations: Further Problems." *Philosophy & Public Affairs* 11, no. 2 (1982): 113–72.

Paterson, Matthew. "Networks and Coordination in Global Climate Governance." In *Paris agreement and beyond: International climate change policy post-2020*, edited by Robert N. Stavins and Robert C. Stowe: Cambridge, MA: Harvard Project on Climate Agreements, 2016.

Paulus, Andreas L. *Die internationale Gemeinschaft im Völkerrecht: eine Untersuchung zur Entwicklung des Völkerrechts im Zeitalter der Globalisierung; The "International Community" in Public International Law: english summary.* Beck, 2001.

———. "International Community." In *Max Planck Encyclopedia of Public International Law [MPEPIL]*, edited by Rüdiger Wolfrum: Oxford University Press, 2013.

———. "Reciprocity Revisited." In *From bilateralism to community interest essays in honour of Bruno Simma*, edited by Ulrich Fastenrath and Bruno Simma: Oxford University Press, 2011.

Pauwelyn, Joost, and Lilliana Andonova. "A 'Legally Binding Treaty' or Not? The Wrong Question for Paris Climate Summit." *EJIL: Talk! Blog of the*

European Journal of International Law, https://www.ejiltalk.org/a-legally-binding-treaty-or-not-the-wrong-question-for-paris-climate-summit/, 4 December 2015.

Pauwelyn, Joost, Ramses A. Wessel, and Jan Wouters. "When Structures Become Shackles: Stagnation and Dynamics in International Lawmaking." *EJIL* 25, no. 3 (2014): 733–63.

Payandeh, Mehrdad. *Internationales Gemeinschaftsrecht: zur Herausbildung gemeinschaftsrechtlicher Strukturen im Völkerrecht der Globalisierung = International community law: the evolution of community structures in the international legal order in the era of globalization; (English Summary)*. Springer, 2010.

PBL Netherlands Environmental Assessment Agency. "China Now No. 1 in CO2 Emissions; USA in Second Position." *News release*, 19 Jun 2007, 2007, http://www.pbl.nl/en/dossiers/Climatechange/Chinanowno1inCO2emissionsUSAinsecondposition.

Pearce, Fred. "Should Polluting Nations Be Liable for Climate Damages?" Yale Environment 360 – Published at the Yale School of Forestry & Environmental Studies, https://e360.yale.edu/features/should_polluting_nations_be_liable_for_climate_damages, 2013.

Pellet, Alain. "Article 38." In *The statute of the international court of justice: A commentary*, edited by Andreas Zimmermann, Christian Tomuschat, Karin Oellers-Frahm and Christian J. Tams: Oxford University Press, 2012.

———. "Conclusions." In *The fundamental rules of the international legal order – Jus cogens and obligations erga omnes*, edited by Tomuschat Christian and Thouvenin Jean-Marc: Brill, 2005.

Perkins, Nancy L. "World Trade Organization: United States – Import Prohibition of Certain Shrimp and Shrimp Products." *International Legal Materials* 38, no. 1 (1999): 118–75.

Perrez, Franz Xaver. *Cooperative sovereignty: From independence to interdependence in the structure of international environmental law*. Kluwer Law International, 2000.

Perry, Michael J. "Are Human Rights Universal? The Relativist Challenge and Related Matters." *Human Rights Quarterly* 19, no. 3 (1997): 461–509.

Peters, Anne. "Fragmentation and Constitutionalization." In *The Oxford handbook of the theory of international law*, edited by Anne Orford, Florian Hoffmann and Martin Clark: Oxford University Press, 2016.

"The Philippines: Supreme Court Decision in Minors Oposa v. Secretary of the Department of Environment and Natural Resources (DENR)." *International Legal Materials* 33, no. 1 (1994): 173–206.

Pogge, Thomas. *Realizing rawls*. Cornell University Press, 1989.

Pomerance, Michla. "The ICJ's Advisory Jurisdiction and the Crumbling Wall between the Political and the Judicial." *AJIL* 99, no. 1 (2005): 26–42.

Preiser, Wolfgang. "History of International Law, Basic Questions and Principles." In *MPEPIL*, edited by Rüdiger Wolfrum: Oxford University Press, 2007.

Pullella, Philip. "Pope Demands 'action now' to Save Planet from Environmental Ruin." *Reuters online* (2015).

Rajamani, Lavanya. "Addressing the 'post-Kyoto' Stress Disorder: Reflections on the Emerging Legal Architecture of the Climate Regime." *International & Comparative Law Quarterly* 58, no. 4 (2009): 803–34.

———. "Ambition and Differentiation in the 2015 Paris Agreement: Interpretative Possibilities and Underlying Politics." *International & Comparative Law Quarterly* 65, no. 02 (2016): 493–514.

———. "The Cancun Climate Agreements: Reading the Text, Subtext and Tea leaves." *International & Comparative Law Quarterly* 60, no. 2 (2011): 499–519.

———. *Differential treatment in international environmental law*. Oxford: Oxford UniversityPress, 2006.

———. "Differentiation and Equity in the Post-Paris Negotiations." In *Paris agreement and beyond: International climate change policy post-2020*, edited by Robert N. Stavins and Robert C. Stowe: Cambridge, MA: Harvard Project on Climate Agreements, 2016.

———. "The Durban Platform for Enhanced Action and the Future of the Climate Regime." *International & Comparative Law Quarterly* 61, no. 2 (2012): 501–18.

———. "From Berlin to Bali and beyond: Killing Kyoto Softly?." *International & Comparative Law Quarterly* 57, no. 4 (2008): 909–39.

———. "The Reach and Limits of the Principle of Common but Differentiated Responsibilities and Respective Capabilities in the Climate Change Regime." In *Handbook of climate change and India: Development, politics and governance*, edited by Navroz Dubash: Earthscan, 2012.

Raskin, Paul, Tariq Banuri, Gilberto Gallopin, Pablo Gutman, Al Hammond, Robert Kates, and Rob Swart. "Great Transition: The Promise and Lure of the Times Ahead. A Report of the Global Scenario Group." In *Stockholm Environment Institute / Tellus Institute*, 2002. https://greattransition.org/documents/Great_Transition.pdf.

Rawls, John. *The law of peoples: With 'the idea of public reason' revisited*. Harvard University Press, 2001.

Rayner, Steve. "How to Eat an Elephant: A Bottom-Up Approach to Climate Policy." *Climate Policy* 10, no. 6 (2010): 615–21.

Rehbinder, Eckard. *Das Vorsorgeprinzip im internationalen Vergleich.* Werner-Verlag, 1991.

Risse, Thomas, Steve C. Ropp, and Kathryn Sikkink. *The persistent power of human rights: From commitment to compliance.* Cambridge University Press, 2013.

Rodhe, Henning, Robert Charlson, and Elisabeth Crawford. "Svante Arrhenius and the Greenhouse Effect." *Ambio* 26, no. 1 (1997): 2.

Rubin, Alfred P. "Actio Popularis, Jus Cogens and Offenses Erga Omnes." *New Eng. L. Rev.* 35 (2000): 265.

———. "Pollution by Analogy: The Trail Smelter Arbitration." *Oregon Law Review* 50, no. 3 (1971): 259–82.

Sand, Peter H. "The Evolution of International Environmental Law." In *The Oxford handbook of international environmental law*, edited by Daniel Bodansky, Jutta Brunnée and Ellen Hey: OUP, 2008.

Sands, Philippe. "Climate Change and the Rule of Law: Adjudicating the Future in International Law." *Journal of Environmental Law* 28, no. 1 (2016): 19–35.

———. "International Courts and the Application of the Concept of 'Sustainable Development'." *Max Planck Yearbook of United Nations Law* 3 (1999): 389–405.

———. *Principles of international environmental law*, 3rd ed.: Cambridge University Press, 2012.

Saran, Shyam. *How India sees the world: Kautilya to the 21st century.* Juggernaut Books, 2017.

Sato, Tetsuo. "Legitimacy of International Organizations and their Decisions: Challenges that International Organizations Face in the 21st Century." *Hitotsubashi Journal of Law and Politics* 37 (2010): 11–30.

Schachter, Oscar. *Sharing the world's resources.* Columbia University Press, 1977.

Schmidt, Andreas, Ana Ivanova, and Mike S. Schäfer. "Media Attention for Climate Change around the World: A Comparative Analysis of Newspaper Coverage in 27 Countries." *Global Environmental Change* 23, no. 5 (2013): 1233–48.

Schröder, Meinhard. "Instrumente des internationalen Umweltrechts unter Berücksichtigung der Noumea-Konvention vom 24./25.11. 1986." *Jahrbuch des Umwelt- und Technikrechts* (1987): 273–96.

———. "Klimaschutz als Problem des internationalen Rechts." *Jahrbuch des Umwelt-und Technikrechts* (1993): 191.

———. "Precautionary Approach/Principle." In *MPEPIL*, edited by Rüdiger Wolfrum: Oxford University Press, 2014.

Scobbie, Lain. "Words My Mother Never Taught Me—'In Defense of the International Court'." *AJIL* 99, no. 1 (2005): 76–88.

Secretariat, UNFCCC. "Historic Paris Agreement on Climate Change: 195 Nations Set Path to Keep Temperature Rise Well Below 2 Degrees Celsius." *News release*, 13 Dec 2015, 2015, https://unfccc.int/news/finale-cop21.

———. "Pope Francis Releases Encyclical on Climate and Environment – UN Leaders React." *News release*, 2015, http://newsroom.unfccc.int/unfccc-newsroom/pope-francis-releases-encyclical-on-climate-and-environment/.

Shelton, Dinah. "Equity." In *The Oxford handbook of international environmental law*, edited by Daniel Bodansky, Jutta Brunnée and Ellen Hey: OUP, 2008.

———. "International Law and 'Relative Normativity'." In *International law*, edited by Malcolm D. Evans: Oxford University Press, 2010.

Simma, Bruno. "From bilateralism to community interest in international law." In *Recueil des Cours*, edited by Académie de Droit International: Martinus Nijhoff, 1994.

———. "Universality of International Law from the Perspective of a Practitioner." *EJIL* 20, no. 2 (2009): 265–97.

Slaughter, Anne-Marie. "The Paris Approach to Global Governance." Project Syndicate, http://www.project-syndicate.org/commentary/paris-agreement-model-for-global-governance-by-anne-marie-slaughter-2015-12, 2015.

Sohn, Louis B. "The Stockholm Declaration on the Human Environment." *Harv. Int'l. LJ* 14, no. 3 (1973): 423.

Stahn, Carsten. "Responsibility to Protect: Political Rhetoric or Emerging Legal Norm?." *AJIL* 101, no. 1 (2007): 99–120.

Stone, Christopher D. "Defending the Global Commons." In *Greening international law*, edited by Philippe Sands: Earthscan, 1993.

Sullivan, Gordan R., and et al. *National Security and the threat of climate change*: The Center for Naval Analysis Corporation, 2007.

Tabuchi, Hiroko, and Lisa Friedman. "U.S. Cities, States and Businesses Pledge to Measure Emissions." *New York Times*, 11 July 2017, 2017.

Tams, Christian. "The 'International Community' as a Legal Concept." In *Fundamental concepts of international law*, edited by Jean D'Aspremont and Sahib Singh: Edward Elgar, Forthcoming (Available at SSRN: https://ssrn.com/abstract=3086270).

Tasioulas, John. "In Defence of Relative Normativity: Communitarian Values and the Nicaragua Case." *Oxford Journal of Legal Studies* 16, no. 1 (1996): 85–128.

Teitel, Ruti G. *Humanity's law*. Oxford University Press, 2011.

Thaker, Jagadish, and Anthony Leiserowitz. "Shifting Discourses of Climate Change in India." *Climate Change* 123, no. 2 (2014): 107.

The Climate Group. "US States, Cities and Businesses Keep US Climate Action on Track." *News release*, 18 Sep 2017, 2017, https://www.theclimategroup.org/news/us-states-cities-and-businesses-keep-us-climate-action-track.

Thirlway, H. W. A. *The sources of international law*. Oxford University Press, 2014.

Thürer, Daniel. "Soft law." In *MPEPIL*, edited by Rüdiger Wolfrum: Oxford University Press, 2009.

Tladi, Dire. "South African Lawyers, Values and New Vision of International Law: The Road to Perdition Is Paved with the Pursuit of Laudable Goals." *S. Afr. YB Int'l L.* 33 (2008): 167–83.

Tomuschat, Christian. "Obligations Arising for States without or against Their Will." In *Recueil des Cours*, edited by Académie de Droit International: Martinus Nijhoff, 1993.

Trachtman, Joel P. *The future of international law: Global government*. Cambridge University Press, 2013. doi: 10.1017/CBO9781139565585.

Trindade, Antônio Augusto Cançado. *International law for humankind – towards a new Jus Gentium*, edited by The Hague Academy of International Law: Martinus Nijhoff Publishers, 2010. doi:https://doi.org/10.1163/ej.9789004184282.i-728.

UNEP. "The Implications of the Common Concern of Mankind Concept on Global Environmental Issues – Note from the UNEP Secretariat to the Meeting of the Group of Legal Experts to Examine the Concept of the Common Concern of Mankind in Relation to Global Environmental Issues, 13–15 Dec 1990." *Revista Instituto Interamericano de Derechos Humanos* 13 (1991): 237–46.

United Nations Commission on Sustainable Development. "Report of the Expert Group Meeting on Identification of Principles of International Law for Sustainable Development." In *Background paper; Geneva, Switzerland, 26–28 September*, 1995.

United States Conference of Catholic Bishops. "Global Climate Change: A Plea for Dialogue Prudence and the Common Good (Statement)", 2001. http://www.usccb.org/issues-and-action/human-life-and-dignity/e...ate-change-a-plea-for-dialogue-prudence-and-the-common-good.cfm

van Aaken, Anne. "Is International Law Conducive to Preventing Looming Disasters?." *Global Policy* 7 (2016): 81–96.

Velders, Guus J. M., Stephen O. Andersen, John S. Daniel, David W. Fahey, and Mack McFarland. "The Importance of the Montreal Protocol in Protecting Climate." *Proceedings of the National Academy of Sciences* 104, no. 12 (2007): 4814–19.

Verdross, Alfred. *Die Verfassung der Völkerrechtsgemeinschaft*. J. Springer, 1926.

Verdross, Alfred, and Bruno Simma. *Universelles Völkerrecht*. Duncker & Humblot, 1984.

Verheyen, Roda. *Climate change damage and international law: Prevention duties and state responsibility*. Martinus Nijhoff Publishers, 2005.

Victor, David G. "Making the Promise of Paris a Reality." In *Paris agreement and beyond: International climate change policy post-2020*, edited by Robert N. Stavins and Robert C. Stowe: Cambridge, MA: Harvard Project on Climate Agreements, 2016.

Vidal, John. "How a 'typo' Nearly Derailed the Paris Climate Deal." *The Guardian*, 16 Dec 2015, 2015.

Villalpando, Santiago. "The Legal Dimension of the International Community: How Community Interests Are Protected in International Law." *EJIL* 21, no. 2 (2010): 387–419.

Viñuales, Jorge E. "The Contribution of the International Court of Justice to the Development of International Environmental Law: A Contemporary Assessment." *Fordham Int'l LJ* 32 (2008): 232.

———. "The Paris Climate Agreement: An Initial Examination." C-EENRG Working Papers: Cambridge Centre for Environment, Energy and Natural Resource Governance, University of Cambridge, 2015.

von Bernstorff, Jochen, and Ingo Venzke. "Ethos, Ethics, and Morality in International Relations." In *Max Planck Encyclopedia of Public International Law [MPEPIL]*, edited by Rüdiger Wolfrum: Oxford University Press, 2011.

Waltz, Kenneth. *Theory of international politics*. Waveland Press, 1979, reissued 2010.

Wang, B. B., Y. T. Sheng, M. Ding, M. Lyv, J. L. Xing, and Q. N. Zhou. "Climate Change in the Chinese Mind." In *Beijing, CT*: China Center for Climate Change Communication, 2017. http://www.efchina.org/Attachments/Report/report-comms-20171108/Climate_Change_in_the_Chinese_Mind_2017.pdf.

Warrick, Joby, and Chris Mooney. "196 Countries Approve Historic Climate Agreement." *The Washington Post*, 12 Dec 2015, 2015.

Weil, Prosper. "Towards Relative Normativity in International Law." *AJIL* 77, no. 3 (1983): 413.

Wendt, Alexander. "Anarchy Is What States Make of It: The Social Construction of Power Politics." *International Organization* 46, no. 02 (1992): 391–425.

Wiener, Antje. *Contestation and constitution of norms in global international relations*. Cambridge University Press, 2018. doi: 10.1017/9781316718599.

Wiener, Jonathan B. "Precaution." In *The Oxford handbook of international environmental law*, edited by Daniel Bodansky, Jutta Brunnée and Ellen Hey: OUP, 2007.

Wiener, Jonathan B., and Michael D. Rogers. "Comparing Precaution in the United States and Europe." *Journal of Risk Research* 5, no. 4 (2002): 317–49.

Willsher, Kim. "Quit the EU for Better Trade Deal, Trump Reportedly Told Macron." *The Guardian*, 29 June 2018, 2018.

Winkler, Harald. "Mitigation (Art. 4)." In *The Paris agreement on climate change: analysis and commentary*, edited by Daniel Klein, María Pía Carazo, Meinhard Doelle, Jane Bulmer and Andrew Higham: Oxford University Press, 2017.

Wirth, David A. "Cracking the American climate negotiators' hidden code: United States law and the Paris agreement." *Climate Law* 6, no. 1 (2016): 152–70.

Wolfrum, Rüdiger. "Common Heritage of Mankind." In *MPEPIL*, edited by Rüdiger Wolfrum: Oxford University Press, 2009.

———. "International Law of Cooperation." In *MPEPIL*, edited by Rüdiger Wolfrum: Oxford University Press, 2010.

World Commission on Environment and Development. *Our common future.* Oxford University Press, 1987.

Zaelke, Durwood, and James Cameron. "Global Warming and Climate Change – An Overview of the International Legal Process." *American University International Law Review* 5, no. 2 (1990): 249.

Ziegler, Charles E. "Contesting the Responsibility to Protect." *International Studies Perspectives* 17, no. 1 (2016): 75–97.

———. "Critical Perspectives on the Responsibility to Protect: BRICS and Beyond." *International Relations* 30, no. 3 (2016): 262–77.

www.ingramcontent.com/pod-product-compliance
Ingram Content Group UK Ltd.
Pitfield, Milton Keynes, MK11 3LW, UK
UKHW021933290926
8980IPUK00016B/1609

9 783631 852354